Workshop on Computational Linguistics for Literature 2012

Held at the 2012 Conference of the North American Chapter of the Association for Computational Linguistics: Human Language Technologies (NAACL-HLT 2012)

Montreal, Quebec, Canada
3 – 8 June 2012

ISBN: 978-1-62276-571-3

Printed from e-media with permission by:

Curran Associates, Inc.
57 Morehouse Lane
Red Hook, NY 12571

CURRAN ASSOCIATES INC. proceedings.com

Some format issues inherent in the e-media version may also appear in this print version.

Printed by Curran Associates, Inc. (2013)

For permission requests, please contact the Association for Computational Linguistics at the address below.

Association for Computational Linguistics
209 N. Eighth Street
Stroudsburg, Pennsylvania 18360

Phone: 1-570-476-8006
Fax: 1-570-476-0860

acl@aclweb.org

Additional copies of this publication are available from:

Curran Associates, Inc.
57 Morehouse Lane
Red Hook, NY 12571 USA
Phone: 845-758-0400
Fax: 845-758-2634
Email: curran@proceedings.com
Web: www.proceedings.com

Proceedings of the NAACL Workshop on Computational Linguistics for Literature:
Preface

"What do you read, my lord?"
"Words, words, words."

It may well be that our generation is the last to be intimately familiar with the printed book. We live in an age when the percentage of digitized literature increases steadily. Older work comes online thanks in part to scanning initiatives such as Project Gutenberg (`gutenberg.org`), Google Books (`books.google.com`) or Million Book Project (`archive.org/details/millionbooks`). New material is often born digital, and becomes available via e-book stores and through non-traditional outlets such as blogging and self-publishing.

Literature is in many ways distinct from genres usually considered in computational linguistics, such as newspaper prose, unstructured Web pages or speech. That is why the growing availability of online literature presents new opportunities and challenges in language processing. How can automatic methods help readers find new literature on a certain topic, understand a text or a genre, identify the author of an anonymous text, or read a book written in another language? How might language analysis techniques go beyond words to help identify the deeper meaning found in literature, no matter the time, place or culture from which it originates?

The vibrant research field at the intersection of computing and the humanities, known as Digital Humanities, emphasizes the skills in applying computational techniques to data in arts, humanities and social sciences. We have organized this workshop to help nurture a dialogue between Digital Humanities and the computational linguistics community, where the cutting-edge work in text understanding occurs. Our main target audience are computer scientists and linguists interested in literature as a genre of study, especially those well versed in the rigours of language understanding and those with experience in the idiosyncrasies of literary text. Our invited speaker, Inderjeet Mani, sets the tone with a talk entitled "Computing and the Literary Landscape" which frames the field in terms of the low- and high-hanging fruit that we as a community may pursue.

The papers in this volume cover quite a range of research interests, so much so that to group them by topic is a tough nut to crack. There are both *corpus-based studies* and *in-depth treatment* of specific literary works.

Intriguingly, we have *two* papers on the *computational treatment of poetry*. Julian Brooke, Adam Hammond and Graeme Hirst present work on stylistic segmentation of T. S. Eliot's influential *The Waste Land*. Justine Kao and Dan Jurafsky contribute an essay in computational aesthetics: an exploration of what could be seen as contributing to the aesthetic merits of a good poem.

Two papers, by Anders Søgaard and by Michael Bendersky and David Smith, look into what makes certain phrases likely to be quoted. We can but hope to read a book a day, and we would need many lifetimes to barely scratch the surface of the available literature. To be able to extract a salient (quotable!) passage of a longer work gives us at least a fighting chance to stay afloat.

Next come several papers which consider the literary applications of more widely considered challenges in language understanding. Choonkyu Lee and Smaranda Muresan study the *usage of referring expressions* and coreference in literary narrative. Wajdi Zaghouani and Mona Diab discuss the pilot experiments in annotating the Koran for *semantic role labelling*. Apoorv Agarwal, Augusto Corvalan, Jacob Jensen and Owen Rambow put *network analysis* to work in search of insight into character interactions in an abridged version of *Alice in Wonderland*. What social networks did Lewis Carroll anticipate? *Authorship attribution* is the theme of the papers by Bei Yu and by Andreas van Cranenburgh. The former tests a procedure based on function words on novels, essays and blogs. The latter works with fragments of parse trees, and tests this form of stylometry on some twenty books by five celebrated authors. Because literature is global in scope, *machine translation* of literary work should be quite important. Two papers offer two different points of view: Qian Yu, Aurélien Max and François Yvon experiment with aligning literary works available in multiple languages, while Rob Voigt and Dan Jurafsky look at the role of referential cohesion in machine translation of literature.

The changes to a language over time present challenges in processing older texts. A paper by Ann Irvine, Laure Marcellesi and Afra Zomorodian investigates how we might digitize literary work of a certain vintage when tools trained on modern language are not quite adequate for language of two centuries ago. In a different mode, Sophie Kushkuley takes a look at *Harper's Bazaar*: How did people write about fashion trends in the nineteenth century?

Last but not least, a position paper by Antonio Roque presents several problems in literary analysis and discusses how language technology may help solve such problems.

We anticipate a lively and wide-ranging discussion between the authors of these diverse contributions. We hope that this workshop, and others like it, will galvanize the area of literary analysis within computational linguistics. Literature is a carrier of our culture and its history, so advances in the application of natural language processing to literature will help unlock and explore the insights found within.

We owe a word of thanks to the many individuals who made this workshop possible. First and foremost, we thank the authors. The number of submissions we received shows that the field of computational linguistics for literature is doing very well indeed. We are deeply indebted to the reviewers for their hard work. They enabled us to select an exciting program and to give valuable feedback to the authors. We also thank Mona Diab and Colin Cherry for their incessant help with the logistics. Finally, many thanks to Google Inc. for their financial support.

Enjoy the workshop!

Anna, David, Stan, and Rada

Organizers:

David K. Elson (Google)
Anna Kazantseva (University of Ottawa)
Rada Mihalcea (University of North Texas)
Stan Szpakowicz (University of Ottawa)

Program Committee:

Cecilia Ovesdotter Alm (Rochester Institute of Technology)
Nicholas Dames (Columbia University)
Hal Daumé III (University of Maryland)
Anna Feldman (Montclair State University)
Mark Finlayson (MIT)
Pablo Gervás (Universidad Complutense de Madrid)
Roxana Girju (University of Illinois at Urbana-Champaign)
Amit Goyal (University of Maryland)
Katherine Havasi (MIT Media Lab)
Matthew Jockers (Stanford University)
James Lester (North Carolina State University)
Inderjeet Mani (Children's Organization of Southeast Asia)
Kathy McKeown (Columbia University)
Saif Mohammad (National Research Council, Canada)
Vivi Nastase (HITS gGmbH)
Rebecca Passonneau (Columbia University)
Livia Polanyi (LDM Associates)
Owen Rambow (Columbia University)
Michaela Regneri (Saarland University)
Reid Swanson (University of California, Santa Cruz)
Marilyn Walker (University of California, Santa Cruz)
Janice Wiebe (University of Pittsburgh)

Invited Speaker:

Inderjeet Mani (Children's Organization of Southeast Asia)

Table of Contents

Workshop Schedule

9:00-9:03	Welcome
9:03-10:00	Invited Talk *Computing and the Literary Landscape* Inderjeet Mani *Abstract* I begin by distinguishing literary from non-literary narrative, and then go onto to describe a framework for narrative computing involving environments for authoring and interacting with literary artifacts as well as searching, analyzing, and translating them. These artifacts concern events whose characters act and react based on their beliefs. I focus here on computational issues related to four facets of narrative structure: story embedding, accessibility relations, time, and plot. I conclude with some recommendations for research strategies.
10:00-10:30	Session A *Computational Analysis of Referring Expressions in Narratives of Picture Books* Choonkyu Lee, Smaranda Muresan and Karin Stromswold
10:30-11:00	Break
11:00-12:30	Session B *A Computational Analysis of Style, Affect, and Imagery in Contemporary Poetry* Justine Kao and Dan Jurafsky *Towards a Literary Machine Translation: The Role of Referential Cohesion* Rob Voigt and Dan Jurafsky *Unsupervised Stylistic Segmentation of Poetry with Change Curves and Extrinsic Features* Julian Brooke, Adam Hammond and Graeme Hirst
12:30-2:00	Lunch
2:00-3:00	Session C1 *Aligning Bilingual Literary Works: a Pilot Study* Qian Yu, Aurélien Max and François Yvon *Function Words for Chinese Authorship Attribution* Bei Yu
3:00-3:30	Session C2 Poster teasers
3:30-4:00	Break

4:00-5:00 Session D

Posters

Mining wisdom
Anders Søgaard
Literary authorship attribution with phrase-structure fragments
Andreas van Cranenburgh
Digitizing 18th-Century French Literature: Comparing transcription methods for a critical edition text
Ann Irvine, Laure Marcellesi and Afra Zomorodian
A Dictionary of Wisdom and Wit: Learning to Extract Quotable Phrases
Michael Bendersky and David Smith
A Pilot PropBank Annotation for Quranic Arabic
Wajdi Zaghouani, Abdelati Hawwari and Mona Diab
Trend Analysis in Harper's Bazaar
Sophie Kushkuley
Social Network Analysis of Alice in Wonderland
Apoorv Agarwal, Augusto Corvalan, Jacob Jensen and Owen Rambow
Towards a computational approach to literary text analysis
Antonio Roque

5:00-5:55 Session E
Open discussion

5:55-6:00 Farewell

Computational Analysis of Referring Expressions in Narratives of Picture Books

Choonkyu Lee
Department of Psychology
Rutgers Center for Cognitive Science
Rutgers University – New Brunswick
choonkyu@eden.rutgers.edu

Smaranda Muresan
Library and Information Science Department
School of Communication and Information
Rutgers University – New Brunswick
smuresan@rci.rutgers.edu

Karin Stromswold
Department of Psychology
Rutgers Center for Cognitive Science
Rutgers University – New Brunswick
karin@ruccs.rutgers.edu

Abstract

This paper discusses successes and failures of computational linguistics techniques in the study of how inter-event time intervals in a story affect the narrator's use of different types of referring expressions. The success story shows that a conditional frequency distribution analysis of proper nouns and pronouns yields results that are consistent with our previous results – based on manual coding – that the narrator's choice of referring expression depends on the amount of time that elapsed between events in a story. Unfortunately, the less successful story indicates that state-of-the-art coreference resolution systems fail to achieve high accuracy for this genre of discourse. Fine-grained analyses of these failures provide insight into the limitations of current coreference resolution systems, and ways of improving them.

1 Introduction

In theories of information structure in extended discourse, various factors of discourse salience have been proposed as determinants of information 'newness' vs. 'givenness' (e.g., Prince, 1981). Based on evidence from speakers' choice of different types of referring expressions in referring back to a previously introduced discourse referent, scholars have discovered effects of (a) 'referential distance' (Givón, 1992), a text-based measure of distance between the antecedent and the re-mention in terms of number of intervening clauses; (b) topic-prominence of the referent in the previous mention (Brennan, 1995); (c) presence of another candidate referent ('competitor') in linguistic or visual context (Arnold and Griffin, 2007), among others. In re-mentioning individuals, one can, for example, simply repeat names or use anaphoric devices, such as definite descriptions and pronouns.

In our work, we have been investigating the role of mental representation of nonlinguistic situational dimensions of the storyline (e.g., Zwaan, 1999) as an additional factor of salience in discourse organization. From the five situational dimensions of the event-indexing model (Zwaan and Radvansky, 1998), we have focused on the time dimension. In a narrative elicitation study (Lee and Stromswold, submitted; Lee, 2012), we presented picture sequences from three wordless picture books in Mercer Mayer's "Boy, Dog, Frog series" (Mayer, 1969; Mayer, 1974; Mayer and Mayer, 1975), and had 8 adults estimate the *inter-event intervals in story time* between consecutive scenes with no linguistic stimuli, and had a different group of native English-speaking adults write stories to go along with the pictures. The 36 adults wrote a total of 58 written narratives, which consisted of 2778 sentences and 38936 word tokens (48 sentences and 671 word tokens per narrative on average). The use of wordless picture books allows fixed target content and clear visual availability of the characters and their actions.

In our previous analysis (Lee and Stromswold, submitted) of the effect of inter-event time intervals on the narrator's referential choice in referring

S1) Finally though, the boy starts to get tired and decides to crawl into bed. His dog joins him and soon they are asleep. The boy forgot to put a lid on the bottle, and Mr. Frog is sneaking out!
S2) When the boy wakes up in the morning, he sees that Mr. Frog is gone. He is very upset that he lost his new friend.

Figure 1. Sample 'Long Interval' Between Scenes S1 and S2 (Mean Estimate: 6h 48m 45s).

S3) After staring at the frog for two minutes he says "Ribbittttttt" and she screams and throws her fork into the air, and falls back in her chair. Charles gets scared by her screaming and jumps off her plate into the air.
S4) Luckily, he lands safely into a man's drink. He is mid-conversation with a beautiful lady and doesn't feel the new addition to his martini.

Figure 2. Sample 'Short Interval' Between Scenes S3 and S4 (Mean Estimate: 3s).

back to characters, we manually annotated critical sentences selected on the basis of the eight longest (mean duration = 1 hour 7 minutes 2 seconds; henceforth, 'Long Intervals') and the eight shortest (mean duration = 10 seconds; henceforth, 'Short Intervals') estimated intervals. Examples of a Long Interval and a Short Interval between scenes are given in Figures 1 and 2, together with sample corresponding narratives. For each of the 58 narratives, we analyzed the first sentence after a Long and Short Interval. Our coding of *referring* expressions involved frequency counts (ranging from 0 to 3) of instances of each of our Referential Types – Proper Names (e.g., *Mr. Frog*), Definite Descriptions (e.g., *the frog*), and Pronouns (e.g., *he*) – per critical sentence. We found a significant interaction between Interval and Referential Type in both a chi-square test of association and an analysis of variance, and the effect generally held across participants. Our finding demonstrated that narrators used Proper Names more after Long Intervals than after Short Intervals in story time, and more singular-referent Pronouns after Short Intervals than after Long Intervals.

Addressing the issue of the effect of inter-event interval on referential choice on a larger scale requires accurate automatic methods for identification of Referential Types and coreference resolution for the narratives. In this paper we first present a simple computational method for analyzing the *entire scene* descriptions after the Long and Short Intervals to study how inter-event intervals affect referential choice, focusing on Proper Nouns and Pronouns. Our results from the automatic methods are consistent with the results obtained using manual coding of the *critical sentences*. Second, we present an annotation study of nine narratives with coreference chains, and also discuss the performance of two state-of-the-art coreference resolution systems on a sample of our data.

2 Inter-event Interval Effect on Referring Expressions: A Basic Computational Approach

In order to address the question of how inter-event intervals affect the choice of referring expressions, we analyzed the frequency of Pronouns and Proper Nouns in scenes following the Long and Short Intervals. The results in Table 1 are consistent with our previous results obtained based on manual coding of the critical sentences only: The 'Long Interval' (LI) scenes and the 'Short Interval' (SI) scenes diverge in relative frequencies of our target part-of-speech tags – Pronouns (nominal (PRP) and possessive (PRP$) forms) vs. Proper Names (NNP).

One can observe that there are generally higher frequencies of Proper Names for the scenes after the Long Intervals compared to the Short Intervals, not only in absolute number but in relative proportion to Pronouns as well. A noticeable exception, Scene 3 of *One Frog Too Many* (Mayer and

Book	Scene#	PRP	PRP$	NNP
Frog Goes to Dinner	4 (LI)	62	56	106
	5 (LI)	54	37	96
	21 (LI)	87	60	120
	9 (SI)	45	22	27
	13 (SI)	50	44	50
	14 (SI)	40	21	40
One Frog Too Many	8 (LI)	33	33	55
	19 (LI)	63	42	90
	20 (LI)	60	29	88
	3 (SI)	70	65	158
	15 (SI)	69	50	73
	23 (SI)	1	2	2
Frog, Where Are You?	2 (LI)	89	70	143
	3 (LI)	70	65	158
	18 (SI)	64	56	86
	19 (SI)	63	42	90

Table 1. Scene-based Frequencies of Pronouns and Proper Names after the 16 Long and Short Intervals.

Mayer, 1975), is a very early scene in the picture book, with many character introductions and discourse-newness (Prince, 1981). Even with this exception included, the association between Interval (Long vs. Short) and Referential Type (Pronouns vs. Proper Names) was significant in a new analysis based on the entire scene descriptions, rather than just the first sentences for these scenes [$\chi^2(1) = 9.50$, $p = .0021$]. The significant effect of Interval reveals that Proper Names were more commonly used after Long Intervals than after Short Intervals, and Pronouns were more commonly used after Short Intervals than after Long Intervals.

The exception in Scene 3 of *One Frog Too Many* suggests, however, that excluding first few mentions in a coreference chain from analysis may reveal a stronger effect of Interval on referential type of re-mentions (although one mention for introducing a character does not always establish discourse-givenness from the narrator's perspective (Clancy, 1980)). Successful automatic coreference resolution would facilitate this analysis as well.

3 Annotation of Referring Expressions in Narratives of Picture Books

In order to provide descriptive statistics of referring expressions in our narratives of pictures books and to test the performance of coreference systems automatically in the future, we annotated 9 narratives manually with coreference chains (3 narratives for each of the 3 pictures books, with each narrative written by a different writer). Only animate entities, or characters in the stories, were considered. We used the MMAX2 annotation tool (Müller and Strube, 2006). A coreference schema is available from the Heidelberg Text Corpus (HTC, Malaka and Zipf, 2000) sample directory included in the MMAX2 package. The HTC schema allows marking a mention in terms of the discourse entity or coreference chain it corresponds to, as well as 'np_form' (what type of (pro)nominal it is), 'grammatical_role' (subject/object/other) and 'semantic_class' (abstract/human/physical object/other). We imported the HTC schema to annotate the mention level in terms of coreference, and also created a 'scene' level for our picture-book narratives.

The narratives were annotated by the authors of this paper independently in the initial version, and with adjudication for the final version. As the referents were very clear in the narratives for the picture books, there was only one case of initial disagreement in the authors' coreference decisions. Table 2 shows statistics related to these 9 narratives.

Narrative ID	# of Mentions	# of Chains	# of Words	Longest Chain	Average Chain Length	Density
1	65	8	280	22	8.13	.23
2	71	5	277	29	14.20	.26
3	52	7	268	15	7.43	.19
4	128	13	562	60	9.85	.23
5	62	12	256	20	5.17	.24
6	78	11	383	25	7.09	.20
7	271	23	1109	58	11.78	.24
8	111	21	514	38	5.29	.22
9	167	26	834	37	6.42	.20

Table 2. Descriptive Statistics for Each Narrative.

The density of referring expressions is very high (~22% of tokens/words in a story are referring expressions). Densities are also consistent across narratives: Narrative #7, which was by far the longest one with 1109 words, also showed a very high density (24%). Numbers of coreference chains are also consistent within each target picture book regardless of writer or narrative length: 8, 5, and 7 for *One Frog Too Many* (Mayer and Mayer, 1975); 13, 12, and 11 for *Frog, Where Are You?* (Mayer, 1969); and 23, 21, and 26 for *Frog Goes to Dinner* (Mayer, 1974). Table 2 also shows that the longest chain contains 60 mentions, and the average chain has about 8 mentions.

4 Performance of Coreference Resolution Systems on Narratives of Picture Books

In computational linguistics, the increasing availability of annotated coreference corpora has led to developments in machine learning approaches to automatic coreference resolution (see Ng, 2010). The task of automatic NP coreference resolution is to determine "which NPs in a text [...] refer to the same real-world entity" (Ng, 2010, p. 1396). Successful coreference resolution often requires real-world knowledge of public figures, entity relationships, and aliases, beyond linguistic parameters such as number and gender features.

In this paper, we have chosen two coreference resolution systems: Stanford's Multi-Pass Sieve Coreference Resolution System (Lee et al., 2011) (henceforth, Stanford dcoref) and ARKref (O'Connor and Heilman, 2011). Stanford dcoref consists of an initial mention-detection module, the main coreference resolution module, and task-specific post-processing. In this system, global information about the text is shared across mentions in the same cluster in the form of attributes such as gender and number. This system received the highest scores at a recent CoNLL shared task (Pradhan et al., 2011), which the authors attributed to the initial high-recall component (in mention detection) followed by high-precision classifiers in the coreference resolution sieves. ARKref is a syntactically rich, rule-based within-document coreference system very similar to (the syntactic components of) Haghighi and Klein (2009).

We analyzed in depth the performance of these systems on one of our narratives for *Frog Goes to Dinner* (Mayer, 1974). We expected automatic coreference resolution systems to show poorer performance when applied to our written narratives than that reported in the literature, because most of these systems have been trained on newswire, blog, or conversation corpora, which – though quite a heterogeneous set in themselves – are not similar to our written narrative data. Some of the most noteworthy particularities of our written narrative collection include (a) fictional content, in which animals occur frequently and are greatly anthropomorphized, (b) an imaginary target audience of a limited age range (six- to eight-year-olds), and (c) clear scene-by-scene demarcation in the writing process, with a new text input box for each new scene in a picture book. The first point, in particular, may limit the utility of named entity recognition (NER) and WordNet relations among nominals in the preprocessing steps prior to coreference resolution. As we discuss below, preprocessing errors in parsing and NER did in fact contribute to coreference precision errors.

Our written narratives had a lot of singleton mentions for secondary characters and plural combinations of characters. We thus evaluated the performance based on the B^3 measure proposed by Bagga and Baldwin (1998), rather than the link-based MUC (Vilain et al., 1995).

We computed the B^3 with equal weighting for all mentions. Stanford dcoref achieved B^3 scores of 0.78 Precision, 0.43 Recall and 0.55 F_1, while ARKref scores were 0.67 for precision, 0.45 for recall, and 0.54 for F_1. Stanford dcoref includes a post-processing module in which singletons are removed, which partially contributes to the low recall score for the system.

4.1 Qualitative analysis of coreference output

In this section, we discuss the errors from both ARKref and Stanford dcoref in depth. The coreference outputs from both ARKref and Stanford dcoref demonstrate that preprocessing errors can lead to errors downstream for coreference resolution. Misparsing is one of the serious issues. For example, in ARKref's output for our sample narrative (for *Frog Goes to Dinner)*, the third-person singular verb *waves* in *Billy waves goodbye* (Scene 6) and *Froggy waves goodbye* (Scene 7) was misparsed as a plural nominal and thus a headword of a mention for a discourse entity, and these two instances were marked as coreferent. Lee et al. also acknowledged misparsing as a major problem for Stanford dcoref.

A few surprising errors in the ARKref output include (a) marking *the woman* and *him* in the same clause as coreferent despite the gender mismatch, and (b) leaving *the lady* as a singleton and starting a new coreference chain for *her* in the same clause. It is strange that the explicitly anaphoric pronoun mention did not lead ARKref to link it to the identified mention *the lady*.

Other noteworthy errors common to both systems' outputs were the following:

(1) inconsistent mention detection and coreference resolution for mentions of the frog character with *Froggy*;

(2) failure to recognize cataphora in *Without knowing Froggy's in [his]$_i$ saxophone, [the saxophone player]$_i$ tries to blow harder*... and linking the pronoun to *Froggy* instead;

(3) starting a new coreference chain at Scene 4 at the mention of *Billy* when the referent (the boy) has been already introduced as *Billy Smith* in Scene 1;

(4) the same type of error for another character (the frog) at an indefinite NP *a frog* in *She is so shocked that there is a frog in her salad.*

With regard to error (1), preprocessing results in the Stanford dcoref output reveal some NER errors in which *Froggy* was mislabeled as an 'organization,' which, along with the absence of *Froggy* in the name gazetteer for the system (Lee et al., 2011), would lead to both precision and recall errors for *Froggy*, as we observed.

Error (3) reveals the potential pitfall of overreliance on headwords for mention/discourse-new detection, which leads these systems to miss the internal structure to people's names – namely, [first name + last name] for the same person,[1] which then can be re-mentioned using just the first name. Although in news articles and other formal writing it is typical to mention a person by the last name (e.g., *Obama* rather than *Barack*) as long as the referent is clear, stories, conversations, and other less formal genres would make more frequent use of first names of individuals for re-mention compared to other genres. Because the importance of coreference resolution is not limited to formal writing, coreference resolution systems need to incorporate name-specific knowledge, either in preprocessing stages such as parsing and NER or in coreference resolution after the preprocessing.

Error (4) is not as undesirable as the other ones: Even for a human annotator, it is more difficult to make a coreference decision for a case like this one, in which the fact that the salad-eating lady was shocked would come about similarly for any frog, not just Froggy. Although there does not seem to be a rule for classifying an indefinite NP as denoting a new entity,[2] training on a large corpus would lead to such a tendency because indefinites usually do indicate discourse-newness introducing a new discourse referent.

In another narrative for the same picture book, there were two definite NPs (*the woman* and *the waiter*) for which the definiteness was due to the visual availability of the referent in the scene or a bridging inference (restaurant – waiter) rather than a previous mention. Definiteness may lead coreference systems to prefer assigning the mention in question to an existing coreference chain rather than creating a new chain, but ARKref processed both of these possibly misleading definite NPs successfully by creating a new coreference chain, and Stanford dcoref got one right and made a recall error for the other. On the other hand, referring to different secondary male characters similarly as *the man* did lead to a spurious coreference chain linking all of these mentions.

5 Conclusion and Future Directions

With the NLP tools discussed above, possibilities abound for interesting research on narratives. Based on scene-based segmentation of narratives written for fixed target picture sequences, one can collect various kinds of linguistic and nonlinguistic data associated with the picture sequences and conduct regression analysis to see which factor has the most predictive value for linguistic variation such as Referential Type choice. Important factors include temporal and thematic (dis)continuity in the target content (McCoy and Strube, 1999; Vonk et al., 1992), and discourse salience factors (Prince, 1981), for which we have collected measures in our previous work.

Our Interval Effect finding lends support to McCoy and Strube's (1999) intuition underlying their referring-expression generation system, for which they used reference time change in discourse as a major predictor of referential type. Gaining further insight into the impact of time change in content on referential choice in naturally occurring discourse can thus lead to a predictive model of referring expressions as well.

In the future, we plan to use 'semantic_class' attributes and features such as ANIMACY in the

[1] Application to East Asian languages would need to adjust to the opposite 'family name + given name' sequence, often even in English transliteration (e.g., *Kim Jong-il*).

[2] According to Lee et al. (2011), Stanford dcoref correctly recognizes coreference in appositive constructions with an indefinite NP *after* the first mention.

HTC schema as our task-specific filters for selecting just story characters. Moreover, we plan to explore other state-of-the-art coreference systems such as CherryPicker (Rahman and Ng, 2009). The NLP tools and techniques discussed above can be applied to cross-document coreference resolution as well (see Bagga and Baldwin, 1998, for discussion of a meta document), although training the systems for narratives like ours would involve much more manual annotation and supervision, particularly because different authors usually assign different names to a given character. In order to limit the amount of manual annotation, unsupervised methods for coreference resolution (Ng, 2008; Poon and Domingos, 2008; Haghighi and Klein, 2007) could be used. This, however, would require a larger number of picture books and human-produced narratives.

Coreference is far from a simple phenomenon, both for theory and application. Nevertheless, ultimately it would be desirable to improve the automatic coreference resolution systems in ways that reflect corpus-linguistic and psycholinguistic findings – e.g., referential distance effects (Givón, 1992), and the privileged status in memory of discourse entities in the immediately preceding clause (Clark and Sengul, 1979). The goal would be to represent as many of the interacting factors in referential choice as possible, with a weighting scheme or a ranking algorithm sensitive to these multiple factors.

References

Jennifer E. Arnold and Zenzi M. Griffin. 2007. The effect of additional characters on choice of referring expression: Everyone counts. *Journal of Memory and Language*, 56: 521-536.

Amit Bagga and Breck Baldwin. 1998. Algorithms for scoring coreference chains. In *Proceedings of LREC Workshop on Linguistic Coreference*, pages 563-566.

Susan Brennan. 1995. Centering attention in discourse. *Language and Cognitive Processes*, 10: 137-167.

Patricia M. Clancy. 1980. Referential choice in English and Japanese narrative discourse. In Wallace L. Chafe, editor, *The Pear Stories: Cognitive, Cultural, and Linguistic Aspects of Narrative Production*. Ablex, Norwood, NJ.

Herbert H. Clark and C. J. Sengul. 1979. In search of referents for nouns and pronouns. *Memory and Cognition*, 7(1): 35-41.

Thomas Givón. 1992. The grammar of referential coherence as mental processing instructions. *Linguistics*, 30:5-55.

Aria Haghighi and Dan Klein. 2007. Unsupervised coreference resolution in a nonparametric Bayesian model. In *Proceedings of ACL 2007*, pages 848–855.

Aria Haghighi and Dan Klein. 2009. Simple coreference resolution with rich syntactic and semantic features. In *Proceedings of EMNLP 2009*, pages 1152–1161.

Choonkyu Lee. 2012. Situation model and salience. The LSA 2012 Special Session on Information Structure and Discourse: In Memory of Ellen F. Prince. Portland, Oregon.

Choonkyu Lee and Karin Stromswold. submitted. Situation model and accessibility: Referring expressions in narrative production.

Heeyoung Lee, Yves Peirsman, Angel Chang, Nathanael Chambers, Mihai Surdeanu, and Dan Jurafsky. 2011. Stanford's multi-pass sieve coreference resolution system at the CoNLL-2011 Shared Task. In *Proceedings of the CoNLL-2011 Shared Task*, pages 28-34.

Rainer Malaka and Alexander Zipf. 2000. Deep Map: Challenging IT research in the framework of a tourist information system. In Daniel R. Fesenmaier, Stefan Klein, and Dimitrios Buhalis, editors, *Information and Communication Technologies in Tourism 2000: Proceedings of the International Conference in Barcelona, Spain*, pages 15-27. Springer, Wien.

Mercer Mayer. 1969. *Frog, Where Are You?* Penguin Books, New York.

Mercer Mayer. 1974. *Frog Goes to Dinner.* Penguin Books, New York.

Mercer Mayer and Marianna Mayer. 1975. *One Frog Too Many.* Penguin Books, New York.

Kathleen F. McCoy and Michael Strube. 1999. Taking time to structure discourse: Pronoun generation beyond accessibility. In *Proceedings of the Twenty-First Annual Conference of the Cognitive Science Society*, pages 378-383. Lawrence Erlbaum Associates, Mahwah, NJ.

Christoph Müller and Michael Strube. 2006. Multi-level annotation of linguistic data with MMAX2. In Sabine Braun, Kurt Kohn, and Joybrato Mukherjee, editors, *Corpus Technology and Language Pedagogy. New Resources, New Tools, New Methods*, pages 197-214. Peter Lang, Frankfurt.

Vincent Ng. 2009. Unsupervised models for coreference resolution. In *Proceedings of EMNLP 2008*, pages 640-649.

Vincent Ng. 2010. Supervised noun phrase coreference research: The first fifteen years. In *Proceedings of ACL 2010*, pages 1396-1411.

Brendan O'Connor and Michael Heilman. 2011. ARKref is a Noun Phrase Coreference System. Website at http://www.ark.cs.cmu.edu/ARKref/

Hoifung Poon and Pedro Domingos. 2008. Joint unsupervised coreference resolution with Markov logic. In *Proceedings of EMNLP 2008*, pages 650-659.

Sameer Pradhan, Lance Ramshaw, Mitchell Marcus, Martha Palmer, Ralph Weischedel, and Nianwen Xue. 2011. CoNLL-2011 Shared Task: Modeling unrestricted coreference in OntoNotes. In *Proceedings of CoNLL 2011*.

Ellen Prince. 1981. Toward a taxonomy of given-new information. In Peter Cole, editor, *Radical Pragmatics*, pages 223-256. Academic Press, New York.

Altaf Rahman and Vincent Ng. 2009. Supervised models for coreference resolution. In *Proceedings of EMNLP 2009*, pages 968-977.

Marc Vilain, John Burger, John Aberdeen, Dennis Connolly, and Lynette Hirschman. 1995. A model-theoretic coreference scoring scheme. In *Proceedings of the 6th Message Understanding Conference*, pages 45-52.

Wietske Vonk, Lettica G. M. M. Hustinx, and Wim H. G. Simons. 1992. The use of referential expressions in structuring discourse. *Language and Cognitive Processes*, 7(3/4): 301-333.

Rolf A. Zwaan. 1999. Situation models: The mental leap into imagined worlds. *Current Directions in Psychological Science*, 8(1):15-18.

Rolf A. Zwaan and Gabriel A. Radvansky. 1998. Situation models in language comprehension and memory. *Psychological Bulletin*, 123(2):162-185.

A Computational Analysis of Style, Affect, and Imagery in Contemporary Poetry

Justine Kao
Psychology Department
Stanford University
Stanford, CA 94305, USA
justinek@stanford.edu

Dan Jurafsky
Linguistics Department
Stanford University
Stanford, CA 94305, USA
jurafsky@stanford.edu

Abstract

What makes a poem beautiful? We use computational methods to compare the stylistic and content features employed by award-winning poets and amateur poets. Building upon existing techniques designed to quantitatively analyze style and affect in texts, we examined elements of poetic craft such as diction, sound devices, emotive language, and imagery. Results showed that the most important indicator of high-quality poetry we could detect was the frequency of references to concrete objects. This result highlights the influence of *Imagism* in contemporary professional poetry, and suggests that concreteness may be one of the most appealing features of poetry to the modern aesthetic. We also report on other features that characterize high-quality poetry and argue that methods from computational linguistics may provide important insights into the analysis of beauty in verbal art.

1 Introduction

Poetry is nerved with ideas, blooded with emotions, held together by the delicate, tough skin of words.

—Paul Engle (1908 -1991)

Many people have experienced the astounding and transformational power of a beautiful poem. However, little empirical research has been done to examine the textual features or mental processes that engender such a sensation. In this paper, we propose a computational framework for analyzing textual features that may be responsible for generating sensations of poetic beauty. We built a poetry corpus consisting of poems by award-winning professional poets and amateur poets, and compared poems in the two categories using various quantitative features. Although there are many reasons why some poems are included in prestigious anthologies and others are never read, such as a poet's fame, we assume that the main distinction between poems in well-known anthologies and poems submitted by amateurs to online forums is that expert editors perceive poems in the former category as more aesthetically pleasing. Given this assumption, we believe that the kind of comparison we propose should be the first step towards understanding how certain textual features might evoke aesthetic sensations more than others.

The next sections review previous computational work on poetry and motivate the features we use; we then introduce our corpus, our analyses, and results.

2 Computational aesthetics

Previous research on the computational analysis of poetry focused on quantifying poetic devices such as rhyme and meter (Hayward, 1996; Greene et al., 2010; Genzel et al., 2010), tracking stylistic influence between authors (Forstall et al., 2011), or classifying poems based on the poet and style (Kaplan & Blei, 2007; He et al., 2007; Fang et al., 2009). These studies showed that computational methods can reveal interesting statistical properties in poetic language that allow us to better understand and categorize great works of literature (Fabb, 2006). However, there has been very little work using computational techniques to answer an important question in both poetics and linguistics (Jakobson, 1960): what makes one poem more aesthetically appealing than another?

One such attempt is the "aesthetic measure" proposed by mathematician G.D. Birkhoff, who formalized beauty as a ratio between order and complexity (Birkhoff, 1933). Birkhoff found interesting correlations between the measure and people's aesthetic judgments of shapes, sounds, and poems. While the aesthetic measure enjoyed some success in the domain of visual arts (Rigau et al., 2008), it ran into problems of semantics when applied to language. Birkhoff's aesthetic measure judges a poem's beauty based solely on phonemic features, such as alliterations and assonance, rhymes, and musical vowels. The formula does not capture the subtlety of word choice or richness of meaning in poetry. Since Birkhoff's measure only considers phonetic features, it fails to fully quantify the aesthetic value of meaningful poetic texts.

In this paper, we aim to combine computational linguistics with computational aesthetics. We introduce a variety of theoretically-motivated features that target both poetic style and content, and examine whether each feature is a distinguishing characteristic of poems that are considered beautiful by modern experts and critics.

3 Elements of Craft

One demands two things of a poem. Firstly, it must be a well-made verbal object that does honor to the language in which it is written. Secondly, it must say something significant about a reality common to us all, but perceived from a unique perspective

—W. H. Auden (1907 - 1973)

We review several elements of craft that creative writers and critics reference in their analysis and appreciation of poetry. For each feature that we consider in our model, we provide theoretical motivation from creative writing and literary criticism. We then describe how we computed the values of each feature using tools from computational linguistics.

3.1 Diction

Aristotle argued that good writing consists of a balance of ordinary words that make the writing comprehensible and strange words that make the writing distinguished (Aristotle, 1998). Several hundred years later, Longinus argued that "noble diction and elevated word arrangement" is one of the primary sources of aesthetic language (Earnshaw, 2007; Longinus, 2001). These early scholars of poetic craft passed down the belief that poetic beauty stems from the level of individual words. In her influential creative writing textbook titled, "Imaginative Writing: The Elements of Craft," Burroway (2007) describes poetry as a high-density form of language. Poetic language is usually intentionally ambiguous and often packs several meanings into a compact passage (Addonizio & Laux, 1997). As a result, each word in a poem carries especially heavy weight and must be carefully selected and digested. Based on these ideas, we decided to examine whether or not good poetry is defined by the use of sophisticated vocabulary.

Diction can be evaluated from two different perspectives: word frequency, a measure of difficulty, and type-token ratio, a measure of diversity.

Word frequency: Psychologists, linguists, and testing agencies often use word frequency to estimate the difficulty and readability of words and sentences (Marks, Carolyn B. et al., 1974; Breland, 1996). Based on these studies, it is reasonable to predict that poems written by professional poets may contain more difficult words and lower average word frequencies than poems written by amateur poets.

We measured average word frequency using a list of top 500,000 most frequent words from the Corpus of Contemporary American English (COCA) (Davies, 2011). An average log word frequency was obtained for each poem by looking up each word in the poem in the word list and summing up the log word frequencies. The total log frequency was then divided by the number of words in the poem to obtain the average.

Type-token ratio: Readability measures and automatic essay grading systems often use the ratio of total word types to total number of words in order to evaluate vocabulary sophistication, with higher type-token ratios indicating more diverse and sophisticated vocabulary (Ben-Simon & Bennett, 2007; Pitler & Nenkova, 2008). We predict that professional poets utilize a larger and more varied vocabulary and avoid using the same word several times throughout a poem. A type-token ratio score was calculated for each poem by counting all the separate instances of words and dividing that number by the total number of words in the poem.

3.2 Sound Device

Poetry has a rich oral tradition that predates literacy, and traces of this aspect of poetic history can be found in sound devices such as rhyme, repetition, and meter. How a poem sounds is critical to how it is perceived, understood, and remembered. Indeed, most contemporary creative writing handbooks devote sections to defining various sound devices and analyzing notable poetry according to interesting patterns of sound (Burroway, 2007; Addonizio & Laux, 1997).

The sound device features described below were computed using Kaplan's 2006 *PoetryAnalyzer*. *PoetryAnalyzer* utilizes the Carnegie Mellon Pronouncing Dictionary to obtain pronunciations of words in each poem and identify patterns indicative of poetic sound devices.

Perfect and slant end rhyme: Rhyme is one of the most well-known and popular sound devices in poetry. The earliest poets used strict rhyme schemes as a mnemonic device to help them memorize and recite long poems. Research in psychology has confirmed poets' intuitions about the powerful effects of rhyme on perception and learning. For example, an aphorism that contains a rhyme is more likely to be perceived as true than a non-rhyming aphorism with the same meaning (McGlone & Tofighbakhsh, 2000). Exposure to rhymes also enhances phonological awareness in young children and can lead to better reading performances (Bryant et al., 1990).

The *PoetryAnalyzer* identifies end rhymes in poems by examining the phoneme sequences at the end of lines. A window of four line endings is analyzed at a time. If two words in the window have different initial consonants but identical phoneme sequences from the stressed vowel phoneme onward, then an instance of a perfect end rhyme instance is recorded. The final count of perfect end rhymes in a poem is normalized by the total number of words. If two words in the window of four line endings have the same stressed vowel but different phonemes following the stressed vowel, then an instance of a slant end rhyme is recorded. The final count of slant end rhymes in a poem is normalized by the total number of words.

Alliteration and consonance: Alliteration is the repetition of consonant sounds at the beginning of words, and consonance is the repetition of consonant sounds elsewhere. In addition to rhyme, alliteration was used as a powerful mnemonic device in ancient epic poetry (Rubin, 1995). Researchers in psychology and discourse analysis have shown that alliteration reactivates readers' memories for previous information that was phonologically similar to the cue (Lea et al., 2008).

The *PoetryAnalyzer* identifies alliteration and consonance as follows. If the initial phoneme of two consecutive words are identical consonants, the alliteration count is incremented. The total count is then divided by the total number of words to obtain a alliteration score for each poem. If there are at least two identical consonant phonemes in a window of nine syllables, the consonance count is incremented. The count is divided by the total number of words in a poem to obtain a consonance score.

Assonance: Assonance is the repetition of vowel sounds. Similar to consonants, different vowel sounds also have their own characteristics and effects. Long vowels take longer to utter and draw out the rhythm and pacing of the line, while short vowels feel brief and urgent (Burroway, 2007).

We calculated an assonance score for each poem in the same fashion as we did for the consonance score, except the target phonemes are vowels instead of consonants.

3.3 Affect

Studies have shown that poetry allows mental health patients to explore and reinterpret their emotions in useful ways. Through reading and writing poetry, patients are able to freely express their thoughts without the constraints of form and logic (Harrower, 1972). On the other hand, critics of poetry therapy have suggested that writing poetry may be harmful to psychological health, because it allows the poet to immerse herself in an inexplicable emotion without having to make sense or order out of it (Stirman & Pennebaker, 2001). For example, Silverman & Will (1986) claimed that Sylvia Plath's poetry may have undermined her control mechanisms and contributed to her death. If reading good poetry is found to be cathartic and therapeutic, do skilled poets make more references to psychological states and explore the emotional world with more depth and intensity?

We examine this question using several existing sentiment lexicons available for sentiment analysis research. One is the Harvard General Inquirer, which consists of 182 word categories, including basic sentiment categories, categories for concrete objects, and categories for abstract concepts (Stone et al., 1966). Another sentiment lexicon is the Linguistic Inquiry and Word Count (LIWC) (Pennebaker et al., 2001). While the General Inquirer was designed for content analysis, LIWC was designed to facilitate the understanding of individuals' cognitive and emotional states through text analysis. As a result, most of the categories in LIWC involve mental activity, with over $4,500$ words related to affective, social, and cognitive processes. Six categories from the Harvard General Inquirer and two categories from LIWC were selected because they are most suitable for our purpose of analyzing elements of poetic craft. These features are summarized in Table 1.

Feature	Examples
Word frequency	–
Type-token ratio	–
Perfect end rhyme	*floor / store*
Slant end rhyme	*bred / end*
Alliteration	*frozen field*
Consonance	*brown skin hung*
Assonance	*shallower and yellowed*
Positive outlook	*able; friend*
Negative outlook	*abandon; enemy*
Positive emotion	*happiness; love*
Negative emotion	*fury; sorrow*
Phys. wellbeing	*alive; eat*
Psych. wellbeing	*calm; adjust*
Object	*boat; leaf*
Abstract	*day; love*
Generalization	*none; all*

Table 1: Summary of features

3.4 Imagery

One of the most important and oft-repeated piece of advice for writers is the following: "Show, don't tell." Burroway (2007) interprets this as meaning: "Use concrete, significant details that address the senses." Effective imagery allows readers to bring in their own associations to understand and truly experience a new emotion, and skilled poets and writers are able to pick out specific sensory details that evoke deeper abstractions and generalizations.

The appeal of concrete imagery may have roots in processes that facilitate learning and memory. Previous research has shown that concrete noun pairs are easier to memorize than abstract noun pairs, which suggests that imagery can enhance the learning of word pairings (Paivio et al., 1966). Other studies have shown that mental imagery facilitates relational association between concepts (Bower, 1970). Furthermore, Jessen et al. (2000) found neural correlates that suggest that concrete nouns are processed differently in the brain than abstract nouns. One of the reasons why we find poetic imagery striking may be due to the psychological power of imagery to evoke rich associations formed by culture and personal experience.

Another reason why imagery is an essential element of poetic craft is that it allows writers to avoid falling into cliche, which is the bane of the creative writer's existence. Burroway (2007) writes, "flat writing is...full of abstractions, generalizations, and judgments. When these are replaced with nouns that call up a sense image and with verbs that represent actions we can visualize, the writing comes alive." Many abstract and common concepts can be embodied or evoked by surprising imagery. In our analysis, we predict that skilled poets are more likely to describe concrete objects and less likely to reference abstract concepts. We measure the degree to which a poem contains concrete details rather than abstractions and generalizations using categories from the Harvard General Inquirer (see Table 1).

4 Methods

4.1 Materials

In order to test the defining features of beautiful poetry described in the section above, we constructed a corpus containing poems that vary in quality and "beauty" by some established standard. One way to do this would be to randomly sample poems from various sources and ask experts to rate them for quality and beauty. However, such a method can be expensive and time-consuming. A more efficient way of achieving a similar effect is to sample poems from pre-existing categories, such as poems written by skilled professional poets versus poems written by amateur poets. We assume that award-winning poets produce poems that experts would consider "better" and more beautiful than poetry written by amateurs. Although there might be exceptions, since for example experts may consider some poems written by amateur poets to be very beautiful and sophisticated, these pre-existing categories for the most part should be a good approximation of expert opinions.

One hundred poems were selected from sixty-seven professional poets whose work was published in a collection of Contemporary American Poetry (Poulin & Waters, 2006). The poets produced most of their work towards the middle and end of the 20th century and are considered some of the best contemporary poets in America (e.g., Louise Gluck, Mary Oliver, Mark Strand, etc.). All of the poets are listed in the website of the Academy of American Poets and many have won prestigious awards. This serves as confirmation that the poets in this collection are widely acclaimed and that their craft is acknowledged and celebrated by poetry experts and literary critics.

We randomly selected one to three poems from each poet, proportionate to the number of poems each poet had in the collection. When an excessively long poem (over 500 words) was selected, we removed it and replaced it with a different poem from the same poet. This served as a rough control for the length of the poems in the corpus. The final selection of one hundred professional poems ranged from 33 to 371 words in length with an average length of 175 words. We believe that these poems are a good representation of work produced by the best and most celebrated poets of our time.

In addition, one hundred poems were selected from amateur poets who submitted their work anonymously to a free and open-to-all website, aptly called "Amateur Writing" (www.amateur-writing.com). At the time of selection, the website had over 2500 amateur poem submissions by registered users. The website contains a diverse set of poems submitted by amateur writers with a wide range of experience and skill levels. We randomly selected one hundred poems from the website and corrected for misspellings and obvious grammatical errors in the poems to control for the effect of basic language skills. The final selection of amateur poems ranged from 21 to 348 words in length with an average length of 136 words.

4.2 Procedures

We implemented the 16 features described in section 3, each of which target one of three separate domains: style, sentiment, and imagery. The sound device scores were computed using *PoetryAnalyzer* (Kaplan & Blei, 2007). For each category taken from the General Inquirer, scores were calculated using the General Inquirer system available on a server (Inquirer, 2011). A score for a certain category is the number of words in a poem that appear in the category normalized by the length of the poem. For the two categories taken from LIWC, scores were calculated by counting the number of words in each poem that match a word stem in the LIWC dictionary and dividing it by the total number of words. A score for each of the features was derived for every poem in the poetry corpus. All scores were then standardized to have zero mean and unit variance across poems.

5 Results and Analysis

To measure the effect of each variable on the likelihood of a poem being written by a professional or an amateur poet, we constructed a logistic regression model in R (R: A Language and Environment for Statistical Computing). For model selection, we used the step-wise backward elimination method. This method begins by building a model using all 16 feature variables. It then recursively eliminates variables that do not significantly contribute to explaining the variance in the data according to the Akaike information criterion (AIC), which measures the amount of information lost when using a certain model. The selection method stops when further eliminating a variable would result in significant loss of information and model fit. The final logistic regression model for the predictors of professional versus amateur poetry is summarized in the formula above (Table 2). Note that the variables included in the final model might not all be statistically significant.

Results show that poem type (professional or am-

Probability(poem type = professional $|X$), where

$X\beta$	$-0.6071 =$	
-0.5039 *	average log word frequency	+
0.6646 *	type token ratio	+
0.4602 *	slant end rhyme frequency	+
-2.1 *	perfect end rhyme frequency	+
-0.6326 *	alliteration frequency	+
-1.0701 *	positive outlook words	+
-0.7861 *	negative emotional words	+
-0.5227 *	psychological words	+
1.3124 *	concrete object words	+
-1.2633 *	abstract concept words	+
-0.836 *	generalization words	

Table 2: Model formula

ateur) is significantly predicted by eight different variables ($p < 0.05$): type token ratio, perfect end rhyme frequency, alliteration frequency, positive outlook words, negative emotional words, concrete object words, abstract concept words, and generalization words. The other nine variables: average log word frequency, slant end rhyme frequency, assonance, consonance, negative outlook words, positive emotional words, physical well-being words, and psychological words did not have significant predictive value. While positive outlook and positive emotion were highly correlated ($r = 0.54$), as were negative outlook and negative emotion ($r = 0.53$), there was no collinearity among the variables in the final logistic regression model selected by the backward elimination method.

The model predicts the likelihood of the poem type (professional or amateur) using the formula described in Table 2. The influence of each feature is represented by the coefficient β for each variable. A positive value for a coefficient increases the likelihood of a poem being written by a professional. For example, type token ratio and concrete object words have positive coefficient values; thus higher type token ratios and more concrete object words increase the likelihood of a poem being a professional poem. A negative value for a coefficient decreases the likelihood of a poem being written by a professional. For example, perfect end rhyme frequency has a negative coefficient value, and thus higher perfect end rhyme frequencies decrease the likelihood of a poem being written by a professional poet. The

Feature variable	Odds	p-value
type token ratio	1.94	0.0308
perfect end rhyme frequency	0.12	$5.06e^{-7}$
alliteration frequency	0.53	0.0188
positive outlook words	0.34	0.0130
negative emotional words	0.46	0.0244
concrete object words	3.72	0.0002
abstract concept words	0.28	0.0027
generalization words	0.43	0.0035

Table 3: Odds ratios and p values of significant predictors of professional poetry

Professional		**Amateur**	
Word	**Count**	**Word**	**Count**
tree	29	thing	40
room	20	wall	12
thing	18	bed	11
grass	17	clock	7
wall	14	room	7
flower	13	tree	6
glass	13	leave	6
floor	13	gift	5
car	12	mirror	4
dirt	11	flower	4
[...]	538	[...]	103
Proportion	4.1%	Proportion	1.5%
Type count	250	Type count	85

Table 4: Concrete words

relative odds and p-values of each significant predictor variable are presented in Table 3.

In summary, professional poems have significantly higher type-token ratios, contain fewer perfect end rhymes, fewer instances of alliteration, fewer positive outlook words, fewer negative emotional words, more references to concrete objects, less references to abstract concepts, and fewer generalizations. From the odds ratios, we can see that the most significant predictors of professional poetry are fewer perfect end rhymes and more references to concrete objects.

6 Discussion

What are skilled poets doing differently from amateurs when they write beautiful poetry? Based on results from our regression model, it appears that Aris-

Professional		Amateur	
Word	**Count**	**Word**	**Count**
day	40	day	54
night	31	time	33
year	25	beauty	25
time	20	soul	16
death	11	night	15
new	9	new	14
morning	8	moment	13
childhood	7	christmas	12
hour	7	think	11
afternoon	7	future	9
[...]	139	[...]	143
Proportion	1.8%	Proportion	2.6%
Type count	82	Type count	75

Table 5: Abstract words

Professional		Amateur	
Word	**Count**	**Word**	**Count**
all	63	all	82
nothing	26	never	46
never	19	always	43
always	14	nothing	21
every	11	every	15
any	10	forever	14
anything	5	anything	7
nobody	5	any	6
everything	5	everything	5
forever	3	everyone	4
Proportion	$< 1\%$	Proportion	1.8%

Table 6: Generalization words

totle may have been wrong about diction, at least for modern poetry. The words in professional poetry are not significantly more unusual or difficult than words used by amateur writers. This suggests that contemporary poets are not interested in flowery diction or obscure words, but are focused on using ordinary words to create extraordinary effects.

However, professional poets do use more distinct word types. The 100 poems written by professional poets contain a total of 18,304 words and 4,315 distinct word types (23.57%). The 100 poems written by amateur poets contain a total of 14,046 words and 2,367 distinct word types (16.85%), a much smaller portion. In aggregate, professional poets have a larger and more varied vocabulary than amateur poets. Moreover, professional poets use a significantly larger number of word types within each poem. Although professional poets do not use more difficult and unusual words, higher type-token ratio is a significant predictor of professional poetry, suggesting that professional poems may be distinguished by a richer set of words.

The results on sound devices provide interesting insight into the current stylistic trends of contemporary professional poetry. While sound devices have a long history in poetry and are considered a feature of poetic beauty, contemporary professional poets now use these devices much less often than amateur poets. Sound devices that were traditionally important in poetry for mnemonic purposes, such as rhyme and alliteration, are more prevalent in amateur poems. Even subtle and sophisticated sound devices like slant rhyme, consonance, and assonance are not significant indicators of professional poetry. These results suggest that repetition of sound is becoming a less aesthetically significant poetic device among contemporary masters of poetry.

In terms of affect, our results suggest that poems by professional poets are not more negatively emotional—at least not explicitly. On the contrary, amateur poets are significantly more likely to reference negative emotions than professional poets. Our results reveal an interesting distinction between words with positive and negative outlooks and connotations versus words that reference positive and negative emotions. While the two pairs of categories are strongly correlated, they capture different aspects of a text's emotional content. The positive and negative outlook categories contain many words that are not emotions but may evoke certain emotional attitudes, such as *clean* and *death*. The fact that professional poets are significantly less likely to use explicitly negative emotion words than amateur poets, but not significantly less likely to use negatively connotative words, suggests that professional poets may evoke more negative sentiment through connotation rather than explicit descriptions.

As predicted, poems written by professional poets contain significantly more words that reference objects and significantly less words about abstract concepts and generalizations. This result suggests that professional poets follow the sacred rule of "show, don't tell" and let images instead of words convey emotions, concepts, and experiences that stick to readers' minds. Professional poets not only use more object words than amateur poets (698 counts versus 205), but they also use a larger and more diverse set of object words (250 types versus 85), as shown in Table 4. Professional poets reference natural objects very often, such as *tree, grass,* and *flower*. On the other hand, the most frequent concrete object word in amateur poems is the extremely vague word *thing*. This suggests that even when amateur poets reference concrete objects, they do not use words that provide specific sensory details.

Our analysis supports the idea that Imagism has strongly influenced the ways in which modern poets and literary critics think about literary writing. Literary critic I.A. Richards argued that image clusters and patterns of imagery are keys to deeper meaning in literary works, and that critics should pay close attention to these patterns in order to understand "the language of art" beneath the surface ordinary language (Richards, 1893). Not only are concrete images able to render the world in spectacular detail, they also provide windows into particular experiences on which readers can project their own perceptions and interpretations.

Consistent with our predictions and with the aesthetic ideals of Imagism, professional poets also make significantly fewer direct references to abstract and intangible concepts (Table 5). If the deeper meaning of a poem is conveyed through imagery, abstract words are no longer needed to reference concepts and experiences explicitly. Moreover, amateur poets use significantly more words concerned with generalizations, as shown in Table 6. While amateur poets embrace the human impulse to generalize, the skilled poet must learn to extract and report unique details that single out each experience from the rest.

Overall, our results suggest that professional poets are more likely to show, while amateur poets have a tendency to tell. This difference marks the most significant distinction between contemporary professional and amateur poetry in our analysis and may be an essential aspect of craft and poetic beauty.

7 Future directions

Categorizing poetry as professional or amateur is a rather coarse measure of quality. In order to identify defining features of more fine-grained levels of poetic skill, future work could compare award-winning poetry with poems written by less prestigious but also professionally trained poets. Experimenting with different databases and lexicons for affect and imagery could also be helpful, such as word-emotion associations (Mohammad & Turney, 2011) and imageability ratings (Coltheart, 1981). In addition, more sophisticated methods that consider sense ambiguities and meaning compositionality in affective words (Socher et al., 2011) should be applied to help enhance and improve upon our current analyses.

While our approach reveals interesting patterns that shed light on elements of poetic sophistication, conclusions from the analysis need to be tested using controlled experiments. For example, does modifying a professional poem to include less concrete words make people perceive it as less beautiful? Investigating these questions using psychology experiments could help identify causal relationships between linguistic elements and sensations of poetic beauty.

In summary, our framework provides a novel way to discover potential features of poetic beauty that can then be experimentally tested and confirmed. By applying both stylistic and content analyses to the quantitative assessment of contemporary poetry, we were able to examine poetic craft on a representative set of poems and reveal potential elements of skill and sophistication in modern poetry.

Acknowledgments

We are deeply grateful for David Kaplan's generosity in sharing the code for the *PoetryAnalyzer* program, on which a substantial part of our analysis is based. We would also like to thank Lera Boroditsky, Todd Davies, and the anonymous reviewers for their extremely helpful feedback.

References

Addonizio, K., & Laux, D. (1997). *The Poet's Companion: A guide to the pleasures of writing poetry*. W. W. Norton and Company.

Aristotle (1998). Poetics. *The Critical Tradition: Classical Texts and Contemporary Trends*.

Ben-Simon, A., & Bennett, R. E. (2007). Toward more substantively meaningful automated essay scoring. *The journal of Technology, Learning, and Assessment*.

Birkhoff, G. (1933). *Aesthetic Measure*. Kessinger Publishing.

Bower, G. (1970). Imagery as a relational organizer in associative learning. *Journal of Verbal Learning and Verbal Behavior*, *9*(5), 529–533.

Breland, H. M. (1996). Word frequency and word difficulty: A comparison of counts in four corpora. *Psychological Science*, *7*(2), pp. 96–99.

Bryant, P., Maclean, M., Bradley, L., & Crossland, J. (1990). Rhyme and alliteration, phoneme detection, and learning to read. *Developmental Psychology*, *26*(3).

Burroway, J. (2007). *Imaginative Writing: The Elements of Craft*. Pearson, 2 ed.

Coltheart, M. (1981). The mrc psycholinguistic database. *The Quarterly Journal of Experimental Psychology*, *33*(4), 497–505.

Davies, M. (2011). Word frequency data from the Corpus of Contemporary American English (COCA). Downloaded from http://www.wordfrequency.info on May 10, 2011.

Earnshaw, S. (Ed.) (2007). *The Handbook of Creative Writing*. Edinburgh University Press.

Fabb, N. (2006). Generated metrical form and implied metrical form. *Formal approaches to poetry*, (pp. 77–91).

Fang, A. C., Lo, F., & Chinn, C. K. (2009). Adapting nlp and corpus analysis techniques to structured imagery analysis in classical chinese poetry. In *Proceedings of the Workshop on Adaptation of Language Resources and Technology to New Domains*, AdaptLRTtoND '09, (pp. 27–34).

Forstall, C., Jacobson, S., & Scheirer, W. (2011). Evidence of intertextuality: investigating paul the deacon's angustae vitae. *Literary and Linguistic Computing*, *26*(3), 285–296.

Genzel, D., Uszkoreit, J., & Och, F. (2010). Poetic statistical machine translation: rhyme and meter. In *Proceedings of the 2010 Conference on Empirical Methods in Natural Language Processing*, (pp. 158–166). Association for Computational Linguistics.

Greene, E., Bodrumlu, T., & Knight, K. (2010). Automatic analysis of rhythmic poetry with applications to generation and translation. In *Proceedings of the 2010 Conference on Empirical Methods in Natural Language Processing*, EMNLP '10, (pp. 524–533).

Harrower, M. (1972). *The therapy of poetry*. Oryx, London.

Hayward, M. (1996). Analysis of a corpus of poetry by a connectionist model of poetic meter. *Poetics*, *24*(1), 1–11.

He, Z., Liang, W., Li, L., & Tian, Y. (2007). Svm-based classification method for poetry style. In *Machine Learning and Cybernetics, 2007 International Conference on*, vol. 5, (pp. 2936–2940). IEEE.

Inquirer, H. G. (2011). How the general inquirer is used and a comparison of general inquirer with other text-analysis procedures.

Jakobson, R. (1960). Closing statement: Linguistics and poetics. *Style in language*, *350*, 377.

Jessen, F., Heun, R., Erb, M., Granath, D. O., Klose, U., Papassotiropoulos, A., & Grodd, W. (2000). The concreteness effect: Evidence for dual coding and context availability. *Brain and Language*, *74*(1), 103 – 112.

Kaplan, D. (2006). Computational analysis and visualized comparison of style in american poetry. Unpublished undergraduate thesis.

Kaplan, D., & Blei, D. (2007). A computational approach to style in american poetry. In *IEEE Conference on Data Mining*.

Lea, R., Rapp, D., Elfenbein, A., Mitchel, A., & Romine, R. (2008). Sweet silent thought: Alliteration and resonance in poetry comprehension. *Psychological Science*, *19*(709).

Longinus (2001). On sublimity. *The Norton Anthology of Theory and Criticism*.

Marks, Carolyn B., Doctorow, Marleen J., & Wittrock, M. C. (1974). Word frequency and reading comprehension. *The Journal of Educational Research*, *67*(6), 259–262.

McGlone, M., & Tofighbakhsh, J. (2000). Birds of a feather flock conjointly (?): Rhyme as reason in aphorisms. *Psychological Science*, *11*, 424–428.

Mohammad, S., & Turney, P. (2011). Crowdsourcing a word–emotion association lexicon. *Computational Intelligence*, *59*(000), 1–24.

Paivio, A., Yuille, J., & Smythe, P. (1966). Stimulus and response abstractness, imagery, and meaningfulness, and reported mediators in paired-asscoiate learning. *Canadian Journal of Psychology*, *20*(4).

Pennebaker, J., Francis, M., & Booth, R. J. (2001). *Linguistic Inquiry and Word Count (LIWC): LIWC2001*. Mahwah, NJ: Erlbaum.

Pitler, E., & Nenkova, A. (2008). Revisiting readability: A unified framework for predicting text quality. In *Empirical Methods in Natural Language Processing*, (pp. 186–195).

Poulin, A., & Waters, M. (2006). *Contemporary American Poetry*. Houghton Mifflin Company, eighth ed.

Richards, I. (1893). *Practical criticism: a study of literary judgment*. Transaction Publishers.

Rigau, J., Feixas, M., & Sbert, M. (2008). Informational aesthetics measures. In *IEEE Computer Graphics and Applications*.

Rubin, D. (1995). *Memory in oral traditions: The cognitive psychology of epic, ballads, and counting-out rhymes*. New York: Oxford University Press.

Silverman, M., & Will, N. (1986). Sylvia plath and the failure of emotional self-repair through poetry. *Psychoanal Q*, *55*, 99–129.

Socher, R., Pennington, J., Huang, E., Ng, A., & Manning, C. (2011). Semi-supervised recursive autoencoders for predicting sentiment distributions. In *Proceedings of the Conference on Empirical Methods in Natural Language Processing*, (pp. 151–161). Association for Computational Linguistics.

Stirman, S. W., & Pennebaker, J. (2001). Word use in the poetry of suicidal and nonsuicidal poets. *Psychosomatic Medicine*, *63*(4), 517–22.

Stone, P., Dunphry, D., Smith, M., & Ogilvie, D. (1966). *The General Inquirer: A Computer Approach to Content Analysis*. Cambridge, MA: MIT Press.

Towards a Literary Machine Translation: The Role of Referential Cohesion

Rob Voigt
Center for East Asian Studies
Stanford University
robvoigt@stanford.edu

Dan Jurafsky
Department of Linguistics
Stanford University
jurafsky@stanford.edu

Abstract

What is the role of textual features above the sentence level in advancing the machine translation of literature? This paper examines how referential cohesion is expressed in literary and non-literary texts and how this cohesion affects translation. We first show in a corpus study on English that literary texts use more dense reference chains to express greater referential cohesion than news. We then compare the referential cohesion of machine versus human translations of Chinese literature and news. While human translators capture the greater referential cohesion of literature, Google translations perform less well at capturing literary cohesion. Our results suggest that incorporating discourse features above the sentence level is an important direction for MT research if it is to be applied to literature.

Introduction

The concept of literary machine translation might seem at first to be a near-contradiction in terms. The field of machine translation has traditionally aimed its sights at the translation of technical or otherwise informative texts, with the strongest focus on newswire and other informative texts relevant to the goals of government funders.

Nevertheless, the prospect of literary MT is appealing. Human translation of literary texts is an extremely time- and money-intensive task, but one that is a crucial element of the global system of transcultural literary exchange. From a technical standpoint, since "by definition, literature is the art that uses language" (Chapman 1973), literary translation represents perhaps the strongest formulation of the machine translation problem. Jonathan Slocum, writing in 1985, essentially rejects the idea of literary MT altogether, noting that it is serendipitous for technical MT that emphasis is placed on semantic fidelity to the source text, whereas literary translation must take into account larger considerations such as style with which "computers do not fare well." Given the explosion of statistical methodologies in MT, are we now at a point where we can hope to begin tackling some of the questions associated with a potential literary machine translation?

This problem is severely understudied. Regardless of the plausibility (or even desirability) of eventually using MT to produce full-fledged translations of literary texts, a serious consideration of the unique difficulties posed by literary translation may well serve to push forward our computational understanding of literature and the language of translation.

In particular, literary translation seems to demand that we address larger-scale textual features beyond the sentence-level approach commonly employed by contemporary MT systems. There is a substantial body of work by scholars in the field of translation studies addressing greater-than-sentence-level textual features from a linguistic and literary-theoretical perspective, and this existing work can offer conceptual understanding and a parallel vocabulary with which to discuss progress in this regard in machine translation.

Eugene Nida (1964), for example, used the terms "formal equivalence" and "dynamic equivalence" to differentiate between translations aiming to replicate the form of their source and those aiming to replicate the source text's effects on its readers. Hatim and Mason (1995) brought the "seven standards of textuality" set forth by Beaugrande and Dressler (1981) into the translation studies context as metrics for evaluating the "expectation-fulfilling" or "expectation-defying" outcome of a translated text.

Cohesion is defined by Beaugrande and Dressler as "concern[ing] the ways in which the components of the textual world, i.e., the configuration of concepts and relations which underlie the surface text, are mutually accessible and relevant." Cohesion considers the limited human capacity for storing the "surface materials" of a text long enough to relate them semantically during the act of reading.

We therefore propose to study referential cohesion (Halliday and Hasan 1976), the relation between co-referring entities in a narrative, as an important component of cohesion. Referential cohesion has a significant literature in natural language processing (Grosz et al. 1995, Mani et al. 1998, Marcu 2000, Karamanis et al. 2004, Kibble and Power 2004, Elsner and Charniak 2008, Barzilay and Lapata 2008, inter alia) as does automatic coreference resolution, which has significantly increased in accuracy in recent years (Bengston and Roth 2008, Haghighi and Klein 2009, Haghighi and Klein 2010, Rahman and Ng 2011, Pradhan et al. 2011, Lee et al. 2011).

We formulate and test two hypotheses in this position paper: First, we anticipate that given stylistic considerations and their fundamental narrative function, prose literary texts are inherently "more cohesive" than news. Second, in light of the aforementioned necessity for "dynamic equivalence" in the literary translation, we anticipate that current machine translation systems, built with newswire texts in mind, will be less successful at conveying cohesion for literary texts than for news.

2. Investigating Literary Cohesion

Our first preliminary experiment examines how referential cohesion in literary texts differs from news text by examining coreference in a monolingual English-language corpus, without considering machine-translated texts.

We created a small corpus of twelve short stories for comparison with twelve recent long-form news stories from the New York Times, Wall Street Journal, The Atlantic, and the news blog The Daily Beast. The stories chosen were written by a variety of authors: Isaac Asimov, J.D. Salinger, Edgar Allen Poe, Tobias Wolff, Vladimir Nabokov, Sir Arthur Conan Doyle, Shirley Jackson, Jack London, Mark Twain, Willa Cather, Ambrose Bierce, and Stephen Crane – in the interest of avoiding over-specificity to any particular genre or style. The corpus thus included 12 short stories with 76,260 words and 12 news articles with 23,490 words, for a total corpus size of 24 documents and 99,750 words.

We used standard publicly-available NLP tools to process the corpus. We used the Stanford CoreNLP suite[1] to tokenize and sentence-split both the human and MT versions of each text and then to run the multi-pass sieve coreference resolution system described in Lee et al. (2011).

This system works by making multiple passes over the text, first doing recall-oriented mention extraction, then resolving coreference through a series of sieves moving from highest to lowest precision. This system is state-of-the-art, with a B^3 F1 score of 68.9 with no gold mention boundaries on the CoNLL 2011 shared task test set. Nevertheless, it is likely to introduce some measure of noise into our results.

For the rest of the paper we use the term "cluster" to refer to clusters agglomerated by the system that co-refer to the same entity, and "mention" to refer to individual instances of each entity in the text.

	Clusters per 100 Tokens	Mentions per 100 Tokens	Density: Mentions per Cluster
Short Stories	3.6	19.3	5.4
News Text	3.9	15.0	3.9

Table 1. Cohesion as measured by coreference in literary vs. non-literary texts. Figures given are the overall average across all documents.

Table 1 reports the numbers of clusters and mentions (normalized per 100 tokens). The literary texts had the same number of clusters (entities) as the news texts (one-tailed t-test, $p = 0.080$), albeit with a trend towards fewer clusters in literature. But literary text had more mentions ($p < 0.001$), and a higher number of mentions per cluster ($p < 0.001$) than the news texts.

The results of this preliminary study suggest that the literary text tended to discuss the same number of entities as the non-fiction, but to

[1] Available online at nlp.stanford.edu/software/corenlp.shtml

Suddenly, the nurse resorted to direct measures. She seized the boy's upper arm in one hand and dipped the other in the milk. She dashed the milk across his lips, so that it dripped down cheeks and receding chin.

...

Always, his frightened eyes were on her, watching, watching for the one false move. She found herself soothing him, trying to move her hand very slowly toward his hair, letting him see it every inch of the way, see there was no harm in it. And she succeeded in stroking his hair for an instant.

...

Instead, she turned on the night light and moved the bed. The poor thing was huddled in the corner, knees up against his chin, looking up at her with blurred and apprehensive eyes.

...

She looked down at those eager brown eyes turned up to hers and passed her hands softly through his thick, curly hair.

Figure 1. Human markup of cohesion throughout Asimov's "The Ugly Little Boy." Recurring entities are color-coded: red is the character Edith Fellowes, grey is her hands, blue is the character Timmie, light green is his eyes, dark green is his chin, yellow is his hair, and magenta is the milk. This sample contains 149 words and 7 recurring entities with a total of 29 mentions.

Two studies have found that weight-loss operations worked much better than the standard therapies for Type 2 diabetes in obese and overweight people whose blood sugar was out of control. Those who had surgery, which stapled the stomach and rerouted the small intestine, were much more likely to have a complete remission of diabetes, or to need less medicine, than people who were given the typical regimen of drugs, diet and exercise.

...

The new studies, published on Monday by The New England Journal of Medicine, are the first to rigorously compare medical treatment with these particular stomach and intestinal operations as ways to control diabetes. Doctors had been noticing for years that weight-loss operations, also called bariatric surgery, could sometimes get rid of Type 2 diabetes. But they had no hard data.

...

One of the studies, conducted at the Catholic University in Rome, compared two types of surgery with usual medical treatment.

Figure 2. Human markup of cohesion throughout a NYT news article. Recurring entities are color-coded, similar to the above. This sample contains 152 words and 7 recurring entities with a total of 21 mentions.

mention each entity more often. In other words, literary text uses more dense reference chains as a way of creating a higher level of cohesion.

Figures 1 and 2 provide representative examples, hand-labeled for coreference, to offer a qualitative intuition for this difference in cohesion. In the literary example in Figure 1 we find seven recurring entities with an average of 4.1 mentions each. In the news example in Figure 2 we find seven recurring entities but only 3.0 average mentions, resulting in qualitatively less dense reference chains in the news sample.

Our results are consistent with Biber (1988), whose factor analysis study found that fiction tended to have a high frequency of third-person personal pronouns. This is true in our corpus; third-person pronouns occur 57.7% more in the fiction as opposed to the non-fiction texts (16.9 vs 10.7 occurrences per 100 words). But even when we count ignoring third-person pronouns, we found a greater density of mentions per cluster for literature than for news (4.0 vs 3.3, $p = 0.015$). The result that literature seems to have more to say about each entity thus extends and explains Biber's finding that literature has more third-person pronouns.

While our results are suggestive, they remain preliminary. A more detailed follow-up will need to look at the specific realization of the mentions and the kind of local coherence relations that link them (Althaus et al. 2004, Poesio et al. 2004, Barzilay and Lapata 2008, Elsner and Charniak 2008), and to investigate the different aspects of referential chains with larger corpora and more varying genres.

3. MT Success at Conveying Cohesion

To evaluate the impact of this difference in expressed cohesion on machine translation systems, we compared coreference output between human and machine translations of literary and informative texts from Chinese. For this task we chose a small dataset of sixteen short stories in Chinese by the early 20th-century author Lu Xun (鲁迅) and their corresponding English translations by Gladys Yang. We chose Lu Xun for his prominence as the "father of modern Chinese literature" and vernacular style, and because Yang's English translations are widely accepted as being of high quality by the literary community. For comparison to news text, we chose a series of six long-form articles from the magazine *Sinorama* and their corresponding English reference translations in the LDC's "Chinese English News Magazine Parallel Text" corpus (LDC2005T10). These magazine texts were chosen because the brief newswire texts often used in MT evaluation are too short to allow for meaningful textual-level comparisons of this sort. Thus our corpus contained 16 human-translated short stories with 90,712 words, 16 machine-translated short stories with 82,475 words, 6 human-translated magazine articles with 45,310 words, and 6 machine-translated magazine articles with 39,743 words, for a total size of 44 documents and 258,240 words.

We used Google Translate as our MT translation engine, first because the large web-based resources behind that system might help to mitigate the inevitable complication of domain specificity in the training data, and second because of its social position internationally as the most likely way average readers might encounter machine translation.

We first used Google Translate to produce machine translations of both the literary and magazine texts, and then used the Lee et al. (2011) coreference system in Stanford CoreNLP as described above to evaluate cohesion on both the human and machine English translations. As acknowledged in the prior section, automatic coreference is likely to introduce some amount of noise, but there is no reason to think that this noise would be biased in any particular direction for MT.

Results from the coreference analysis of the literary and magazine texts are shown in Table 2. The results in the two rows labeled "Human" substantiate our findings from the previous section. The human translations of the short stories have a significantly ($p = 0.003$) higher referential chain density (5.2) than the human translations of the magazine pieces (4.2). Translators, or at least Gladys Yang in these translations, seem to act similarly to source-text writers in creating more dense referential chains in literature than in non-fiction genres.

In order to study the success of machine translation in dealing with cohesion, we took the human translations as a gold standard in each case, using this translation to normalize the number of clusters and mentions to the length of the reference documents to address the length variance caused by the MT system.

	Clusters per 100 Tokens	Mentions per 100 Tokens	Density: Mentions per Cluster
Short Story			
Human	3.7	19.0	5.2
Machine	4.1	16.4	3.8
Magazine			
Human	3.9	16.0	4.2
Machine	3.9	14.0	3.7

Table 2. Cohesion as measured by coreference in human and machine translations of Lu Xun short stories and *Sinorama* magazine articles. The first two columns are normalized to the length of the human "gold" translations, and figures given are the overall average across all documents.

The results in Table 2 show little underclustering for the MT output. The number of clusters (entities) in the machine translations (4.1 and 3.9) do not differ from the human translations (3.7 and 3.9), ($p = 0.074$), although there is a trend toward underclustering for literature.

The main difference we see is in referential chain density (mentions per cluster). Whereas these experiments reconfirm the trend towards more mentions per cluster in literature than informative text, referential chains in the MT output do not differ between the two genres. The machine translation only captures 79.4% (13,846 vs. 17,438) of the human-translated mentions in the literary texts.

In the literary genre the automatic coreference system finds more than one additional mention per cluster in the human translations as compared to MT ($p < 0.001$), while in the magazine case the human and MT translations are the same, though there is a similar trend towards less dense referential chains in MT output ($p = 0.055$).

4. Examples and Discussion

It is worth first acknowledging the somewhat surprising ability of MT to maintain cohesion in both domains. The fact that a system operating almost exclusively on a sentence-by-sentence basis is able to maintain upwards of three-quarters of the mentions in the difficult and linguistically distant context of Chinese-to-English

MT is remarkable in and of itself, and speaks to the relative success of modern MT. There is, of course, no guarantee that these mentions found by the coreference system are in fact all the correct ones, so the true figure is likely somewhat lower, but a qualitative examination of the system's output shows that they are largely accurate.

What is actually causing the discrepancies in cohesion noted above as regards our two domains? Below we look at some specific cases of reduced cohesion in our results from the Lu Xun story "Flight to the Moon." In these examples the human translator was forced to rely on greater-than-sentence-level features of the text to effect an appropriately cohesive translation that the MT system was unable to convey.

Zero Anaphora

Zero anaphora is a well-documented and common linguistic phenomena in Chinese (Li and Thompson 1979, Huang 1989). Kim (2000) investigated subject drop in Chinese and English, finding that English overtly specifies subjects in 96% of cases, while the figure for Chinese is only 64%, and a significant amount of prior work has focused on the computational identification and resolution of zero anaphora in Chinese (see Yeh and Chen 2001, Converse 2006, Zhao and Ng 2007, Kong and Zhou 2010). The following example sentences demonstrate this difficulty.

Human Translation

When the big game was finished **they** ate wild boars, rabbits and pheasants. **He** was such a fine archer, **he** could shoot as much as **he** pleased.

Machine Translation

Later large animal shot down, ate wild boar, rabbit pheasant; shooting method and high strength, many as **you** want.

Original Chinese

后来大动物射完了，就吃野猪兔山鸡射法又高强，要多少有多少。

Figure 3. Reduced cohesion via zero anaphora in MT output. Relevant mentions are hand-annotated in bold.

In a qualitative analysis of our results, problems such as these were by far the most common cause of cohesion errors, and as the reader will notice, they often lead to an output that loses crucial elements for maintaining the cohesion of the narrative, such as in this case the distinction between the husband/wife couple, "they," and the husband individually, "he."

Inconsistent Reference

Having no process for maintaining consistency of reference to entities in the narrative, the following non-consecutive coreferencing sentences illustrate how in the MT version of the text the cohesiveness of the "hen" cluster in the original is lost.

Human Translation

-"Who are you? Why have you shot my best black laying **hen**?"
-"What! A **hen**?" he echoed nervously. "I thought **it** was a **wood pigeon**."
-"Imagine mistaking a **hen** for a **wood pigeon**!"
-"I am Yi." While saying this he saw that his arrow had pierced the **hen's** heart, killing it outright.
-"What about this **hen**?"
-"**She** was my best: **she** laid me an egg every day."
-"I'll give you these for your **hen**"

Machine Translation

-"Who are you what? How good black **hen** shot to the top of my house?"
-"Ah! **Chicken**? I only said a **wood pigeon partridge**," he said in dismay.
-"**hens** do not know, will be treated as the **wood pigeon partridge**"
-"I Yi Yi." He said, to see his shot arrows, is being consistently the heart of the **hen**, of course, died
-"**Chicken** how to do it?"
-"Lost my best **hen** every day to lay eggs."
-"they brought lost your **chicken**."

Original Chinese

-"你是谁哪？怎么把我家的顶好的黑母鸡射死了？"
-"阿呀！鸡么？我只道是一只鹁鸪。"他惶恐地说。

-"连母鸡也不认识，会当作鹁鸪！"
-"我就是夷羿。"他说着，看看自己所射的箭，是正贯了母鸡的心，当然死了
-"这鸡怎么办呢？"
-"这是我家最好的母鸡，天天生蛋。"
-"就拿来赔了你的鸡"

Figure 4. Reduced cohesion via inconsistent reference in MT output. Relevant mentions are hand-annotated in bold.

The reader will notice that in the original Chinese, *ji* (鸡, lit. "chicken") is used here as a shortened version of *muji* (母鸡, lit. "hen") in colloquial speech, which the human translator clearly notes and translates each mention consistently to maintain cohesion. Similarly, being that number is not explicitly marked in Chinese, the MT system translates *lian muji* (连母鸡, lit. "even hen") as "hens" instead of catching that here 母鸡 refers back to the entity being discussed.

De (的) Drops

It is common in Chinese for the noun head of a nominalization formed by the particle *de* (的) to be implicit, yet in many cases the human translator will add it for clarity and, presumably, to maintain cohesion.

Human Translation
"There are those who know **my name**."

Machine Translation
"Some people is one to know."

Original Chinese
"有 些 人 是 一 听 就 知道 的。"
Exist some people be one hear then know NOM

Figure 5. Reduced cohesion via *de* dropping in MT output. Relevant mentions are hand-annotated in bold.

This phenomenon reminds of translation theorist Mona Baker's (1996) concept of "explicitation": "an overall tendency to spell things out rather than leave them implicit in translation." Indeed, Olohan and Baker (2000) demonstrate this empirically using the Translational English Corpus, finding a strong tendency in translated texts to explicitly mark the "that"-connective following words such as "say," "tell," "promise," and so on where it could have been omitted.

5. Implications and Future Research

We found in two separate analyses that literary texts had more dense reference chains than informative texts. This result supports our hypothesis that literary texts are indeed more cohesive in general than informative texts; that is to say, the stylistic and narrative demands of literature lead to prose being more cohesively "about" its subjects than news. It remains to replicate this experiment on a large, carefully sampled cross-genre corpus to confirm these preliminary findings, perhaps integrating a more complex measure of cohesion as in Barzilay and Lapata (2008).

We also found that MT systems had difficulty in conveying the cohesion in literary texts. Of course these results are preliminary and may be confounded by the nature of the training data used by modern MT systems. The uses of Google Translate as an MT system and longer-form magazine articles as our informative texts were aimed at mitigating these concerns to some extent, but for now these results primarily serve as indicative of the need for further research in this area.

Cohesion, as well, is only one of the seven "standards of textuality" put forth by Beaugrande and Dressler (1981) and taken up by Hatim and Mason (1997) in the translation context. Some of these have an existing literature addressing their computational identification and analysis (eg. Morris and Hirst 1991), in which cases we might apply existing methods to identify genre effects in literary text. For others, such as situationality, it remains to investigate appropriate computational analogues for large-scale automatic analysis and application to literary text. Studies addressing relevant textual-level concerns in literature show increasing promise, such as Elson et al. (2010)'s work in automatically extracting social networks from fiction.

Once these sorts of genre effects in literature are more clearly understood, they can be addressed on a large scale for comparisons between machine- and human-translated literary texts in the manner carried out in this paper, in order to identify further potential stumbling blocks for machine translation on the textual level as regards literary texts. Our preliminary work as presented here suggests, at the very least, the potential value and necessity of such analyses if we are to make progress towards a true literary machine translation.

Acknowledgements

Thanks to Heeyoung Lee for help with the coreference system, three anonymous reviewers for their careful reading and helpful comments, and the U.S. Department of Education for the Foreign Language and Area Studies grant that helped fund this research.

References

Althaus, Ernst, Nikiforos Karamanis, and Alexander Koller. 2004. Computing locallycoherent discourses. In *ACL.*

Baker, Mona. 1996. Corpus-based translation studies: The challenges that lie ahead. In *Terminology, LSP and Translation: Studies in language engineering.* John Benjamins, Amsterdam.

Barzilay, Regina and Mirella Lapata. 2008. Modeling Local Coherence: An Entity-based Approach. *Computational Linguistics*, 34(1).

Beaugrande, Robert and Wolfgang Dressler. 1981. *Introduction to Text Linguistics.* Longman, London.

Bengston, E. and Dan Roth. 2008. Understanding the value of features for coreference resolution. In *EMNLP.*

Biber, Douglas. 1988. *Variation across speech and writing.* Cambridge University Press, Cambridge.

Chapman, Raymond. 1973. *Linguistics and Literature*. Edward Arnold, London.

Converse, Susan. 2006. *Pronominal anaphora resolution for Chinese.* Ph.D. thesis.

Elsner, Micha and Eugene Charniak. 2008. Coreference-inspired Coherence Modeling. In *Proceedings of ACL 2008.*

Elson, David, Nicholas Dames, and Kathleen McKeown. 2010. Extracting social networks from literary fiction. In *ACL.*

Grosz, Barbara, Aravind K. Joshi, and Scott Weinstein. 1995. Centering: A framework for modeling the local coherence of discourse. *Computational Linguistics*, 21(2).

Haghighi, Aria and Dan Klein. 2009. Simple coreference resolution with rich syntactic and semantic features. In *EMNLP.*

Haghighi, Aria and Dan Klein. 2010. Coreference resolution in a modular, entity-centered model. In *HLT-NAACL*.

Halliday, M. A. K. and Ruqaiya Hasan. 1976. *Cohesion in English.* Longman, London.

Hatim, Basil and Ian Mason. 1997. *The Translator as Communicator.* Routledge, London.

Huang, James C.-T. 1989. Pro drop in Chinese, a generalized control approach. In O, Jaeggli and K. Safir, editors, *The Null Subject Parameter.* D. Reidel Dordrecht.

Karamanis, Nikiforos, Massimo Poesio, Chris Mellish, and Jon Oberlander. 2004. Evaluating centering-based metrics of coherence for text structuring using a reliably annotated corpus. In *ACL.*

Kibble, Rodger and Richard Power. 2004. Optimizing Referential Coherence in Text Generation. *Computational Linguistics* 30(4).

Kim, Young-Joo. 2000. Subject/object drop in the acquisition of Korean: A cross-linguistic comparison. *Journal of East Asian Linguistics*, 9(4).

Kong, Fang and Guodong Zhou, 2010. A Tree Kernel-based Unified Framework for Chinese Zero Anaphora Resolution. In *EMNLP.*

Lee, Heeyoung, Yves Peirsman, Angel Chang, Nathanael Chambers, Mihai Surdeanu, Dan Jurafsky. Stanford's Multi-Pass Sieve Coreference Resolution System at the CoNLL-2011 Shared Task. 2011. In *Proceedings of the CoNLL-2011 Shared Task.*

Li, Charles and Sandra Thompson. 1979. Third-person pronouns and zero-anaphora in Chinese discourse. *Syntax and Semantics*, 12:311-335.

Ma, Xiaoyi. 2005. Chinese English News Magazine Parallel Text. LDC2005T10.

Mani, Inderjeet, Barbara Gates, and Eric Bloedorn. 1998. Using Cohesion and Coherence Models for Text Summarization. In *AAAI.*

Marcu, Daniel. 2000. *The Theory and Practice of Discourse Parsing and Summarization.* MIT Press, Cambridge, MA.

Morris, Jane and Graeme Hirst. 1991. Lexical Cohesion Computed by Thesaural Relations as an Indicator of the Structure of Text. *Computational Linguistics,* 17(1).

Nida, Eugene. 1964. *Towards a Science of Translating.* Brill, Leiden.

Olohan, Maeve and Mona Baker. 2000. Reporting *that* in translated English: Evidence for subconscious processes of explicitation? *Across Languages and Cultures* 1.

Poesio, Massimo, Rosemary Stevenson, Barbara di Eugenio, and Janet Hitzeman, 2004. Centering: A Parametric theory and its instantiations. *Computational Linguistics*, 30(3).

Pradhan, Sameer, Lance Ramshaw, Mitchell Marcus, Martha Palmer, Ralph Weischedel, and Nianwen Xue. 2011. CoNLL-2011 Shared Task: Modeling Unrestricted Coreference in OntoNotes. In *CoNLL.*

Rahman, Altaf and Vincent Ng. 2011. Coreference resolution with world knowledge. In *ACL*.

Slocum, Jonathan. 1985. A Survey of Machine Translation: its History, Current Status, and Future Prospects. *Computational Linguistics*, 11(1).

Zhao, Shanheng and Hwee Tou Ng. 2007. Identification and Resolution of Chinese Zero Pronouns: A Machine Learning Approach. In *Proceedings of EMNLP CoNLL Joint Conference.*

Unsupervised Stylistic Segmentation of Poetry with Change Curves and Extrinsic Features

Julian Brooke
Dept of Computer Science
University of Toronto
jbrooke@cs.toronto.edu

Adam Hammond
Dept of English
University of Toronto
adam.hammond@utoronto.ca

Graeme Hirst
Dept of Computer Science
University of Toronto
gh@cs.toronto.edu

Abstract

The identification of stylistic inconsistency is a challenging task relevant to a number of genres, including literature. In this work, we carry out stylistic segmentation of a well-known poem, *The Waste Land* by T.S. Eliot, which is traditionally analyzed in terms of numerous voices which appear throughout the text. Our method, adapted from work in topic segmentation and plagiarism detection, predicts breaks based on a curve of stylistic change which combines information from a diverse set of features, most notably co-occurrence in larger corpora via reduced-dimensionality vectors. We show that this extrinsic information is more useful than (within-text) distributional features. We achieve well above baseline performance on both artificial mixed-style texts and *The Waste Land* itself.

1 Introduction

Most work in automated stylistic analysis operates at the level of a text, assuming that a text is stylistically homogeneous. However, there are a number of instances where that assumption is unwarranted. One example is documents collaboratively created by multiple authors, in which contributors may, either inadvertently or deliberately (e.g. Wikipedia vandalism), create text which fails to form a stylistically coherent whole. Similarly, stylistic inconsistency might also arise when one of the 'contributors' is actually not one of the purported authors of the work at all — that is, in cases of plagiarism. More-deliberate forms of stylistic dissonance include satire, which may first follow and then flout the stylistic norms of a genre, and much narrative literature, in which the author may give the speech or thought patterns of a particular character their own style distinct from that of the narrator. In this paper, we address this last source of heterogeneity in the context of the well-known poem *The Waste Land* by T.S. Eliot, which is often analyzed in terms of the distinct voices that appear throughout the text.

T.S. Eliot (1888–1965), recipient of the 1948 Nobel Prize for Literature, is among the most important twentieth-century writers in the English language. Though he worked in a variety of forms — he was a celebrated critic as well as a dramatist, receiving a Tony Award in 1950 — he is best remembered today for his poems, of which *The Waste Land* (1922) is among the most famous. The poem deals with themes of spiritual death and rebirth. It is notable for its disjunctive structure, its syncopated rhythms, its wide range of literary allusions, and its incorporation of numerous other languages. The poem is divided into five parts; in total it is 433 lines long, and contains 3533 tokens, not including the headings.

A prominent debate among scholars of *The Waste Land* concerns whether a single speaker's voice predominates in the poem (Bedient, 1986), or whether the poem should be regarded instead as dramatic or operatic in structure, composed of about twelve different voices independent of a single speaker (Cooper, 1987). Eliot himself, in his notes to *The Waste Land*, supports the latter view by referring to "characters" and "personage[s]" in the poem.

One of the poem's most distinctive voices is that of the woman who speaks at the end of its second section:

I can't help it, she said, pulling a long face,
It's them pills I took, to bring it off, she said
[158–159]

Her chatty tone and colloquial grammar and lexis distinguish her voice from many others in the poem, such as the formal and traditionally poetic voice of a narrator that recurs many times in the poem:

Above the antique mantel was displayed
As though a window gave upon the sylvan scene
The change of Philomel
[97–99]

While the stylistic contrasts between these and other voices are apparent to many readers, Eliot does not explicitly mark the transitions between them. The goal of the present work is to investigate whether computational stylistic analysis can identify the transition between one voice and the next.

Our unsupervised approach, informed by research in topic segmentation (Hearst, 1994) and intrinsic plagiarism detection (Stamatatos, 2009), is based on deriving a curve representing stylistic change, where the local maxima represent likely transition points. Notably, our curve represents an amalgamation of different stylistic metrics, including those that incorporate external (extrinsic) knowledge, e.g. vector representations based on larger corpus co-occurrence, which we show to be extremely useful. For development and initial testing we follow other work on stylistic inconsistency by using artificial (mixed) poems, but the our main evaluation is on *The Waste Land* itself. We believe that even when our segmentation disagrees with expert human judgment, it has the potential to inform future study of this literary work.

2 Related work

Poetry has been the subject of extensive computational analysis since the early days of literary and linguistic computing (e.g., Beatie 1967). Most of the research concerned either authorship attribution or analysis of metre, rhyme, and phonetic properties of the texts, but some work has studied the style, structure, and content of poems with the aim of better understanding their qualities as literary texts. Among research that, like the present paper, looks at variation with a single text, Simonton (1990) found quantitative changes in lexical diversity and semantic classes of imagery across the components of Shakespeare's sonnets, and demonstrated correlations between some of these measures and judgments of the "aesthetic success" of individual sonnets. Duggan (1973) developed statistical measures of formulaic style to determine whether the eleventh-century epic poem *Chanson de Ronald* manifests primarily an oral or a written style. Also related to our work, although it concerned a novel rather than a poem, is that of McKenna and Antonia (2001), who used principal component analysis of lexical frequency to discriminate different voices (dialogue, interior monologue, and narrative) and different narrative styles in sections of *Ulysses* by James Joyce.

More general work on identifying stylistic inconsistency includes that of Graham et al. (2005), who built artificial examples of style shift by concatenating Usenet postings by different authors. Feature sets for their neural network classifiers included standard textual features, frequencies of function words, punctuation and parts of speech, lexical entropy, and vocabulary richness. Guthrie (2008) presented some general methods for identifying stylistically anomalous segments using feature vector distance, and tested the effectiveness of his unsupervised method with a number of possible stylistic variations. He used features such as simple textual metrics (e.g. word and sentence length), readability measures, obscure vocabulary features, frequency rankings of function words (which were not found to be useful), and context analysis features from the General Inquirer dictionary. The most effective method ranked each segment according to the city-block distance of its feature vector to the feature vector of the textual complement (the union of all other segments in the text). Koppel et al. (2011) used a semi-supervised method to identify segments from two different books of the Bible artificially mixed into a single text. They first demonstrated that, in this context, preferred synonym use is a key stylistic feature that can serve as high-precision bootstrap for building a supervised SVM classifier on more general features (common words); they then used this classifier to provide an initial prediction for each verse and smooth the results over adjacent segments. The method crucially relied on properties of the King James Version translation of the text in order to identify synonym preferences.

The identification of stylistic inconsistency or heterogeneity has received particular attention as a component of intrinsic plagiarism detection — the task of "identify[ing] potential plagiarism by analyzing a document with respect to undeclared changes in writing style" (Stein et al., 2011). A typical approach is to move a sliding window over the text looking for areas that are outliers with respect to the style of the rest of the text, or which differ markedly from other regions in word or character-trigram frequencies (Oberreuter et al., 2011; Kestemont et al., 2011). In particular, Stamatatos (2009) used a window that compares, using a special distance function, a character trigram feature vector at various steps throughout the text, creating a style change function whose maxima indicate points of interest (potential plagarism).

Topic segmentation is a similar problem that has been quite well-explored. A common thread in this work is the importance of lexical cohesion, though a large number of competing models based on this concept have been proposed. One popular unsupervised approach is to identify the points in the text where a metric of lexical coherence is at a (local) minimum (Hearst, 1994; Galley et al., 2003). Malioutov and Barzilay (2006) also used a lexical coherence metric, but applied a graphical model where segmentations are graph cuts chosen to maximize coherence of sentences within a segment, and minimize coherence among sentences in different segments. Another class of approaches is based on a generative model of text, for instance HMMs (Blei and Moreno, 2001) and Bayesian topic modeling (Utiyama and Isahara, 2001; Eisenstein and Barzilay, 2008); in such approaches, the goal is to choose segment breaks that maximize the probability of generating the text, under the assumption that each segment has a different language model.

3 Stylistic change curves

Many popular text segmentation methods depend crucially on a reliable textual unit (often a sentence) which can be reliably classified or compared to others. But, for our purposes here, a sentence is both too small a unit — our stylistic metrics will be more accurate over larger spans — and not small enough — we do not want to limit our breaks to sentence boundaries. Generative models, which use a bag-of-words assumption, have a very different problem: in their standard form, they can capture *only* lexical cohesion, which is not the (primary) focus of stylistic analysis. In particular, we wish to segment using information that goes beyond the distribution of words in the text being segmented. The model for stylistic segmentation we propose here is related to the TextTiling technique of Hearst (1994) and the style change function of Stamatatos (2009), but our model is generalized so that it applies to any numeric metric (feature) that is defined over a span; importantly, style change curves represent the change of a set of very diverse features.

Our goal is to find the precise points in the text where a stylistic change (a voice switch) occurs. To do this, we calculate, for each token in the text, a measure of stylistic change which corresponds to the distance of feature vectors derived from a fixed-length span on either side of that point. That is, if $\mathbf{v}_{ij}$ represents a feature vector derived from the tokens between (inclusive) indices i and j, then the stylistic change at point c_i for a span (window) of size w is:

$$c_i = Dist(\mathbf{v}_{(i-w)(i-1)}, \mathbf{v}_{i(i+w-1)})$$

This function is not defined within w of the edge of the text, and we generally ignore the possibility of breaks within these (unreliable) spans. Possible distance metrics include cosine distance, euclidean distance, and city-block distance. In his study, Guthrie (2008) found best results with city-block distance, and that is what we will primarily use here. The feature vector can consist of any features that are defined over a span; one important step, however, is to normalize each feature (here, to a mean of 0 and a standard deviation of 1), so that different scaling of features does not result in particular features having an undue influence on the stylistic change metric. That is, if some feature is originally measured to be f_i in the span i to $i+w-1$, then its normalized version f'_i (included in $\mathbf{v}_{i(i+w-1)}$) is:

$$f'_i = \frac{f_i - \overline{f}}{\sigma_f}$$

The local maxima of c represent our best predictions for the stylistic breaks within a text. However, stylistic change curves are not well behaved; they may contain numerous spurious local maxima if a local maximum is defined simply as a higher value between two lower ones. We can narrow our definition, however, by requiring that the local maximum be maximal within some window w'. That is, our breakpoints are those points i where, for all points j in the span $x - w'$, $x + w'$, it is the case that $g_i > g_j$. As it happens, $w' = w/2$ is a fairly good choice for our purposes, creating spans no smaller than the smoothed window, though w' can be lowered to increase breaks, or increased to limit them. The absolute height of the curve at each local minimum offers a secondary way of ranking (and eliminating) potential breakpoints, if more precision is required; however, in our task here the breaks are fairly regular but often subtle, so focusing only on the largest stylistic shifts is not necessarily desirable.

4 Features

The set of features we explore for this task falls roughly into two categories: surface and extrinsic. The distinction is not entirely clear cut, but we wish to distinguish features that use the basic properties of the words or their PoS, which have traditionally been the focus of automated stylistic analysis, from features which rely heavily on external lexical information, for instance word sentiment and, in particular, vector space representations, which are more novel for this task.

4.1 Surface Features

Word length A common textual statistic in register and readability studies. Readability, in turn, has been used for plagiarism detection (Stein et al., 2011), and related metrics were consistently among the best for Guthrie (2008).

Syllable count Syllable count is reasonably good predictor of the difficulty of a vocabulary, and is used in some readability metrics.

Punctuation frequency The presence or absence of punctuation such as commas, colons, semicolons can be very good indicator of style. We also include periods, which offer a measure of sentence length.

Line breaks Our only poetry-specific feature; we count the number of times the end of a line appears in the span. More or fewer line breaks (that is, longer or shorter lines) can vary the rhythm of the text, and thus its overall feel.

Parts of speech Lexical categories can indicate, for instance, the degree of nominalization, which is a key stylistic variable (Biber, 1988). We collect statistics for the four main lexical categories (noun, verb, adjective, adverb) as well as prepositions, determiners, and proper nouns.

Pronouns We count the frequency of first-, second-, and third-person pronouns, which can indicate the interactiveness and narrative character of a text (Biber, 1988).

Verb tense Past tense is often preferred in narratives, whereas present tense can give a sense of immediacy.

Type-token ratio A standard measure of lexical diversity.

Lexical density Lexical density is the ratio of the count of tokens of the four substantive parts of speech to the count of all tokens.

Contextuality measure The contextuality measure of Heylighen and Dewaele (2002) is based on PoS tags (e.g. nouns decrease contextuality, while verbs increase it), and has been used to distinguish formality in collaboratively built encyclopedias (Emigh and Herring, 2005).

Dynamic In addition to the hand-picked features above, we test dynamically including words and character trigrams that are common in the text being analyzed, particularly those not evenly distributed throughout the text (we exclude punctuation). To measure the latter, we define *clumpiness* as the square root of the index of dispersion or variance-to-mean ratio (Cox and Lewis, 1966) of the (text-length) normalized differences between successive occurrences of a feature, including (importantly) the difference between the first index of the text and the first occurrence of the feature as well as the last occurrence and the last index; the measure varies between 0 and 1, with 0 indicating perfectly even distribution. We test with the top n features based on the ranking of the product of the feature's frequency in the text (*tf*) or product of the frequency and its clumpiness (*tf-cl*); this is similar to a *tf-idf* weight.

4.2 Extrinsic features

For those lexicons which include only lemmatized forms, the words are lemmatized before their values are retrieved.

Percent of words in Dale-Chall Word List A list of 3000 basic words that is used in the Dale-Chall Readability metric (Dale and Chall, 1995).

Average unigram count in 1T Corpus Another metric of whether a word is commonly used. We use the unigram counts in the 1T 5-gram Corpus (Brants and Franz, 2006). Here and below, if a word is not included it is given a zero.

Sentiment polarity The positive or negative stance of a span could be viewed as a stylistic variable. We test two lexicons, a hand-built lexicon for the SO-CAL sentiment analysis system which has shown superior performance in lexicon-based sentiment analysis (Taboada et al., 2011), and SentiWordNet (SWN), a high-coverage automatic lexicon built from WordNet (Baccianella et al., 2010). The polarity of each word over the span is averaged.

Sentiment extremity Both lexicons provide a measure of the degree to which a word is positive or negative. Instead of summing the sentiment scores, we sum their absolute values, to get a measure of how extreme (subjective) the span is.

Formality Average formality score, using a lexicon of formality (Brooke et al., 2010) built using latent semantic analysis (LSA) (Landauer and Dumais, 1997).

Dynamic General Inquirer The General Inquirer dictionary (Stone et al., 1966), which was used for stylistic inconsistency detection by Guthrie (2008), includes 182 content analysis tags, many of which are relevant to style; we remove the two polarity tags already part of the SO-CAL dictionary, and select others dynamically using our *tf-cl* metric.

LSA vector features Brooke et al. (2010) have posited that, in highly diverse register/genre corpora, the lowest dimensions of word vectors derived using LSA (or other dimensionality reduction techniques) often reflect stylistic concerns; they found that using the first 20 dimensions to build their formality lexicon provided the best results in a near-synonym evaluation. Early work by Biber (1988) in the Brown Corpus using a related technique (factor analysis) resulted in discovery of several identifiable dimensions of register. Here, we investigate using these LSA-derived vectors directly, with each of the first 20 dimensions corresponding to a separate feature. We test with vectors derived from the word-document matrix of the ICWSM 2009 blog dataset (Burton et al., 2009) which includes 1.3 billion tokens, and also from the BNC (Burnard, 2000), which is 100 million tokens. The length of the vector depends greatly on the frequency of the word; since this is being accounted for elsewhere, we normalize each vector to the unit circle.

5 Evaluation method

5.1 Metrics

To evaluate our method we apply standard topic segmentation metrics, comparing the segmentation boundaries to a gold standard reference. The measure P_k, proposed by Beeferman et al. (1997), uses a probe window equal to half the average length of a segment; the window slides over the text, and counts the number of instances where a unit (in our case, a token) at one edge of the window was predicted to be in the same segment (according to the reference) as a unit at the other edge, but in fact is not; or was predicted not to be in the same segment, but in fact is. This count is normalized by the total number of tests to get a score between 0 and 1, with 0 being a perfect score (the lower, the better). Pevzner and Hearst (2002) criticize this metric because it penalizes false positives and false negatives differently and sometimes fails to penalize false positives altogether; their metric, *WindowDiff* (WD), solves these problems by counting an error whenever there is a difference between the number of segments in the prediction as compared to the reference. Recent work in topic segmentation (Eisenstein and Barzilay, 2008) continues to use both metrics, so we also present both here.

During initial testing, we noted a fairly serious shortcoming with both these metrics: all else being equal, they will usually prefer a system which predicts fewer breaks; in fact, a system that predicts no breaks at all can score under 0.3 (a very competitive result both here and in topic segmentation), if the variation of the true segment size is reasonably high. This is problematic because we do not want to be trivially 'improving' simply by moving towards a model that is too cautious to guess anything at all. We therefore use a third metric, which we call BD (break difference), which sums all the distances, calculated as fractions of the entire text, between each true break and the nearest predicted break. This metric is also flawed, because it can be trivially made 0 (the best score) by guessing a break everywhere. However, the relative motion of the two kinds of metric provides insight into whether we are simply moving along a precision/recall curve, or actually improving overall segmentation.

5.2 Baselines

We compare our method to the following baselines:

Random selection We randomly select boundaries, using the same number of boundaries in the reference. We use the average over 50 runs.

Evenly spaced We put boundaries at equally spaced points in the text, using the same number of boundaries as the reference.

Random feature We use our stylistic change curve method with a single feature which is created by assigning a uniform random value to each token and averaging across the span. Again, we use the average score over 50 runs.

6 Experiments

6.1 Artificial poems

Our main interest is *The Waste Land*. It is, however, prudent to develop our method, i.e. conduct an initial investigation of our method, including parameters and features, using a separate corpus. We do this by building artificial mixed-style poems by combining stylistically distinct poems from different authors, as others have done with prose.

6.1.1 Setup

Our set of twelve poems used for this evaluation was selected by one of the authors (an English literature expert) to reflect the stylistic range and influences of poetry at the beginning of the twentieth century, and *The Waste Land* in particular. The titles were removed, and each poem was tagged by an automatic PoS tagger (Schmid, 1995). Koppel et al. built their composite version of two books of the Bible by choosing, at each step, a random span length (from a uniform distribution) to include from one of the two books being mixed, and then a span from the other, until all the text in both books had been included. Our method is similar, except that we first randomly select six poems to include in the particular mixed text, and at each step we randomly select one of poems, reselecting if the poem has been used up or the remaining length is below our lower bound. For our first experiment, we set a lower bound of 100 tokens and an upper bound of 200 tokens for each span; although this gives a higher average span length than that of *The Waste Land*, our first goal is to test whether our method works in the (ideal) condition where the feature vectors at the breakpoint generally represent spans which are purely one poem or another for a reasonably high w (100). We create 50 texts using this method. In addition to testing each individual feature, we test several combinations of features (all features, all surface features, all extrinsic features), and present the best results for greedy feature removal, starting with all features (excluding dynamic ones) and choosing features to remove which minimize the sum of the three metrics.

6.1.2 Results

The Feature Sets section of Table 1 gives the individual feature results for segmentation of the artificially-combined poems. Using any of the features alone is better than our baselines, though some of the metrics (in particular type-token ratio) are only a slight improvement. Line breaks are obviously quite useful in the context of poetry (though the WD score is high, suggesting a precision/recall trade-off), but so are more typical stylistic features such as the distribution of basic lexical categories and punctuation. The unigram count and formality score are otherwise the best two individual features. The sentiment-based features did more modestly, though the extremeness of polarity was useful when paired with the coverage of SentiWordNet. Among the larger feature sets, the GI was the least useful, though more effective than any of the

Table 1: Segmentation accuracy in artificial poems

Configuration	**Metrics**		
	WD	P_k	BD
Baselines			
Random breaks	0.532	0.465	0.465
Even spread	0.498	0.490	0.238
Random feature	0.507	0.494	0.212
Feature sets			
Word length	0.418	0.405	0.185
Syllable length	0.431	0.419	0.194
Punctuation	0.412	0.401	0.183
Line breaks	0.390	0.377	0.200
Lexical category	0.414	0.402	0.177
Pronouns	0.444	0.432	0.213
Verb tense	0.444	0.433	0.202
Lexical density	0.445	0.433	0.192
Contextuality	0.462	0.450	0.202
Type-Token ratio	0.494	0.481	0.204
Dynamic (*tf*, *n*=50)	0.399	0.386	0.161
Dynamic (*tf-cl*, 50)	0.385	0.373	0.168
Dynamic (*tf-cl*, 500)	0.337	0.323	0.165
Dynamic (*tf-cl*, 1000)	0.344	0.333	0.199
Dale-Chall	0.483	0.471	0.202
Count in 1T	0.424	0.414	0.193
Polarity (SO-CAL)	0.466	0.487	0.209
Polarity (SWN)	0.490	0.478	0.221
Extremity (SO-CAL)	0.450	0.438	0.199
Extremity (SWN)	0.426	0.415	0.182
Formality	0.409	0.397	0.184
All LSA (ICWSM)	0.319	0.307	0.134
All LSA (BNC)	0.364	0.352	0.159
GI (*tf*, *n*=5)	0.486	0.472	0.201
GI (*tf-cl*, 5)	0.449	0.438	0.196
GI (*tf-cl*, 50)	0.384	0.373	0.164
GI (*tf-cl*, 100)	0.388	0.376	0.163
Combinations			
Surface	0.316	0.304	0.150
Extrinsic	0.314	0.301	0.124
All	0.285	0.274	0.128
All w/o GI, dynamic	0.272	0.259	0.102
All greedy (Best)	**0.253**	**0.242**	**0.099**
Best, *w*=150	0.289	0.289	0.158
Best, *w*=50	0.338	0.321	0.109
Best, Diff=euclidean	0.258	0.247	0.102
Best, Diff=cosine	0.274	0.263	0.145

individual features, while dynamic word and character trigrams did better, and the ICWSM LSA vectors better still; the difference in size between the ICWSM and BNC is obviously key to the performance difference here. In general using our *tf-cl* metric was better than *tf* alone.

When we combine the different feature types, we see that extrinsic features have a slight edge over the surface features, but the two do complement each other to some degree. Although the GI and dynamic feature sets do well individually, they do not combine well with other features in this unsupervised setting, and our best results do not include them. The greedy feature selector removed 4 LSA dimensions, type-token ratio, prepositions, second-person pronouns, adverbs, and verbs to get our best result. Our choice of *w* to be the largest fully-reliable size (100) seems to be a good one, as is our use of city-block distance rather than the alternatives. Overall, the metrics we are using for evaluation suggest that we are roughly halfway to perfect segmentation.

6.2 *The Waste Land*

6.2.1 Setup

In order to evaluate our method on *The Waste Land*, we first created a gold standard voice switch segmentation. Our gold standard represents an amalgamation, by one of the authors, of several sources of information. First, we enlisted a class of 140 undergraduates in an English literature course to segment the poem into voices based on their own intuitions, and we created a combined student version based on majority judgment. Second, our English literature expert listened to the 6 readings of the poem included on *The Waste Land* app (Touch Press LLP, 2011), including two readings by T.S. Eliot, and noted places where the reader's voice seemed to change; these were combined to create a reader version. Finally, our expert amalgamated these two versions and incorporated insights from independent literary analysis to create a final gold standard.

We created two versions of the poem for evaluation: for both versions, we removed everything but the main body of the text (i.e. the prologue, dedication, title, and section titles), since these are not produced by voices in the poem. The 'full' version contains all the other text (a total of 68 voice switches), but our 'abridged' version involves removing all segments (and the corresponding voice switches, when appropriate) which are 20 or fewer tokens in length and/or which are in a language other than English, which reduces the number of voice switches to 28 (the token count is 3179). This version allows us to focus on the segmentation for which our method has a reasonable chance of succeeding and ignore the segmentation of non-English spans, which is relatively trivial but yet potentially confounding. We use $w = 50$ for the full version, since there are almost twice as many breaks as in the abridged version (and our artificially generated texts).

6.2.2 Results

Our results for *The Waste Land* are presented in Table 2. Notably, in this evaluation, we do not investigate the usefulness of individual features or attempt to fully optimize our solution using this text. Our goal is to see if a general stylistic segmentation system, developed on artificial texts, can be applied successfully to the task of segmenting an actual stylistically diverse poem. The answer is yes. Although the task is clearly more difficult, the results for the system are well above the baseline, particularly for the abridged version. One thing to note is that using the features greedily selected for the artificial system (instead of just all features) appears to hinder, rather than help; this suggests a supervised approach might not be effective. The GI is too unreliable to be useful here, whereas the dynamic word and trigram features continue to do fairly well, but they do not improve the performance of the rest of the features combined. Once again the LSA features seem to play a central role in this success. We manually compared predicted with real switches and found that there were several instances (corresponding to very clear voices switches in the text) which were nearly perfect. Moreover, the model did tend to predict more switches in sections with numerous real switches, though these predictions were often fewer than the gold standard and out of sync (because the sampling windows never consisted of a pure style).

Table 2: Segmentation accuracy in *The Waste Land*

Configuration	**Metrics**		
	WD	P_k	BD
Full text			
Baselines			
Random breaks	0.517	0.459	0.480
Even spread	0.559	0.498	0.245
Random feature	0.529	0.478	0.314
System (w=50)			
Table 1 Best	0.458	0.401	0.264
GI	0.508	0.462	0.339
Dynamic	0.467	0.397	0.257
LSA (ICWSM)	0.462	0.399	0.280
All w/o GI	**0.448**	0.395	0.305
All w/o dynamic, GI	0.456	**0.394**	**0.228**
Abridged text			
Baselines			
Random breaks	0.524	0.478	0.448
Even spread	0.573	0.549	0.266
Random feature	0.525	0.505	0.298
System (w=100)			
Table 1 Best	0.370	0.341	0.250
GI	0.510	0.492	0.353
Dynamic	0.415	0.393	0.274
LSA (ICWSM)	0.411	0.390	0.272
All w/o GI	0.379	0.354	0.241
All w/o dynamic, GI	**0.345**	**0.311**	**0.208**

7 Conclusion

In this paper we have presented a system for automatically segmenting stylistically inconsistent text and applied it to *The Waste Land*, a well-known poem in which stylistic variation, in the form of different 'voices', provides an interesting challenge to both human and computer readers. Our unsupervised model is based on a stylistic change curve derived from feature vectors. Perhaps our most interesting result is the usefulness of low-dimension LSA vectors over surface features such as words and trigram characters as well as other extrinsic features such as the GI dictionary. In both *The Waste Land* and our development set of artificially combined poems, our method performs well above baseline. Our system could probably benefit from the inclusion of machine learning, but our main interest going forward is the inclusion of additional features — in particular, poetry-specific elements such as alliteration and other more complex lexicogrammatical features.

Acknowledgments

This work was financially supported by the Natural Sciences and Engineering Research Council of Canada.

References

Stefano Baccianella, Andrea Esuli, and Fabrizio Sebastiani. 2010. SentiWordNet 3.0: An enhanced lexical resource for sentiment analysis and opinion mining. In *Proceedings of the 7th conference on International Language Resources and Evaluation (LREC'10)*, Valletta, Malta, May.

Bruce A. Beatie. 1967. Computer study of medieval German poetry: A conference report. *Computers and the Humanities*, 2(2):65–70.

Calvin Bedient. 1986. *He Do the Police in Different Voices: The Waste Land and its protagonist*. University of Chicago Press.

Doug Beeferman, Adam Berger, and John Lafferty. 1997. Text segmentation using exponential models. In *In Proceedings of the Second Conference on Empirical Methods in Natural Language Processing (EMNLP '97)*, pages 35–46.

Douglas Biber. 1988. *Variation Across Speech and Writing*. Cambridge University Press.

David M. Blei and Pedro J. Moreno. 2001. Topic segmentation with an aspect hidden Markov model. In *Proceedings of the 24th annual international ACM SIGIR conference on Research and Development in Information Retrieval*, SIGIR '01, pages 343–348.

Thorsten Brants and Alex Franz. 2006. *Web 1T 5-gram Corpus Version 1.1*. Google Inc.

Julian Brooke, Tong Wang, and Graeme Hirst. 2010. Automatic acquisition of lexical formality. In *Proceedings of the 23rd International Conference on Computational Linguistics (COLING '10)*.

Lou Burnard. 2000. User reference guide for British National Corpus. Technical report, Oxford University.

Kevin Burton, Akshay Java, and Ian Soboroff. 2009. The ICWSM 2009 Spinn3r Dataset. In *Proceedings of the Third Annual Conference on Weblogs and Social Media (ICWSM 2009)*, San Jose, CA.

John Xiros Cooper. 1987. *T.S. Eliot and the politics of voice: The argument of The Waste Land*. UMI Research Press, Ann Arbor, Mich.

David R. Cox and Peter A.W. Lewis. 1966. *The Statistical Analysis of Series of Events*. Monographs on Statistics and Applied Probability. Chapman and Hall.

Edgar Dale and Jeanne Chall. 1995. *Readability Revisited: The New Dale-Chall Readability Formula*. Brookline Books, Cambridge, MA.

Joseph J. Duggan. 1973. *The Song of Roland: Formulaic style and poetic craft*. University of California Press.

Jacob Eisenstein and Regina Barzilay. 2008. Bayesian unsupervised topic segmentation. In *Proceedings of the Conference on Empirical Methods in Natural Language Processing (EMNLP '08*, EMNLP '08, pages 334–343.

William Emigh and Susan C. Herring. 2005. Collaborative authoring on the web: A genre analysis of online encyclopedias. In *Proceedings of the 38th Annual Hawaii International Conference on System Sciences (HICSS '05)*, Washington, DC.

Michel Galley, Kathleen McKeown, Eric Fosler-Lussier, and Hongyan Jing. 2003. Discourse segmentation of multi-party conversation. In *Proceedings of the 41st Annual Meeting of the Association for Computational Linguistics (ACL '03)*, ACL '03, pages 562–569.

Neil Graham, Graeme Hirst, and Bhaskara Marthi. 2005. Segmenting documents by stylistic character. *Natural Language Engineering*, 11(4):397–415.

David Guthrie. 2008. *Unsupervised Detection of Anomalous Text*. Ph.D. thesis, University of Sheffield.

Marti A. Hearst. 1994. Multi-paragraph segmentation of expository text. In *Proceedings of the 32nd Annual Meeting of the Association for Computational Linguistics (ACL '94)*, ACL '94, pages 9–16.

Francis Heylighen and Jean-Marc Dewaele. 2002. Variation in the contextuality of language: An empirical measure. *Foundations of Science*, 7(3):293–340.

Mike Kestemont, Kim Luyckx, and Walter Daelemans. 2011. Intrinsic plagiarism detection using character trigram distance scores. In *Proceedings of the PAN 2011 Lab: Uncovering Plagiarism, Authorship, and Social Software Misuse*.

Moshe Koppel, Navot Akiva, Idan Dershowitz, and Nachum Dershowitz. 2011. Unsupervised decomposition of a document into authorial components. In *Proceedings of the 49th Annual Meeting of the Association for Computational Linguistics (ACL '11)*.

Thomas K. Landauer and Susan Dumais. 1997. A solution to Plato's problem: The latent semantic analysis theory of the acquisition, induction, and representation of knowledge. *Psychological Review*, 104:211–240.

Igor Malioutov and Regina Barzilay. 2006. Minimum cut model for spoken lecture segmentation. In *Proceedings of the 44th Annual Meeting of the Association for Computational Linguistics (ACL '06)*, pages 25–32.

C. W. F. McKenna and A. Antonia. 2001. The statistical analysis of style: Reflections on form, meaning, and ideology in the 'Nausicaa' episode of *Ulysses*. *Literary and Linguistic Computing*, 16(4):353–373.

Gabriel Oberreuter, Gaston L'Huillier, Sebastián A. Ríos, and Juan D. Velásquez. 2011. Approaches for intrinsic and external plagiarism detection. In *Proceedings of the PAN 2011 Lab: Uncovering Plagiarism, Authorship, and Social Software Misuse*.

Lev Pevzner and Marti A. Hearst. 2002. A critique and improvement of an evaluation metric for text segmentation. *Computational Linguistics*, 28:19–36, March.

Helmut Schmid. 1995. Improvements in part-of-speech tagging with an application to German. In *Proceedings of the ACL SIGDAT Workshop*, pages 47–50.

Dean Keith Simonton. 1990. Lexical choices and aesthetic success: A computer content analysis of 154 Shakespeare sonnets. *Computers and the Humanities*, 24(4):251–264.

Efstathios Stamatatos. 2009. Intrinsic plagiarism detection using character *n*-gram profiles. In *Proceedings of the SEPLN'09 Workshop on Uncovering Plagiarism, Authorship and, Social Software Misuse (PAN-09)*, pages 38–46. CEUR Workshop Proceedings, volume 502.

Benno Stein, Nedim Lipka, and Peter Prettenhofer. 2011. Intrinsic plagiarism analysis. *Language Resources and Evaluation*, 45(1):63–82.

Philip J. Stone, Dexter C. Dunphy, Marshall S. Smith, and Daniel M. Ogilivie. 1966. *The General Inquirer: A Computer Approach to Content Analysis*. MIT Press.

Maite Taboada, Julian Brooke, Milan Tofiloski, Kimberly Voll, and Manifred Stede. 2011. Lexicon-based methods for sentiment analysis. *Computational Linguistics*, 37(2):267–307.

Touch Press LLP. 2011. *The Waste Land* app. http://itunes.apple.com/ca/app/the-waste-land/id427434046?mt=8 .

Masao Utiyama and Hitoshi Isahara. 2001. A statistical model for domain-independent text segmentation. In *Proceedings of the 39th Annual Meeting of the Association for Computational Linguistics (ACL '01)*, pages 499–506.

Aligning Bilingual Literary Works: a Pilot Study

Qian Yu and **Aurélien Max** and **François Yvon**
LIMSI/CNRS and Univ. Paris Sud
rue John von Neumann F-91 403 Orsay, France
{fistname.lastname}@limsi.fr

Abstract

Electronic versions of literary works abound on the Internet and the rapid dissemination of electronic readers will make electronic books more and more common. It is often the case that literary works exist in more than one language, suggesting that, if properly aligned, they could be turned into useful resources for many practical applications, such as writing and language learning aids, translation studies, or data-based machine translation. To be of any use, these bilingual works need to be aligned as precisely as possible, a notoriously difficult task. In this paper, we revisit the problem of sentence alignment for literary works and explore the performance of a new, multi-pass, approach based on a combination of systems. Experiments conducted on excerpts of ten masterpieces of the French and English literature show that our approach significantly outperforms two open source tools.

1 Introduction

The alignment of *bitexts*, *i.e.* of pairs of texts assumed to be mutual translations, consists in finding correspondences between logical units in the input texts. The set of such correspondences is called an *alignment*. Depending on the logical units that are considered, various levels of granularity for the alignment are obtained. It is usual to align paragraphs, sentences, phrases or words (see (Wu, 2010; Tiedemann, 2011) for recent reviews). Alignments are used in many fields, ranging from Translation Studies and Computer Assisted Language Learning (CALL) to Multilingual Natural Language Processing (NLP) applications (Cross-Lingual Information Retrieval, Writing Aids for Translators, Multilingual Terminology Extraction and Machine Translation (MT)). For all these applications, sentence alignments have to be computed.

Sentence alignment is generally thought to be fairly easy and many efficient sentence alignment programs are freely available[1]. Such programs rely on two main assumptions: (i) the relative order of sentences is the same on the two sides of the bitext, and (ii) sentence parallelism can be identified using simple surface cues. Hypothesis (i) warrants efficient sentence alignment algorithms based on dynamic programming techniques. Regarding (ii), various surface similarity measures have been proposed: on the one hand, *length-based* measures (Gale and Church, 1991; Brown et al., 1991) rely on the fact that the translation of a short (resp. long) sentence is short (resp. long). On the other hand, *lexical matching* approaches (Kay and Röscheisen, 1993; Simard et al., 1993) identify sure anchor points for the alignment using bilingual dictionaries or surface similarities of word forms. Length-based approaches are fast but error-prone, while lexical matching approaches seem to deliver more reliable results. Most state-of-the-art approaches use both types of information (Langlais, 1998; Simard and Plamondon, 1998; Moore, 2002; Varga et al., 2005; Braune and Fraser, 2010).

In most applications, only high-confidence one-to-one sentence alignments are considered useful and kept for subsequent processing stages. Indeed, when the objective is to build subsentential align-

[1] See, for instance, the Uplug toolbox which integrates several sentence alignment tools in a unified framework: http://sourceforge.net/projects/uplug/

ments (at the level of words, terms or phrases), other types of mappings between sentences are deemed to be either insufficiently reliable or inappropriate. As it were, the one-to-one constraint is viewed as a proxy to literalness/compositionality of the translation and warrants the search of finer-grained alignments. However, for certain types of bitexts[2], such as literary texts, translation often departs from a straight sentence-by-sentence alignment and using such a constraint can discard a significant proportion of the bitext. For MT, this is just a regrettable waste of potentially useful training material (Uszkoreit et al., 2010), all the more so as parallel literary texts constitute a very large reservoir of parallel texts online. For other applications implying to mine, visualize or read the actual translations in their context (second language learning (Nerbonne, 2000; Kraif and Tutin, 2011), translators training, automatic translation checking (Macklovitch, 1994), etc.), the entire bitext has to be aligned. Furthermore, areas where the translation is only partial or approximative need to be identified precisely.

The work reported in this study aims to explore the quality of existing sentence alignment techniques for literary work and to explore the usability of a recently proposed multiple-pass approach, especially designed for recovering many-to-one pairings. In a nutshell, this approach uses sure one-to-one mappings detected in a first pass to train a discriminative sentence alignment system, which is then used to align the regions which remain problematic. Our experiments on the BAF corpus (Simard, 1998) and on a small literary corpus consisting of ten books show that this approach produces high quality alignments and also identifies the most problematic passages better than its competitors.

The rest of this paper is organized as follows: we first report the results of a pilot study aimed at aligning our corpus with existing alignment methods (Section 2). In Section 3, we briefly describe our two-pass method, including some recent improvements, and present experimental performance on the BAF corpus. Attempts to apply this technique to our larger literary corpus are reported and discussed in Section 4. We discuss further prospects and conclude in Section 5.

2 Book alignment with off-the-shelf tools

2.1 A small bilingual library

The corpus used in this study contains a random selection of ten books written mostly in the 19th and in the early 20th century: five are English classics translated into French, and five are French classics translated into English. These books and their translation are freely available[3] from sources such as the Gutenberg project[4] or wikisource[5], and are representative of the kinds of collections that can be easily collected from the Internet. These texts have been preprocessed and tokenized using in-house tools, yielding word and sentence counts in Table 1.

2.2 Baseline sentence alignments

2.2.1 Public domain tools

Baseline alignments are computed using two open-source sentence alignment packages, the sentence alignment tool of Moore (2002)[6], and Hunalign (Varga et al., 2005). These two tools were chosen as representative of the current state-of-the-art in sentence alignment. Moore's approach implements a two-pass, coarse-to-fine, strategy: a first pass, based on sentence length cues, computes a first alignment according to the principles of length-based approaches (Brown et al., 1991; Gale and Church, 1991). This alignment is used to train a simplified version of IBM model 1 (Brown et al., 1993), which provides the alignment system with lexical association scores; these scores are then used to refine the measure of association between sentences. This approach is primarily aimed at delivering high confidence, one-to-one, sentence alignments to be used as training material for data-intensive MT. Sentences that cannot be reliably aligned are discarded from the resulting alignment.

[2] Actual literary bitexts are not so easily found over the Internet, notably due to (i) issues related to variations in the source text and (ii) issues related to the variations, over time, of the very notion of what a translation should be like.

[3] Getting access to more recent books (or their translation) is problematic, due to copyright issues: literary works fall in the public domain 70 years after the death of their author.

[4] http://www.gutenberg.org

[5] http://wikisource.org

[6] http://research.microsoft.com/en-us/downloads/aafd5dcf-4dcc-49b2-8a22-f7055113e656/

		French side		English side	
		# sents	# words	# sents	# words
English books and their French translation					
Emma, J. Austen	EM	5,764	134,950	7,215	200,223
Jane Eyre, C. Brontë	JE	9,773	240,032	9,441	237,487
The last of the Mohicans, F. Cooper	LM	6,088	189,724	5,629	177,303
Lord Jim, J. Conrad	LJ	7962	175,876	7,685	162,498
Vanity fair, W. Thackeray	VF	14,534	395,702	12,769	372,027
French books and their English translation					
Les confessions, J.J. Rousseau	CO	9,572	324,597	8,308	318,658
5 semaines en ballon, J. Verne	5S	7,250	109,268	7,894	121,231
La faute de l'Abbé Mouret, E. Zola	AM	8,604	156,514	7,481	156,692
Les travailleurs de la mer, V. Hugo	TM	10,331	170,015	9,613	178,427
Du côté de chez Swann, M. Proust	SW	4,853	208,020	4,738	232,514
	Total	84,731	2,104,698	80,773	2,157,060

Table 1: A small bilingual library

Hunalign[7], with default settings, also implements a two-pass strategy which resembles the approach of Moore. Their main difference is that Hunalign also produces many-to-one and one-to-many alignment links, which are needed to ensure that all the input sentences appear in the final alignment.

Both systems also deliver confidence measures for the automatic alignment: a value between 0 and 1 for Moore's tool, which can be interpreted as a posterior probability; the values delivered by Hunalign are less easily understood, and range from -1 to some small positive real values (greater than 1).

2.2.2 Evaluation metrics

Sentence alignment tools are usually evaluated using standard recall [R] and precision [P] measures, combined in the F-measure [F], with respect to some manually defined gold alignment (Véronis and Langlais, 2000). These measures can be computed at various levels of granularity: the level of alignment links, of sentences, of words, and of characters. As gold references only specify alignment links, the other references are automatically derived in the most inclusive way. For instance, if the reference alignment links state that the pair of source sentences $\mathbf{f}_1$, $\mathbf{f}_2$ is aligned with target $\mathbf{e}$, the reference sentence alignment will contain both $(\mathbf{f}_1, \mathbf{e})$ and $(\mathbf{f}_2, \mathbf{e})$; likewise, the reference word alignment will contain all the possible word alignments between tokens in the source and the target side. For such metrics, missing the alignment of a large "block" of sentences gets a higher penalty than missing a small one; likewise, misaligning short sentences is less penalized than misaligning longer ones. As a side effect, all metrics, but the more severe one, *ignore null alignments*. Our results are therefore based on the link-level and sentence-level F-measure, to reflect the importance of correctly predicting unaligned sentences in our applicative scenario.

2.2.3 Results

Previous comparisons of these alignment tools on standard benchmarks have shown that both typically yield near state-of-the-art performance. For instance, experiments conducted using the literary subpart of the BAF corpus (Simard, 1998), consisting of a hand-checked alignment of the French novel *De la Terre à la Lune* (*From the Earth to the Moon*), by Jules Verne, with a slightly abridged translation available from the Gutenberg project[8], have yielded the results in Table 2 (Moore's system was used with its default parameters, Hunalign with the `--realign` option).

All in all, for this specific corpus, Moore's strategy delivers slightly better sentence alignments than

[7] ftp://ftp.mokk.bme.hu/Hunglish/src/hunalign; we have used the version that ships with Uplug.

[8] http://www.gutenberg.org/ebooks/83

	P	R	F	% 1-1 links
Alignment based metrics				
Hunalign	0.51	0.60	0.55	0.77
Moore	0.85	0.65	0.74	1.00
Sentence based metrics				
Hunalign	0.76	0.70	0.73	-
Moore	0.98	0.62	0.76	-

Table 2: Baseline alignment experiments

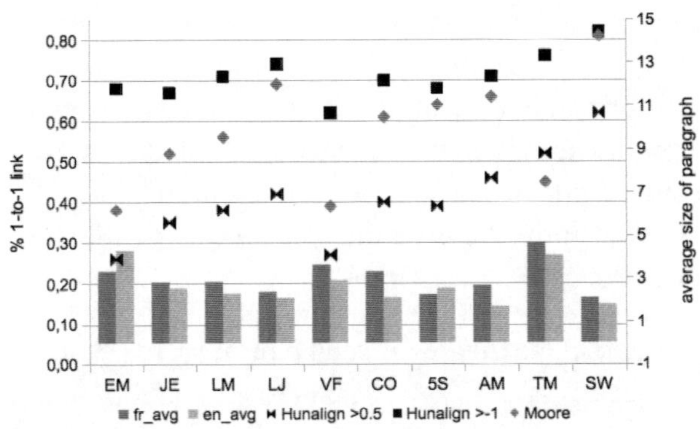

Figure 1: Percentage of one-to-one links and pseudo-paragraph size for various baselines

Hunalign does; in particular, it is able to identify 1-to-1 links with a very high precision.

2.3 Aligning a small library

In a first series of experiments, we simply run the two alignment tools on our small collection to see how much of it can be aligned with a reasonable confidence. The main results are reproduced in Figure 1, where we display both the number of 1-to-1 links extracted by the baselines (as dots on the Figure), as well as the average size of pseudo-paragraphs (see definition below) in French and English. As expected, less 1-to-1 links almost always imply larger blocks.

As expected, these texts turn out to be rather difficult to align: in the best case (*Swann's way* (SW)), only about 80% of the total sentences are aligned by Moore's system; in the more problematic cases (*Emma* (EM) and *Vanity Fair* (VF)), more than 50% of the book content is actually thrown away when one only looks at Moore's alignments. Hunalign's results look more positive, as a significantly larger number of one-to-one correspondences is found. Given that this system is overall less reliable than Moore's approach, it might be safe to filter these alignments and keep only the surer ones (here, keeping only links having a score greater than 0.5). The resulting number of sentences falls way below what is obtained by Moore's approach.

To conclude, both systems seem to have more difficulties with the literary material considered here than with other types of texts. In particular, the proportion of one-to-one links appears to be significantly smaller than what is typically reported for other genres; note, however, that even in the worst case, one-to-one links still account for about 50% of the text. Another finding is that the alignment scores which are output are not very useful: for Moore, filtering low scoring links has very little effect; for Hunalign, there is a sharp transition (around a threshold of 0.5): below this value, filtering has little effect; above this value, filtering is too drastic, as shown on Figure 1.

3 Learning sentence alignments

In this section, we outline the main principles of the approach developed in this study to improve the sentence alignments produced by our baseline tools, with the aim to salvage as many sentences as possible, which implies to come up with a way for better detecting many-to-one and one-to-many correspondences. Our starting point is the set of alignments delivered by Moore's tool. As discussed above, these alignments have a very high precision, at the expense of an unsatisfactory recall. Our sentence alignment method considers these sentence pairs as being parallel and uses them to train a binary classifier for detecting parallel sentences. Using the predictions of this tool, it then attempts to align the remaining portions of the bitext (see Figure 2).

In Figure 2, Moore's links are displayed with solid lines; these lines delineate parallel pseudo-paragraphs in the bitexts (appearing in boxed areas), which we will try to further decompose. Note that two configurations need to be distinguished: (i) one side of a paragraph is empty: no further analysis is performed and a 0-to-many alignment is output; (ii) both sides of a paragraph are non-empty and define a i-to-j alignment that will be processed by the block alignment algorithm described below.

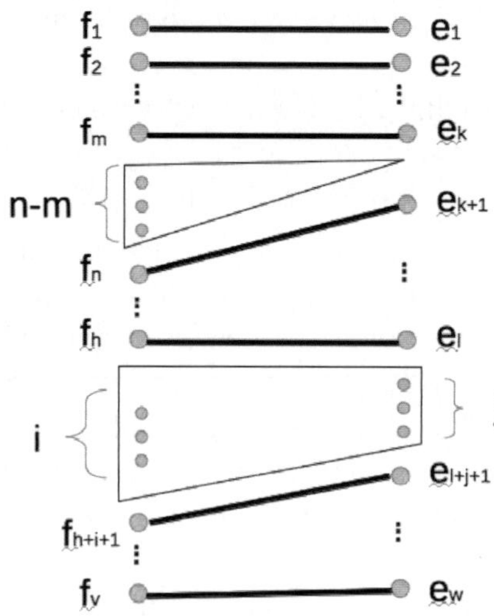

Figure 2: Filling alignment gaps

3.1 Detecting parallelism

Assuming the availability of a set of example parallel sentences, the first step of our approach consists in training a function for scoring candidate alignments. Following (Munteanu and Marcu, 2005), we train a Maximum Entropy classifier[9] (Rathnaparkhi, 1998); in principle, many other binary classifiers would be possible here. Our motivation for using a maxent approach was to obtain, for each possible pair of sentences (**f**,**e**), a link posterior probability $P(link|\mathbf{f}, \mathbf{e})$.

We take the sentence alignments of the first step as positive examples. Negative examples are artificially generated as follows: for all pairs of positive instances $(\mathbf{e}, \mathbf{f})$ and $(\mathbf{e}', \mathbf{f}')$ such that $\mathbf{e}'$ immediately follows $\mathbf{e}$, we select the pair $(\mathbf{e}, \mathbf{f}')$ as a negative example. This strategy produced a balanced corpus containing as many negative pairs as positive ones. However, this approach may give too much weight on the length ratio feature and it remains to be seen whether alternative approaches are more suitable.

Formally, the problem is thus to estimate a conditional model for deciding whether two sentences $\mathbf{e}$ and $\mathbf{f}$ should be aligned. Denoting Y the corresponding binary variable, this model has the following form:

$$P(Y = 1|\mathbf{e}, \mathbf{f}) = \frac{1}{1 + exp[-\sum_{k=1}^{K} \theta_k F_k(\mathbf{e}, \mathbf{f})]},$$

where $\{F_k(\mathbf{e}, \mathbf{f}), k = 1 \ldots K\}$ denotes a set of feature functions testing arbitrary properties of $\mathbf{e}$ and $\mathbf{f}$, and $\{\theta_k, k = 1 \ldots K\}$ is the corresponding set of parameter values.

Given a set of training sentence pairs, the optimal values of the parameters are set by optimizing numerically the conditional likelihood; optimization is performed here using L-BFGS (Liu and Nocedal, 1989); a Gaussian prior over the parameters is used to ensure numerical stability of the optimization.

In this study, we used the following set of feature functions:

- **lexical features**: for each pair of words[10] (e, f) occurring in $V_e \times V_f$, there is a corresponding feature $F_{e,f}$ which fires whenever $e \in \mathbf{e}$ and $f \in \mathbf{f}$.
- **length features**: denoting $l_{\mathbf{e}}$ (resp. $l_{\mathbf{f}}$) the length of the source (resp. target) sentence, measured in number of characters, we include features related to length ratio, defined as $F_r(\mathbf{e}, \mathbf{f}) = \frac{|l_{\mathbf{e}} - l_{\mathbf{f}}|}{max(l_{\mathbf{e}}, l_{\mathbf{f}})}$. Rather than taking the numerical value, we use a simple discretization scheme based on 6 bins.
- **cognate features**: we loosely define cognates[11] as words sharing a common prefix of length at least 3. This gives rise to 4 features, which are respectively activated when the number of cognates in the parallel sentence is 0, 1, 2, or greater than 2.
- **copy features**: an extreme case of similarity is when a word is copied verbatim from the source to the target. This happens with proper nouns, dates, etc. We again derive 4 features, depending on whether the number of identical words in **f** and **e** is 0, 1, 2 or greater than 2.

[9]Using the implementation available from http://homepages.inf.ed.ac.uk/lzhang10/maxent_toolkit.html.

[10]A word is an alphabetic string of characters, excluding punction marks.

[11]Cognates are words that share a similar spelling in two or more different languages, as a result of their similar meaning and/or common etymological origin, e.g. (English-Spanish): *history - historia*, *harmonious - armonioso*.

3.2 Filling alignment gaps

The third step uses the posterior alignment probabilities computed in the second step to fill the gaps in the first pass alignment. The algorithm can be glossed as follows. Assume a bitext block comprising the sentences from index i to j in the source side of the bitext, and from k to l in the target side such that sentences $\mathbf{e}_{i-1}$ (resp. $\mathbf{e}_{j+1}$) and $\mathbf{f}_{k-1}$ (resp. $\mathbf{e}_{l+1}$) are aligned[12].

The first case is when $j < i$ or $k > l$, in which case we create a null alignment for $f_{k:l}$ or for $e_{i:j}$. In all other situations, we compute:

$$\forall i', j', k', l', i \leq i' \leq j' \leq j, k \leq k' \leq l' \leq l,$$
$$a_{i',j',k',l'} = P(Y = 1|\mathbf{e}_{i':j'}, \mathbf{f}_{k':l'}) - \alpha S(i', j', k', l')$$

where $\mathbf{e}_{i':j'}$ is obtained by concatenation of all the sentences in the range $[i':j']$, and $S(i, j, k, l) = (j - i+1)(l-k+1)-1$ is proportional to the block size. The factor $\alpha S(i', j', k', l')$ aims at penalizing large blocks, which, for the sentence-based metrics, yield much more errors than the small ones. This strategy implies to compute $O(|j - i + 1|^2 \times |k - l + 1|^2)$ probabilities, which, given the typical size of these blocks (see above), can be performed very quickly.

These values are then iteratively visited by decreasing order in a greedy fashion. The top-scoring block $i' : j', k' : l'$ is retained in the final alignment; all overlapping blocks are subsequently deleted from the list and the next best entry is then considered. This process continues until all remaining blocks imply null alignments, in which case these $n - 0$ or $0 - n$ alignments are also included in our solution.

This process is illustrated in Figure 3: assuming that the best matching link is $\mathbf{f}_2$-$\mathbf{e}_2$, we delete all the links that include $\mathbf{f}_2$ or $\mathbf{e}_2$, as well as links that would imply a reordering of sentences, meaning that we also delete links such as $\mathbf{f}_1$-$\mathbf{e}_3$.

3.3 Experiments

In this section, we report the results of experiments run using again Jules Verne's book from the BAF corpus. Figures are reported in Table 3 where we contrast our approach with two simple baselines: (i) keep only Moore's links; (ii) complete Moore's links with one single many-to-many alignment for each block. For the maxent-based approach, we also report the precision on just those links that are not predicted by Moore. A more complete set of experiments conducted with other portions of the BAF are reported elsewhere (Yu et al., 2012) and have shown to deliver state-of-the-art results.

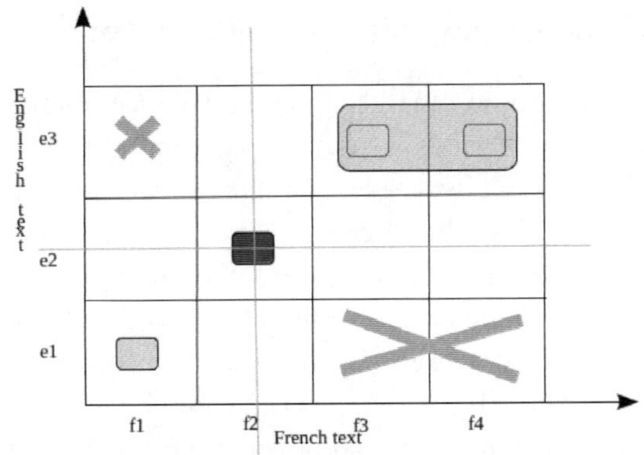

Figure 3: Greedy alignment search

	P		R	F
	(maxent)	(all)	(all)	(all)
link based				
Moore only	-	0.85	0.65	0.74
Moore+all links	-	0.78	0.75	0.76
Maxent, $\alpha = 0$	0.44	0.74	0.81	0.77
Maxent, $\alpha = 0.06$	0.42	0.72	0.82	0.77
sentence based				
Moore only	-	0.98	0.62	0.76
Moore+all links	-	0.61	0.88	0.72
Maxent, $\alpha = 0$	0.80	0.93	0.80	0.86
Maxent, $\alpha = 0.06$	0.91	0.97	0.79	0.87

Table 3: Performance of maxent-based alignments

As expected, complementing the very accurate prediction of Moore's systems with our links significantly boosts the sentence-based alignment performance: recall rises from 0.62 to 0.80 for $\alpha = 0$, which has a clear effect on the corresponding F-measure (from 0.76 to 0.86). The performance differences with the default strategy of keeping those blocks unsegmented are also very clear. Sentence-wise, maxent-based alignments are also quite precise, especially when the value of α is chosen with care (P=0.91 for α=0.06); however, this optimization has a very small overall effect, given that only a limited number of alignment links are actually computed by the maxent classifier.

[12] We enclose the source and target texts between begin and end markers to enforce alignment of the first and last sentences.

4 Sentence alignment in the real world

In this section, we analyze the performance obtained with our combined system, using excerpts of our small corpus as test set. For this experiment, the first two to three hundreds sentences in each book, corresponding to approximately two chapters, were manually aligned (by one annotator), using the same guidelines that were used for annotating the BAF corpus. Except for two books (EM and VF), producing these manual alignments was found to be quite straightforward. Results are in Table 4.

A first comment is that both baselines are significantly outperformed by our algorithm for almost all conditions and books. For several books (LM, AM, SW), the obtained sentence alignments are almost as precise as those predicted by Moore and have a much higher recall, resulting in very good overall alignments. The situation is, of course, much less satisfactory for other books (EM, VF, 5S). All in all, our method salvages many useful sentence pairs that would otherwise be left unaligned.

Moore's method remains remarkably accurate throughout the whole collection, even for the most difficult books. It also outputs a significant proportion of wrong links, which, for lack of reliable confidence estimators, are difficult to spot and contribute to introduce noise into the maxent training set.

The variation of performance can mostly be attributed to idiosyncrasies in the translation. For instance, *Emma* (EM) seems very difficult to align, which can be attributed to the use of an old translation dating back to 1910 (by P. de Puliga), and which often looks more like an adaptation than a translation. Some passages even question the possibility of producing any sensible (human) alignment between source and target[13]:

(en) *Her sister, though comparatively but little removed by matrimony, being settled in London, only sixteen miles off, was much beyond her daily reach; and many a long October and November evening must be struggled through at Hartfield, before Christmas brought the next visit from Isabella and her husband, and their little children, to fill the house, and give her pleasant society again.*

(fr) *La sœur d'Emma habitait Londres depuis son mariage, c'est-à-dire, en réalité, à peu de distance; elle se trouvait néanmoins hors de sa portée journalière, et bien des longues soirées d'automne devraient être passées solitairement à Hartfield avant que Noël n'amenât la visite d'Isabelle et de son mari.*

Les confessions (CO) is much most faithful to the content, yet, the translator has significantly departed from Rousseau's style[14], mostly made up of short sentences, and it is often the case that several French sentences align with one single English sentence, which is detrimental to Moore, and by ricochet, to the quality of maxent predictions. A typical excerpt:

(fr) *Pendant deux ans entiers je ne fus ni témoin ni victime d'un sentiment violent. Tout nourrissait dans mon coeur les dispositions qu'il reçut de la nature.*

(en) *Everything contributed to strengthen those propensities which nature had implanted in my breast, and during the two years I was neither the victim nor witness of any violent emotions.*

The same goes for Thackeray (VF), with a lot of restructurations of the sentences as demonstrated by the uneven number of sentences on both sides of the bitext. *Lord Jim* (LJ) poses another type of difficulty: approximately 100 sentences are missing on the French side, the rest of the text being fairly parallel (more than 82% of the reference links are actually 1-to-1). *Du côté de chez Swann* (SW) represents the other extreme of the spectrum, where the translation sticks as much as possible to the very peculiar style of Proust: nearly 90% of the reference alignments are 1-to-1, which explains the very good F-measure for this book.

It is difficult to analyze more precisely our errors; however, a fairly typical pattern is the inference of a 1-to-1 link rather than a 2-to-1 link made up of a short and a long sentence. An example from Hugo (TM), where our approach prefers to leave the second English sentence unaligned, even though the corresponding segment (*un enfant...*) is the in French sentence:

(fr) *Dans tout le tronçon de route qui sépare la première tour de la seconde tour, il n'y avait que trois passants, un enfant, un homme et une femme.*

(en) *Throughout that portion of the highway which separates the first from the second tower, only three foot-passengers could be seen. These were a child, a man, and a woman.*

A possible walk around for this problem would be to also add a penalty for null alignments.

[13] In this excerpt, in addition to several approximations, the end of the last sentence (*and their children...*) is not translated in French.

[14] Compare the number of sentences in Table 1.

				Moore				*Hunalign*		*Moore+maxent*				
				links	P	R	F	links	F	$S \neq 0$	$S = 0$	P	R	F
	fr	en	links	*link based*										
EM	160	217	164	84	0.76	0.39	0.52	173	0.43	72	10	0.52	0.53	0.52
JE	229	205	174	104	0.86	0.51	0.64	198	0.40	95	5	0.64	0.75	0.69
LM	232	205	197	153	0.97	0.76	0.85	203	0.63	64	2	0.79	0.87	0.83
LJ	580	682	515	403	0.94	0.73	0.82	616	0.60	155	15	0.82	0.81	0.76
VF	321	248	219	129	0.92	0.54	0.68	251	0.39	133	3	0.58	0.70	0.63
CO	326	236	213	104	0.86	0.42	0.56	256	0.28	135	3	0.62	0.70	0.66
5S	182	201	153	107	0.76	0.53	0.62	165	0.52	72	10	0.60	0.74	0.66
AM	258	226	222	179	1.00	0.81	0.90	222	0.71	55	0	0.88	0.93	0.90
TM	404	388	358	284	0.89	0.71	0.79	374	0.69	86	16	0.79	0.85	0.82
SW	492	495	463	431	0.94	0.87	0.90	474	0.80	59	9	0.85	0.92	0.88
	fr	en	links	*sentence based*										
EM	160	217	206	84	0.85	0.34	0.49	199	0.60	124	0	0.62	0.63	0.62
JE	229	205	270	104	0.92	0.36	0.52	235	0.60	125	0	0.90	0.76	0.82
LM	232	205	238	153	0.99	0.64	0.78	234	0.79	62	0	0.97	0.88	0.92
LJ	580	682	645	403	0.96	0.60	0.74	625	0.78	212	0	0.85	0.81	0.83
VF	321	248	363	129	0.98	0.35	0.52	318	0.62	163	0	0.88	0.71	0.79
CO	326	236	380	104	0.94	0.26	0.41	306	0.48	226	0	0.88	0.76	0.82
5S	182	201	260	107	0.98	0.40	0.57	224	0.70	81	0	0.93	0.67	0.78
AM	258	226	264	179	1.00	0.68	0.81	262	0.84	72	0	0.98	0.94	0.96
TM	404	388	445	284	0.96	0.61	0.75	418	0.82	134	0	0.93	0.87	0.90
SW	492	495	532	431	0.99	0.80	0.88	512	0.88	55	0	0.99	0.90	0.94

Table 4: Evaluating alignment systems on a sample of "real-world" books
For each book, we report the number of French and English test sentences, the number of reference links and standard performance measures. For the maxent approach, we also report separately the number of empty ($S = 0$) and non-empty ($S \neq 0$) paragraphs.

5 Conclusions and future work

In this paper, we have presented a novel two-pass approach aimed at improving existing sentence alignment methods in contexts where (i) all sentences need to be aligned and/or (ii) sentence alignment confidence need to be computed. By running experiments with several variants of this approach, we have been able to show that it was able to significantly improve the bare results obtained with the sole Moore alignment system. Our study shows that the problem of sentence alignment for literary texts is far from being solved and additional work is needed to obtain alignments that could be used in real applications, such as bilingual reading aids.

The maxent-based approach proposed here is thus only a first step, and we intend to explore various extensions: an obvious way to go is to use more resources (larger training corpora, bilingual dictionaries, etc.) and add more features, such as part-of-speech, lemmas, or alignment features as was done in (Munteanu and Marcu, 2005). We also plan to provide a much tighter integration with Moore's algorithm, which already computes such alignments, so as to avoid having to recompute them. Finally, the greedy approach to link selection can easily be replaced with an exact search based on dynamic programming techniques, including dependencies with the left and right alignment links.

Regarding applications, a next step will be to produce and evaluate sentence alignments for a much larger and more diverse set of books, comprising more than 100 novels, containing books in 7 languages (French, English, Spanish, Italian, German, Russian, Portuguese) from various origins. Most were collected on the Internet from Gutenberg, wikisource and GoogleBooks[15], and some were collected in the course of the Carmel project (Kraif et al., 2007). A number of these books are translated in more than one language, and some are raw OCR outputs and have not been cleaned from errors.

Acknowledgments

This work has been partly funded through the "Google Digital Humanities Award" program.

[15] http://books.google.com

References

Fabienne Braune and Alexander Fraser. 2010. Improved unsupervised sentence alignment for symmetrical and asymmetrical parallel corpora. In *Coling 2010: Posters*, pages 81–89, Beijing, China. Coling 2010 Organizing Committee.

Peter F. Brown, Jennifer C. Lai, and Robert L. Mercer. 1991. Aligning sentences in parallel corpora. In *Proceedings of the 29th annual meeting on Association for Computational Linguistics, 1991, Berkeley, California*, pages 169–176.

Peter F. Brown, Stephen A. Della Pietra, Vincent J. Della Pietra, and Robert L. Mercer. 1993. The mathematics of statistical machine translation: Parameter estimation. *Computational Linguistics*, 19(2):263–311.

William A. Gale and Kenneth W. Church. 1991. A program for aligning sentences in bilingual corpora. In *Proceedings of the 29th annual meeting of the Association for Computational Linguistics*, pages 177–184, Berkeley, California.

Martin Kay and Martin Röscheisen. 1993. Text-translation alignement. *Computational Linguistics*, 19(1):121–142.

Olivier Kraif and Agnès Tutin. 2011. Using a bilingual annotated corpus as a writing aid: An application for academic writing for efl users. In In Natalie Kübler (Ed.), editor, *Corpora, Language, Teaching, and Resources: From Theory to Practice. Selected papers from TaLC7, the 7th Conference of Teaching and Language Corpora*. Peter Lang, Bruxelles.

Olivier Kraif, Marc El-Bèze, Régis Meyer, and Claude Richard. 2007. Le corpus Carmel: un corpus multilingue de récits de voyages. In *Proceedings of Teaching and Language Corpora : TaLC'200*, Paris.

Philippe Langlais. 1998. A System to Align Complex Bilingual Corpora. Technical report, CTT, KTH, Stockholm, Sweden, Sept.

Dong C. Liu and Jorge Nocedal. 1989. On the limited memory BFGS method for large scale optimization. *Mathematical Programming*, 45:503–528.

Elliot Macklovitch. 1994. Using bi-textual alignment for translation validation: the TransCheck system. In *Proceedings of the First Conference of the Association for Machine Translation in the Americas (AMTA)*, pages 157–168, Columbia.

Robert C. Moore. 2002. Fast and accurate sentence alignment of bilingual corpora. In Stephen D. Richardson, editor, *Proceedings of the annual meeting of tha Association for Machine Translation in the Americas (AMTA'02)*, Lecture Notes in Computer Science 2499, pages 135–144, Tiburon, CA, USA. Springer Verlag.

Dragos Stefan Munteanu and Daniel Marcu. 2005. Improving machine translation performance by exploiting non-parallel corpora. *Computational Linguistics*, 31(4):477–504.

John Nerbonne, 2000. *Parallel Texts in Computer-Assisted Language Learning*, chapter 15, pages 354–369. Text Speech and Language Technology Series. Kluwer Academic Publishers.

Ardwait Rathnaparkhi. 1998. *Maximum Entropy Models for Natural Language Ambiguity Resolution*. Ph.D. thesis, University of Pennsylvania.

Michel Simard and Pierre Plamondon. 1998. Bilingual sentence alignment: Balancing robustness and accuracy. *Machine Translation*, 13(1):59–80.

Michel Simard, George F. Foster, and Pierre Isabelle. 1993. Using cognates to align sentences in bilingual corpora. In Ann Gawman, Evelyn Kidd, and Per-Åke Larson, editors, *Proceedings of the 1993 Conference of the Centre for Advanced Studies on Collaborative Research, October 24-28, 1993, Toronto, Ontario, Canada, 2 Volume*, pages 1071–1082.

Michel Simard. 1998. The BAF: a corpus of English-French bitext. In *First International Conference on Language Resources and Evaluation*, volume 1, pages 489–494, Granada, Spain.

Jörg Tiedemann. 2011. *Bitext Alignment*. Number 14 in Synthesis Lectures on Human Language Technologies, Graeme Hirst (ed). Morgan & Claypool Publishers.

Jakob Uszkoreit, Jay M. Ponte, Ashok C. Popat, and Moshe Dubiner. 2010. Large scale parallel document mining for machine translation. In *Proceedings of the 23rd International Conference on Computational Linguistics*, COLING '10, pages 1101–1109, Beijing, China.

Dániel Varga, László Németh, Péter Halácsy, András Kornai, Viktor Trón, and Viktor Nagy. 2005. Parallel corpora for medium density languages. In *Proceedings of RANLP 2005*, pages 590–596, Borovets, Bulgaria.

Jean Véronis and Philippe Langlais. 2000. Evaluation of Parallel Text Alignment Systems. In Jean Véronis, editor, *Parallel Text Processing*, Text Speech and Language Technology Series, chapter X, pages 369–388. Kluwer Academic Publishers.

Dekai Wu. 2010. Alignment. In Nitin Indurkhya and Fred Damerau, editors, *CRC Handbook of Natural Language Processing*, number 16, pages 367–408. CRC Press.

Qian Yu, Aurélien Max, and François Yvon. 2012. Revisiting sentence alignment algorithms for alignment visualization and evaluation. In *Proceedings of the Language Resource and Evaluation Conference (LREC)*, Istambul, Turkey.

Function Words for Chinese Authorship Attribution

Bei Yu
School of Information Studies
Syracuse University
byu@syr.edu

Abstract

This study explores the use of function words for authorship attribution in modern Chinese (C-FWAA). This study consists of three tasks: (1) examine the C-FWAA effectiveness in three genres: novel, essay, and blog; (2) compare the strength of function words as both genre and authorship indicators, and explore the genre interference on C-FWAA; (3) examine whether C-FWAA is sensitive to the time periods when the texts were written.

1 Introduction

Function words are an important feature set for Authorship Attribution (hereafter "AA") because they are considered *topic-independent* or *context-free*, and that they are largely used in an unconscious manner (Holmes, 1994; Stamatatos, 2009; Koppel et al., 2009). The *Federalist Papers* (Mostellar and Wallace, 1964) may be the most famous example of AA in English. Mostellar and Wallace (1964) conducted a detailed study of searching and testing function words to distinguish Hamilton and Madison as the authors of the disputed Federalist Papers.

Although Function Word based Authorship Attribution (hereafter "FWAA") has been successful in many studies (Stamatatos, 2009), Juola (2008) argued that FWAA are mainly applied in English texts, and it may not be appropriate for other highly inflected languages, like Finnish and Turkish. This may not be the case in that it is the content words, not the function words, that are inflected in those languages. However, function words are indeed rarely used for AA in non-English texts. It was left out in the comprehensive authorship analysis of *The Quiet Don* (in Russian) by Kjetsaa et al. (1984). The literature review for this study found several examples of FWAA in Modern Greek (Mikros and Argiri, 2003) and Arabic (Abbasi and Chen, 2005). Overall, the effectiveness of FWAA has not been tested on many languages.

Some studies on FWAA also reported negative results. Holmes (1994), in his comprehensive survey on authorship attribution, cited doubts given by (Damerau, 1975) and (Oakman, 1980), and called for further investigation on the stability of function word use within an author's work and between works by the same author.

Another problem for FWAA is to explain exactly what authorial characteristics are captured by function words, since function words may also characterize other textual properties like genre, author gender, and even topic, although function words are generally considered *topic-independent* or *context-free* (Stamatatos, 2009; Herring and Paolillo, 2006; Clement and Sharp 2003; Mikros and Argiri, 2007).

Clement and Sharp (2003) found that function words worked as well as content words in identifying document topics. Their further investigation showed that author and topic are not arbitrarily orthogonal to each other. Using the significance level of two-way ANOVA test as measure, Mikros and Argiri (2007) found that some function words in Modern Greek can distinguish both topic and author, providing further evidence for possible topic-author correlation based on function word dimensions.

Function words are also used as indicators for author gender (Argamon et al., 2002; Koppel et al., 2003) and text genre (Biber, 1993). Koppel et al. (2003) found gender preference on certain personal pronouns and prepositions. Herring and Paolillo (2006) repeated Argamon and Koppel's experiment by mixing genre and gender in the data set, and discovered that the same gender indicators actually captured genre characteristics.

In summary, related work has shown that function words may contribute to distinguishing topic, authorship, author gender, and genre. A question soon emerges: which dimension do function words characterize the most saliently? In other words, given a document set of mixed author, topic, and genre, would they interfere with each other in classification tasks? Answer to this question would help guide experiment design for AA tasks, and explain the real authorial characteristics captured by function words.

This paper aims to study the use of function words for Chinese authorship attribution (C-FWAA), since FWAA has not been well-studied in Chinese. Existing studies of C-FWAA are limited to the analysis of famous authorship dispute cases like whether Gao E or Cao Xueqin wrote the last 40 chapters of *the Dream of the Red Chamber*, and no consensus was reached among these C-FWAA studies (Zeng and Zhu, 2006). Therefore no baseline was available yet for general-purpose C-FWAA studies.

This study consists of three tasks. First, examine the effectiveness of C-FWAA in three genres of creative writing: novel, essay, and blog. Second, compare the strength of function words as both genre and authorship indicators, and explore the genre interference on C-FWAA. Third, examine whether C-FWAA is sensitive to the time periods when the texts were written.

The third task is proposed for a unique reason that the influence of ancient Chinese (文言文) on modern Chinese (白话文) may affect function word use. For example, "also" corresponds to "亦" in ancient Chinese, and "也" in modern Chinese. "的" ("'s" or "of"), "地" ("-ly"), and "得" ("so") are only used in modern Chinese. The government of Republic of China (RoC, 1912-1949) and the government of People's Republic of China (PRC, 1949-) both made changes to the Chinese language. Hence the hypothesis is that Chinese function word use may also reflect the time period of literary works.

2 Experiment set up

2.1 Constructing Chinese function word list

Various function word lists have been used in AA tasks in English, and the selection process usually follows arbitrary criteria (Stamatatos, 2009). To construct the Chinese function word list, this study chose 300 most frequent characters from Jun Da's Modern Chinese Character Frequency List (Du, 2005), removing the characters that contain solid meaning, e.g. "来" ("to come"), and removing all personal pronouns, e.g. "我" ("myself") in that they have been known as genre/register indicators (Biber, 1993). This screening process resulted in 35 function words (see Table 1). Detailed English translation can be found in (Du, 2005).

Every text document was then converted to a vector of 35 dimensions, each corresponding to one function word. The value for each dimension is the corresponding function word's number of occurrences per thousand words.

的 / of	是 / be,yes	不 / no	了/*
在 / at/in	有 / exist	这 / this	为 / for
地 / -ly	也 / also	得 / so	就 / then
那 / that	以 /**	着 / ***	之 / of
可 / can	么 / question	而 / but	然 / so
没 / no	于 / at	还 / also	只 / only
无 / no	又 / also	如 / if	但 / but
其 / it	此 / this	与 / and	把 / hold
全 / all	被 / passive	却 / but	

Note: * completion mark; ** according to; *** on-going status mark

Table 1: Chinese function word list

2.2 EM clustering algorithm

This study chose EM clustering algorithm as the main method to evaluate the effectiveness of C-FWAA. Most AA studies use supervised learning methods in that AA is a natural text categorization problem. However, training data may not be available in many AA tasks, and unsupervised learning methods are particularly useful in such cases. In addition, this study aims to examine the clusters emerging from the data and explain whether they represent authors, genres, or time periods.

This study uses Weka's Simple EM algorithm for all experiments. This algorithm first runs k-Means 10 times with different random seeds, and then chooses the partition with minimal squared error to start the expectation maximization iteration. Weka calculates the clustering accuracy as follows: after clustering the data, Weka determines the majority class in each cluster and prints a confusion matrix showing how many errors there would be if the clusters were used instead of the true class (Witten et al., 2011).

2.3 Selecting writers and their works

To exclude gender's affect, all writers chosen in this study are males. Parallel analysis for female writers will be conducted in future work.

Representative writers from three different time periods were selected to examine the relationship between time period and function word use. The first time period (TP1) is the 1930-40s, when modern Chinese replaced ancient Chinese to be the main form of writing in China, and before the PRC was founded. The second time period (TP2) is the 1980-90s, after the Cultural Revolution was over. The third time period (TP3) is the 2000s, when the publishing business has been strongly affected by the free-market economy. Three representative writers were chosen for each time period. The time period from the foundation of PRC (1949) to the end of the Cultural Revolution was excluded from this study because during that time most literary works were written under strong political guidelines. Tables 2 and 3 listed the representative writers and their selected works. Two long novels are separated into chapters in order to test whether C-FWAA is able to assign all chapters in a book to one cluster. Common English translations of the titles are found through Google Search. Chinese Pin Yin was provided for hard-to-translate titles.

All writers have to meet the requirements that their works cross at least two genres: fiction (novel) and non-fiction (essay). The TP3 (2000s) writers should have well-maintained blogs as well. Therefore this study will examine C-FWAA effectiveness in three genres: novel, essay, and blog.

All electronic copies of the selected works were downloaded from online literature repositories such as YiFan Public Library[1] and TianYa Book[2].

Time period	Authors
TP1 (1930-40s)	沈从文(Shen CongWen, SCW) 钱钟书(Qian ZhongShu, QZS) 汪曾祺(Wang ZengQi, WZQ)
TP2 (1980-90s)	王朔(Wang Shuo, WS) 王小波(Wang XiaoBo, WXB) 贾平凹(Jia PingWa, JPW)
TP3 (2000s)	郭敬明(Guo JingMing, GJM) 韩寒(Han Han, HH) 石康(Shi Kang, SK)

Table 2: selected writers in three time periods

TP	Writer	#Novels	essays	blogs
1	汪曾祺[3] WZQ	5	6	
	钱钟书 QZS	14*	10	
	沈从文 SCW	11**	7	
2	王朔 WS	5	16	30
	王小波 WSB	3	10	
	贾平凹 JPW	3	10	
3	郭敬明 GJM	8	6	
	韩寒 HH	5	11	92
	石康 SK	4	14	30

Note: *one long novel 围城(*Fortress Besieged*) is separated into 10 chapters. **one long novel 边城 (*Border Town*) is separated into 7 chapters.

Table 3: statistics of selected works

3 Experiment and result

3.1 Test the effectiveness of EM algorithm for FWAA

The first experiment was to test the effectiveness of the EM algorithm for FWAA. The famous *Federalist Papers* data set was used as the test case. The *Federalist Papers* experiment was repeated using the function words provided in (Mostellar and Wallace, 1964). The original *Ferderalist Papers* and their author identifications were downloaded from the Library of Congress website[4]. Function words were extracted using a Perl script and the word frequencies (per thousand words) were calculated. The 85 essays consist of 51 by Hamilton, 15 by Madison, 3 jointly by Hamilton

[1] URL http://www.shuku.net:8082/novels/cnovel.html

[2] URL http://www.tianyabook.com/

[3] 汪曾祺(Wang Zengqi) is an exception in that his writing career started in the 1930s but peaked in the 1980s.

[4] URL: http://thomas.loc.gov/home/histdox/fedpapers.html

and Madison, 5 by Jay, and 11 with disputed authorship. Mosteller and Wallace (1964) supported the opinion that Madison wrote all 11 disputed essays, which is also the mainstream opinion among historians.

In the first round of experiment, Jay's five essays and the three jointly-written ones were excluded, making the task easier. The cluster number was set to two. EM returned results similar to that in (Mostellar and Wallace, 1964) by assigning all disputed papers to Madison (Table 4). However it did make several mistakes by assigning 3 Hamilton's essays to Madison and one Madison's essay to Hamilton, resulting in an overall accuracy of (66-4)/66=94% in the not-disputed subset.

	C0 (Hamilton)	C1 (Madison)
Hamilton	48	**3**
Madison	**1**	14
Disputed	0	11

Table 4: Hamilton vs. Madison (clustering errors in bold)

In the second round Jay's five essays were added to the test data. The cluster number was then changed to three. The EM algorithm successfully attributed the essays to their real authors with only one error (assigning one Madison's essay to Jay, see the confusion matrix in Table 5). It also assigned all disputed essays to Madison. The 3-author AA result in Table 4 seems even better than the 2-author AA result, but the difference is small.

	C 0	C1	C 2
Hamilton	51	0	0
Madison	0	14	**1**
Jay	0	0	5
Disputed	0	11	0

Table 5: Hamilton vs. Madison vs. Jay

In the third round the three jointly-written essays were added to the test data. These jointly-written essays may resemble either Hamilton or Madison, which would result in 3 clusters still, or they may exhibit a unique style and thus form a new cluster. The test result shows that these three jointly-authored essays did confuse the algorithm no matter if the cluster number is set to three or four. When setting the cluster number to three (Table 6), all three joint essays were assigned to C2, which also attracted 11 Hamilton's, 2 Madison's, 2 Jay's, and 1 disputed essays. Increasing the cluster number to 4 does not reduce the confusion: Hamilton still dominated Cluster 0 with 40 out of 51 essays in it; C1 is still dominated by Madison (13 out of 15) and the disputed essays (9 out 11). Jay's essays were split into C1 and C2. This result actually shows that function words are highly sensitive to noise like the jointly-written essays.

	C0	C1	C2
H-M	0	0	3
Hamilton	40	0	11
Madison	0	13	2
Jay	0	3	2
disputed	1	9	1

Table 6: impact of the jointly-written essays

3.2 Chinese FWAA with genre and time period controlled

This section describes the experiments and results for task 1: evaluating the effectiveness of C-FWAA using EM and the 35 Chinese function words as features. Controlling the time period and genre, the same experiment was repeated for each genre and each TP.

In the first round, the authors within each TP were paired up in the novel genre to distinguish them, which is expected to be easier than distinguishing multiple authors. The results in Table 7 show that the authors of TP1 and TP2 novels are perfectly distinguishable, but those in TP3 are not.

Compared to the writers of TP1 and TP2, writers in TP3 face a new market-driven economy. Writing-for-profit becomes acceptable and even necessary for many writers. TP3 writers like Han Han (HH) and Guo JingMing (GJM) obtained huge financial success from the publication market. Both of them also received doubts regarding the authenticity of their works.

Guo Jingming was found to plagiarize in his book *Meng Li Hua Luo Zhi Duo Shao*, which was also not assigned to his main cluster by C-FWAA. Guo JingMing founded a writing studio and hired employees to publish and market his books. He publicly admits the existence of "group writing" practice in his studio because his name is used more as a brand than as an author.

C-FWAA also encountered difficulty in distinguishing Han Han and Shi Kang's novels. This finding is consistent with the fact that Han Han publicly acknowledged that his *Xiang Shao Nian La Fei Chi* mimicked Shi Kang's style. Since the beginning of 2012, a huge debate surged in Chinese social media over whether Han Han's books and blogs were ghost-penned by his father and others. In this striking "crowd-sourcing Shelock Holmes" movement, numerous doubts were raised based on netizens' amateur content analysis on contradicting statements in Han Han's public videos and different book versions. A separate study is undergoing to analyze the stylistic similarity between Han Han and the candidate pens.

As described in Section 3.1, FWAA is highly sensitive to noise like joint authorship. This may explain the low performance of C-FWAA in TP3 when plagiarism, group writing, and ghostwriting are involved.

After C-FWAA on the novel genre, the same experiment was then repeated on the other two genres: essay and blog. The results in Table 7 show an average accuracy .87 for essays and .83 for blogs. Overall, this round of experiment demonstrates that C-FWAA is effective in distinguishing two authors in all genres and time periods.

	Author pair	Novel	Essay	Blog
TP1	WZQ-SCW	1	.77	
	SCW-QZS	1	.94	
	WZQ-QZS	1	.81	
TP2	WS-JPW	1	1.00	
	WS-WXB	1	.96	
	WXB-JPW	1	.85	
TP3	GJM-HH	.77	1	
	GJM-SK	.75	.65	
	HH-SK	.56	.84	.84
TP2-3	HH-WS			.77
	SK-WS			.88
avg		.90	.87	.83

Table 7: pair-wise C-FWAA

In the second round C-FWAA was tested on the task of distinguishing three authors, also starting from the novel genre and TP1. In the 3-cluster result (Table 8), C0 is devoted to SCW's novel 边城 (*Border Town*), a masterpiece in Chinese literature, C1 captured all other SCW novels, and WZQ and QZS remain in C2 together. WZQ and QZS were further separated after increasing the cluster number to four (with only two errors, highlighted in Table 8, of assigning QZS's two works *God's Dream* and the Foreword of *Fortress Besieged* to SCW). Two long novels that are separated into chapters are also successfully assigned into same clusters except for the Foreword of *Fortress Besieged*.

The 3-author experiment was then repeated on TP2 and obtained 100% accurate results.

The 3-author AA result for TP3 is similar to its 2-author result: HH and SK remain in one cluster. When increasing the cluster number to 4, GJM still dominated C0 and C1, but now HH and SK were separated into C2 and C3 respectively.

The C-FWAA accuracy was then calculated by choosing the better result from 3-cluster and 4-cluster experiments (Table 8). Overall, C-FWAA is able to distinguish three authors in the novel genre effectively.

30s-40s	cluster num = 3			cluster num = 4			
	C0	C1	C2	C0	C1	C2	C3
SCW	7	4	0	7	4	0	0
WZQ	0	0	5	0	0	5	0
QZS	0	0	14	0	**2**	0	12

2000s	cluster num = 3			cluster num = 4			
	C0	C1	C2	C0	C1	C2	C3
GJM	4	3	1	4	3	**1**	**0**
HH	1	0	4	**1**	0	3	**1**
SK	0	1	3	0	**1**	0	3

TP	Accuracy
TP1	28/30=.93
TP2	11/11=1.00
TP3	13/17=.76
Avg	.90

Table 8: 3-author C-FWAA on Chinese novels

The above experiment was then repeated on the essay and blog genres. In the essay genre, the average 3-author C-FWAA accuracy is .83, .89, .84 for TP1, TP2, and TP3 respectively (Table 9), average accuracy .85. For blogs the accuracy is .68 (Table 10).

30s-40s	TP1		
	C0	C1	C2
SCW	5	**2**	0
WZQ	0	6	0
QZS	0	**2**	8

2000s	TP2		
	C0	C1	C2
GJM	6	0	0
HH	0	11	0
SK	**1**	**4**	9

80s-90s	cluster num = 3			cluster num = 4			
	C0	C1	C2	C0	C1	C2	C3
WS	16	0	0	15	0	**1**	0
WXB	0	10	0	0	8	**1**	**1**
JPW	2	4	4	0	0	**1**	9

Time period	Accuracy
1930s-1940s	19/23=.83
1980s-1990s	32/36=.89
2000s	26/31=.84
Average	.85

Table 9: 3-author C-FWAA on Chinese essays

Acc=104/152=.68	C0	C1	C2	C3	C4
HH	63	**7**	**8**	**2**	**12**
WS	**11**	13	**1**	0	**5**
SK	**1**	**1**	28	0	0

Table 10: 3-author C-FWAA on Chinese blogs

Comparing the C-FWAA accuracy on three genres, we can see that function words are quite effective in distinguish writers in all three genres. It is the most effective in novels, then essays, and blogs are the hardest. One possible explanation is that novels are the longest, essays are shorter, and blogs are the shortest. Hence novels provide the largest amount of data for precise measure of authorial characteristics. Further examination is needed to test this hypothesis. Another possible explanation is that blogs pose less constraint on the writers with regard to the writing format, and thus writers may write in much freer and more informal style. Overall, C-FWAA reached over 80% accuracy in distinguishing two or three authors in all three genres. This concludes the task #1.

3.3 Function words as genre indicators with author and time period controlled

This section reports a series of experiments that aim to evaluate the effectiveness of function words as genre indicators and the genre interference on C-FWAA. The first round of experiment examines whether the function words can distinguish novels from essays in each TP. The cluster number was set to two and the clustering result was compared against the genre labels. The error analysis also reveals which genre is less cohesive (failing to hold all of its instances in one cluster).

TP	Author	Accuracy	Which genre is less cohesive?
TP1	WZQ	.73	Essay (3->novel)
	SCW	.78	Essay (3->novel)
	QZS	1	
TP2	JPW	.54	Essay (7->novel)
	WS	1	
	WXB	.85	Essay (2->novel)
TP3	GJM	.71	Novel (4->essay)
	HH	.63	Both (5 essay->novel; 1 novel->essay)
	SK	.66	Essay (2->novel)
	avg	.77	

Table 11: function words as genre indicator (novel vs. essay)

The results in Table 11 show that the average accuracy (over 9 authors) is .77 to distinguish an author's novels and essays, demonstrating that function words are also strong genre indicators. For some authors QZS, WS, and WXB, their novels and essays are highly separable based on function word use. Interestingly, for all writers, their novels hold together perfectly except for GJM, but the essays often spread across two clusters. Again, the explanation may still be that novels are longer than essays, and thus provide more precise style estimation. If so, novels and essays may not be a fair comparison. However, the lengths of essays and blogs are similar. Therefore, the above experiment was repeated to distinguish essays and blogs from same authors. The results in Table 12 show that this task is not easier. The average accuracy is .71, which is a little worse than .77 in distinguishing novels and essays. Once again, one genre, this time it is the essay, that hold together very well, and blogs spread across clusters.

Combining the results in Section 3.2 and this section, we can see that function words are indicators of both authorship and genre, and the C-FWAA performance is affected by genre: it is the easiest for novel, then essay, and hardest for blogs.

Author	Acc	#E->B	#B->E
WS	.80	0/16	9/30
HH	.56	0/11	58/92
SK	.78	5/14	5/31
Avg	.71	.12	.36

Table 12: function words as genre indicator (essay vs. blog)

3.4 Which one do function words characterize more saliently, genre or authorship?

In the experiments reported in this section TP was still controlled, but in each TP the three authors and two genres are mixed together. The experiment was repeated for each TP. Each experiment consists of two steps. First, the cluster number was set to two, and the clustering result was compared against the genre labels. Second, the cluster number was set to three, and the result was compared against the author labels. If genre plays stronger impact on function word use, we should see high accuracy in the 2-cluster result, and if authorship is more salient, the 3-cluster result should be better. The results show that for all three TPs, the author-genre mix decreased the performance of authorship clustering (column #3 “AA in mixed genres” vs. column #4 “AA in novel” and column #5 “AA in essay”), indicating clear genre interference to authorship attribution. In comparison, the genre clustering in mixed authors (column #1) was worse than genre clustering in single author (column #6) in TP1 only. In TP2 and TP3 genre clustering in mixed-authors yielded higher accuracy than that in single-author, showing that mixing authors may increase or decrease genre identification performance.

To better understand the interference between authorship and genre, the 3-cluster result for each TP was visualized in Figures 1-3. The clusters in TP1 (Figure 1) include authorship cluster C0 (bottom row: SCW), genre cluster C2 (top: essay), and mixed cluster C1 (middle: WZQ, QZS, novels, and essays), demonstrating competing influence of authorship and genre on function words. The clusters in TP2 (Figure 2) are more genre-oriented, with C0 dominated by novels and C1 and C2 by essays. The clusters in TP3 (Figure 3) are also as mixed as in TP1, but more authorship-oriented, with C0 dominated by Shi Kang, C1 by Guo JingMing, and C2 by Han Han. In summary, function words characterize authors more saliently in TP1 and TP3, and genres more saliently in TP2. Therefore, we conclude for task #2 that the level of genre interference on authorship attribution is not arbitrary but is actually dependent on individual data set.

	2-genre clustering	3-author clustering	Novel AA	Essay AA	N-E genre
TP1	.51	.64	.93	.83	.84
TP2	.89	.70	1.00	.89	.80
TP3	.70	.75	.76	.84	.67

Table 13: genre vs. authorship

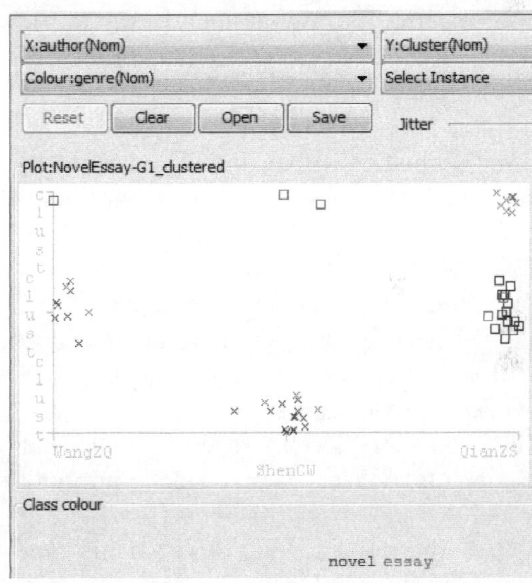

Figure 1: mixing authorship and genre in TP1

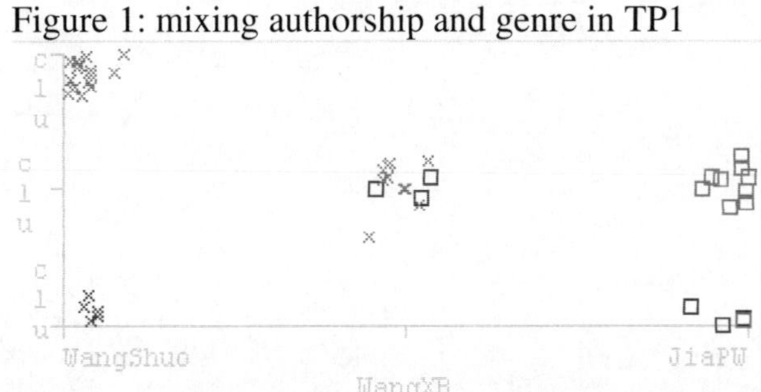

Figure 2: mixing authorship and genre in TP2

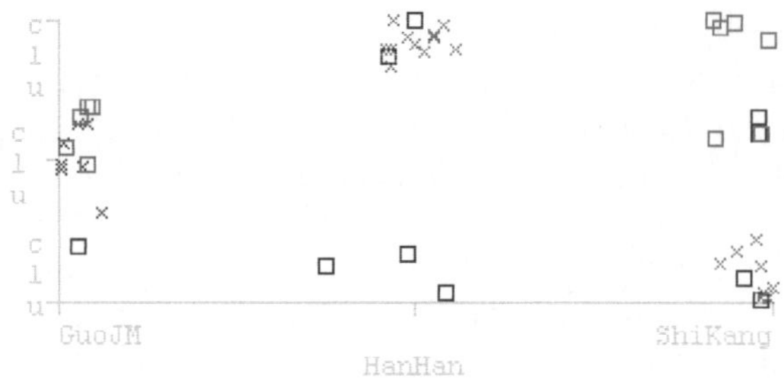

Figure 3: mixing authorship and genre in TP3

3.5 Is C-FWAA dependent on time period?

The task #3 is to examine whether C-FWAA is dependent on time period. The hypothesis is that writers of different times may use the function words differently because of the drastic change in Mandarin Chinese throughout the 20th century. When mixing the novels written in TP1, TP2, and TP3, the algorithm may be more sensitive to the time period than individual authorship. If the hypothesis is true, we should see the clustering result aligns with the time period, not authorship or genre. This time the cluster number is set to -1, which allows EM to use cross validation to automatically determine the optimal number of clusters (Smyth, 1996; McGregor et al., 2004).

EM returns 4 clusters: C0 is dominated by QZS (1940s), C1 by WZQ, WS, and JPW (1980-90s), C2 by SCW (1930s) and WXB (1980-90s), C3 by GJM (2000s). Therefore no obvious relationship is observed between the clusters and the time periods. Further, all TP1 and TP2 writers share one thing in common – their works stay in one cluster, but TP3 writers' works spread across multiple clusters: GJM 2, SK 3, and HH 4. This result is consistent with two facts that Han Han publicly acknowledged that (1) his *Xiang Shao Nian La Fei Chi* mimicked Shi Kang's style, and (2) his *San Chong Men* mimicked Qian ZhongShu's *Wei Cheng*.

Figure 4: clustering all novels from 9 authors

Repeating the experiment on essays resulted in only two clusters. Most writers' essays remain in one cluster with few exceptions (e.g. SCW, QZS, WXB and JPW in C0, and WZQ, WS and GJM in C1), while HH and SK's essays spread across the two clusters. The clusters do not seem to relate to the time periods either. What do these two clusters mean then? An examination of the cluster assignment of HH's essays reveals that his essay books *Du*, *Jiu Zhe Yang Piao Lai Piao Qu*, and *Ke Ai De Hong Shui Meng Shou* belong to C1, all written in casual and conversational style, and the more formal essays like *Qiu Yi*, *Shu Dian*, *Bei Zhong Kui Ren*, and *Yi Qi Chen Mo* belong to C1. Interestingly, most essays in C1 are doubted to be penned by his father. This result suggests that the clustering result actually captured two sub-genres in essays. However, further analysis is needed to test this hypothesis. In summary, no solid relationship was found between time period and Chinese function word use.

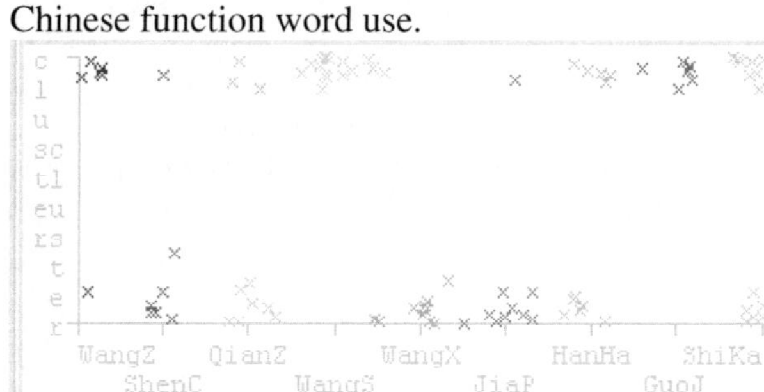

Figure 5: clustering all essays from 9 authors

4 Conclusion and limitations

This study made three contributions. First, it examined the effectiveness of using function words for Chinese authorship attribution (C-FWAA) in three different genres: novel, essay, and blog. Overall C-FWAA is able to distinguish three authors in each genre with various level of success. C-FWAA is the most effective in distinguishing authors of novels (averaged accuracy 90%), followed by essay (85%), and blog is the hardest (68%). Second, this study confirmed that Chinese function words are strong indicators of both genre and authorship. When the data set mixed authors and genres, these two factors may interfere with each other, and in such cases it depends on the data set which factor do function words characterize more saliently. Third, this study examined the hypothesized relationship between time period and

Chinese function word use in novels and essays between 1930s and 2000s, but did not find evidence to support this hypothesis.

This study has several limitations that need to be improved in future work. First, the data set is small and not quite balanced. More authors and works will be added in the future. Second, the random seed for EM is set to the default value 100 in Weka. However, EM clustering result may vary to some extent with different random seeds. More rigorous design is needed for robust performance comparison. One design is to run each clustering experiment multiple times, each time with a different random seed. The clustering accuracy will be averaged over all runs. This new design will allow for performance comparison based on paired-sample t-test significance. Third, the Cultural Revolution time period is excluded from this study due to strong political influence on writers. One reviewer pointed out that this time period should be valuable for examining the relationship between authorship, genre, and time period. Relevant data will be collected in future study.

5 Acknowledgment

Sincere thanks to Peiyuan Sun for his assistance in data collection and the anonymous reviewers for the insightful comments.

References

Ahmed Abbasi & Hsinchun Chen. 2005. Applying Authorship Analysis to Extremist-Group Web Forum Messages. *IEEE Intelligent Systems*, September/October 2005, 67-76.

Shlomo Argamon, Moshe Koppel, Jonathan Fine and Anat Rachel Shimoni. 2003.Gender, genre, and writing style in formal written texts. *Text* 23: 321–346.

Ross Clement and David Sharp. 2003. Ngram and Bayesian Classification of Documents for Topic and Authorship. Literary and Linguistic Computing, 18(4):423-447

Jun Da. Modern Chinese Character Frequency List. 2005. http://lingua.mtsu.edu/chinese-computing/statistics/char/list.php?Which=MO

Fred J. Damerau. 1975. The use of function word frequencies as indicators of style. *Computers and Humanities*, 9:271-280

Susan C. Herring and John C. Paolillo. 2006. Gender and Genre Variation in Weblogs. Journal of Sociolinguistics, 10(4):439-459.

David I. Holmes. 1994. Authorship Attribution. Computers and Humanities, 28:87-106.

Patrick Juola. 2008. Authorship Attribution. Foundations and Trends in Information Retrieval, 1(3):233-334.

Geir Kjetsaa, Sven Gustavsson, Bengt Beckman, and Steinar Gil. 1984. *The Authorship of The Quiet Don.* Solum Forlag A.S.: Oslo; Humanities Press: New Jersey.

Moshe Koppel, Shlomo Argomon, and Anat Rachel Shimoni. 2002. Automatically Categorizing Written Texts by Author Gender. *Literary and Linguistic Computing* 17:401–412.

Moshe Koppel, Jonathan Schler, and Shlomo Argamon. 2009. Computational Methods for Authorship Attribution. *JASIST*, 60(1):9-26.

Anthony McGregor, Mark Hall, Perry Lorier, and James Brunskill. 2004. Flow Clustering Using Machine Learning Techniques. *PAM 2004, LNCS 3015*, 205-214. Springer-Verlag: Berlin.

George K. Mikros & Eleni K. Argiri. 2007. Investigating topic influence in authorship attribution. *Proceedings of the SIGIR'07 Workshop on Plagiarism Analysis, Authorship Identification, and Near-Duplicate Detection*, 29–35.

Frederick Mosteller and David L. Wallace. 1964. *Inference and Disputed Authorship: The Federalist.* CSLI Publications.

Robert L. Oakman. 1980. *Computer Methods for Literary Research.* University of South Carolina Press, Columbia, SC.

Efstathios Stamatatos. 2009. A Survey of Modern Authorship Attribution Methods. *JASIST*, 60(3):538-556.

Padhraic Smyth. 1996. Clustering Using Monte Carlo Cross-Validation. *Proceedings of KDD'96*, 126-133.

Ian Witten, Eibe Frank, and Mark A. Hall. 2011. *Data Mining: Practical Machine Learning Tools and Techniques.* 3rd edition. Morgan-Kaufmann.

Yi-ping Zeng and Xiao-wen Zhu. 2006. Application of computational methods to the Study of Stylistics in China. *Journal of Fujian Normal University (Philosophy and Social Science Edition)*, 136 (1): 14-17.

Mining wisdom

Anders Søgaard
Center for Language Technology
University of Copenhagen
DK-2300 Copenhagen S
soegaard@hum.ku.dk

Abstract

Simple text classification algorithms perform remarkably well when used for detecting famous quotes in literary or philosophical text, with f-scores approaching 95%. We compare the task to topic classification, polarity classification and authorship attribution.

1 Introduction

Mark Twain famously said that 'the difference between the right word and the almost-right word is the difference between lightning and a lightning bug.' Twain's quote is also about the importance of quotes. A great quote can come in handy when you are looking to inspire people, make them laugh or persuade people to believe in a particular point of view. Quotes are emblems that serve to remind us of philosophical or political stand-points, world views, perspectives that comfort or entertain us. Famous quotes such as 'Cogito ergo sum' (Descartes) and 'God is dead' (Nietzsche) occur millions of times on the Internet.

The importance of quotes has motivated publishing houses to create and publish large collections of quotes. In this process, the editor typically spends years reading philosophy books, literature, and interviews to find good quotes, but this process is both expensive and cumbersome. In this paper, we consider the possibility of automatically learning what is a good quote, and what is not.

1.1 Related work

While there seems to have been no previous work on identifying quotes, the task is very similar to widely studied tasks such as topic classification, polarity classification, (lexical sample) word sense disambiguation (WSD) and authorship attribution. In most of these applications, texts are represented as bags-of-words, i.e. a text is represented as a vector $\mathbf{x} = \langle x_1, \ldots, x_N \rangle$ where each x_i encodes the presence and possibly the frequency of an n-gram. It is common to exclude stop words or closed class items such as pronouns and adpositions from the set of n-grams when constructing the bags-of-words. Sometimes lemmatization or word clustering is also used to avoid data sparsity.

Topic classification is the classic problem in text classification of distinguishing articles on a particular topic from other articles on other topics, say sports from international politics and letters to the editor. Several resources exist for evaluating topic classifiers such as Reuters 20 Newsgroups. Common baselines are Naive Bayes, logistic regression, or SVM classifiers trained on bag-of-words representations of n-grams with stop words removed.

While newspaper articles typically consist of tens or hundreds of sentences, famous quotes typically consist of one or two sentences, and it is interesting to compare quotation mining to work on applying topic classification techniques to short texts or sentences (Cohen et al., 2003; Wang et al., 2005; Khoo et al., 2006). Cohen et al. (2003) and Khoo et al. (2006) classify sentences in email wrt. their role in discourse. Khoo et al. (2006) argue that extending a bag-of-words representation with frequency counts is meaningless in small text and restrict themselves to binary representations. They show empirically that excluding stop words and lemmatization both lead to impoverished results. We also observe that stop words are extremely useful for quotation mining.

Polarity classification is the task of determining whether an opinionated text about a particular topic, say a user review of a product, is positive or negative. Polarity classification is different from quotation mining in that there is a small set of strong predictors of polarity (pivot features) (Wang et al., 2005; Blitzer et al., 2007), e.g. the polarity words listed in subjectivity lexica, including opinionated adjectives such as *good* or *awful*. The meaning of polarity words is context-sensitive, however, so context is extremely important when modeling polarity.

Some quotes are expressions of opinion, and there has been some previous research on polarity classification in direct quotations (not famous quotes). Balahur et al. (2009) present work on polarity classification of newspaper quotations, for example. They use an SVM classifier on a bag-of-words representation of direct quotes in the news, but using only words taken from subjectivity lexica as features. Drury et al. (2011) present a strategy for polarity classification of direct quotations from financial news. They use a Naive Bayes classifier on a bag-of-words models of unigrams, but learn group-specific models for analysts and CEOs.

WSD. The lexical sample task in WSD is the task of determining the meaning of a specific target word in context. Mooney (1996) argues that Naive Bayes classification and perceptron classifiers are particularly fit for lexical sample word sense disambiguation problems, because they combine weighted evidence from *all* features rather than select a subset of features for early discrimination. This of course also holds for logistic regression and SVMs. Whether a sentence is a good quotation or not also depends on many aspects of the sentence, and experiments on held-out data comparing Naive Bayes with decision tree-based learning algorithms, also mentioned in Sect. 5, clearly demonstrated that early discrimination based on single features is a bad idea. In this respect, quotation mining is more similar to lexical sample WSD than to topic and polarity classification where there is a small set of pivot features.

Authorship attribution is the task of determining which of a given set of authors wrote a particular text. One of the insights from authorship attribution

Positives
Two lives that once part are as ships that divide.
My appointed work is to awaken the divine nature that is within.
Discussion in America means dissent.
Negatives
The business was finished, and Harriet safe.
But how shall I do? What shall I say?
I am quite determined to refuse him.

Figure 1: Examples.

is that stop words are important when you want to learn stylistic differences. Stylistic differences can be identified from the distribution of closed class words (Arun et al., 2009). As already mentioned, we observe the same holds for quotation mining.

In conclusion, early-discrimination learning algorithms do not seem motivated for applications such as mining quotes where pivot features are hard to choose *a priori*. Furthermore, we hypothesize that it is better *not* to exclude stop words. Quotation mining can thus in our view be thought of as an application that is similar to sentence classification in that famous quotes are relatively small, and similar to authorship attribution in that style is an important predictor of whether a sentence is a famous quote.

2 Data

We obtain the database of famous quotes from a popular on-line collection of quotes[1] and use philosophical and literary text sampled from the Gutenberg corpus as negative data. In particular we use the portion of Gutenberg documents that is distributed in the corpora collection at NLTK.[2] This gives us a total of 44,385 positive data points (famous quotes) and 247,115 negative data points (ordinary sentences). In our experiments we use the top 4,000 data points in each sample, i.e. a total of 8,000 data points, except for when we derive a learning curve later on, which uses up to $2 \times 20,000$ data points. Some sample data points are presented in Figure 1.

3 Experiment

Each data point is represented as a binary bag-of-words - or bag-of-n-grams, really. Our initial hypothesis was to include stop words and keep infor-

[1] http://quotationsbook.com
[2] http://nltk.org

mation about case (capital letters). Stop words are extremely important to distinguish between literary styles, and we speculated that quotes can be distinguished from ordinary text in part by their style. We also speculated that there would be a tendency to capitalize some words in quotes, e.g. 'God', 'the Other', or 'the World'. Finally, we hypothesized that including more context would be beneficial. Our intuition was that sometimes larger chunks such as 'He who' may indicate that a sentence is a quote without the component words being indicative of that in any way.

To evaluate these hypotheses we considered a logistic regression classifier over bag-of-word representations of the quotes and our neutral sentences. We used a publicly available implementation[3] of limited memory L-BFGS to find the weights that maximize the log-likelihood of the training data:

$$\hat{\mathbf{w}} = \arg\max_{\mathbf{w}} \sum_i y(i) \log \frac{1}{1+e^{-\mathbf{w}\cdot\mathbf{x}}} + (1-y^{(i)})$$

$$\log \frac{e^{-\mathbf{w}\cdot\mathbf{x}}}{1+e^{-\mathbf{w}\cdot\mathbf{x}}}$$

where $\mathbf{w}\cdot\mathbf{x}$ is the dot product of weights and binary features in the usual way. We prefer logistic regression over Naive Bayes, since logistic regression is more resistant to possible dependencies between variables. The conditional likelihood maximization in logistic regression will adjust its parameters to maximize the fit even when the resulting parameters are inconsistent with the Naive Bayes assumption. Finally, logistic regression is less sensitive to parameter tuning than SVMs, so to avoid expensive parameter optimization we settled for logistic regression.

To test the importance of case, we did experiments with and without lowercasing of all words. To test the importance of stop words, we did experiments where stop words had been removed from the texts in advance. We also considered models with bigrams and trigrams to test the impact of bigger units of text (context). Finally, we varied the size of the dataset to obtain a learning curve suggesting how our model would perform in the limit.

[3]http://mallet.cs.umass.edu/

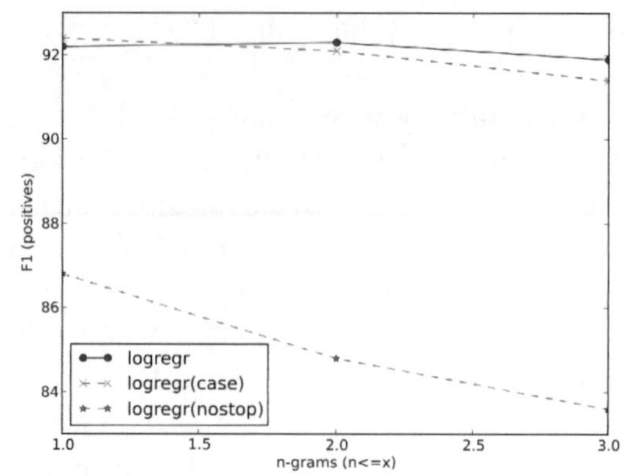

Figure 2: Results with n-grams of different sizes w/o lower-casing and w/o stop words.

4 Results

We report f-scores obtained by 10-fold cross-validation over a balanced 8,000 data points in Figure 2. The green line is our hypothesis model using n-grams of up to different lengths (1, 2 and 3). In this model features are *not* lower-cased (case is preserved), and stop words are *included*. This corresponds to our hypotheses about what would work best for quotation mining. The green line tells us that our unigram model is considerably better than our bigram and trigram models. This is probably because the bigrams and trigrams are too sparsely distributed in our data selection.

The blue line represents results with lowercased features. This means that features will be less sparse, and we now see that the bigram model is slightly better than the unigram model.

The red line represents results where stop words have been removed. This would be a typical model for topic classification. We see that this performs radically worse than the other two models, suggesting that our hypothesis about the usefulness of stop words for quotation mining was correct. The observation that the bigram and trigram models without stop words are much worse than the unigram model without stop words is most likely due to the extra sparsity introduced by open class trigrams.

Our main result is that with sufficient training data the f-score for detecting famous quotes in philosophical and literary text approaches 95%. The learning curves in Figure 3 are the results of our hypothesis

Source	Quote
Bill Clinton's Inaugural 1992	Powerful people maneuver for position and worry endlessly about who is in and who is out, who is up and who is down, forgetting those people whose toil and sweat sends us here and paves our way.
Bill Clinton's Inaugural 1997	But let us never forget : The greatest progress we have made, and the greatest progress we have yet to make, is in the human heart.
PTB CoNLL 2007 test	When the dollar is in a free-fall , even central banks can't stop it .
Europarl 01-17-00	Our citizens can not accept that the European Union takes decisions in a way that is, at least on the face of it, bureaucratic .
Europarl 01-18-00	If competition policy is to be made subordinate to the aims of social and environmental policy , real efficiency and economic growth will remain just a dream .
Europarl 01-19-00	For Europe to become the symbol of peace and fraternity , we need a bold and generous policy to come to the aid of the most disadvantaged .

Figure 4: The sentence with highest probability of being a quote in each corpus according to our 20K logistic regression unigram model).

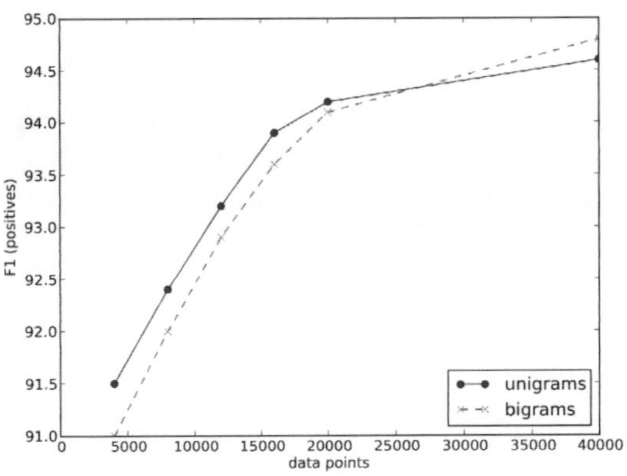

Figure 3: Learning curves for unigram and bigram models without lower-casing and with stop words.

model (green line in Figure 2) obtained with varying amounts of training data, from 4,000 to 40,000 data points. The learning curves also confirm that the bigram model was suffering from sparsity with smaller data selections, and we observe that the bigram model becomes superior to the unigram model with about 30,000 data points. The learning curves show that F-scores for positive class approach 95% as we add more training data.

5 Discussion

To confirm Mooney's hypothesis that it is better to combine weighted evidence from *all* features rather than select a subset of features for early discrimination, also in the case of mining quotes, we ran a decision tree algorithm on the same data sets used above. The f-score for detecting quotes was consistently below 65%.

The decision tree algorithm tries to find good features for early discrimination. Interestingly, one of the most discriminative features picked up by the decision tree from trigram data with case preserved was the bigram 'He who'. This feature was used to split 500 sentences, leaving only 11 in the minority class. Other discriminative features include 'People', 'we are', 'if you have', and 'Nothing is more'.

Similarly, we can observe remarkable differences in marginal distributions by considering the most frequent words in positive and negative texts. Words such as "who", "all", "word", and "things" occur much more frequently in quotes than in more balanced literary philosophical text. Interestingly '–' is also a very good predictor of a sentence being a potential quote.

Finally, we ran a model on other corpora to identify novel candidates of famous quotes (Figure 4). We ran it on texts where you would expect to find potential famous quotes (e.g. inaugurals), as well as on texts where you would not expect that.

6 Conclusion

Simple text classification algorithms perform remarkably well when used for detecting famous quotes in literary or philosophical text, with f-scores approaching 95%. We compare the task to topic classification, polarity classification and authorship attribution and observe that unlike in topic classification, stop words are extremely useful for quotation mining.

References

R Arun, R Saradha, V Suresh, M Murty, and C Madhavan. 2009. Stopwords and stylometry: a latent Dirichlet allocation approach. In *NIPS workshop on Applications for Topic Models*.

Alexandra Balahor, Ralf Steinberger, Erik van der Goot, Bruno Pouliquen, and Mijail Kabadjov. 2009. Opinion mining on newspaper quotations. In *IEEE/WIC/ACM Web Intelligence*.

John Blitzer, Mark Dredze, and Fernando Pereira. 2007. Biographies, bollywood, boom-boxes and blenders: Domain adaptation for sentiment classification. In *ACL*.

William Cohen, Vitor Carvalho, and Tom Mitchell. 2003. Learning to classify email into "speech acts". In *EMNLP*.

Brett Drury, Gaël Dias, and Luis Torgo. 2011. A contextual classification strategy for polarity analysis of direct quotations from financial news. In *RANLP*.

Anthony Khoo, Yuval Marom, and David Albrecht. 2006. Experiments with sentence classification. In *ALTW*.

Raymond Mooney. 1996. Comparative experiments on disambiguating word senses. In *EMNLP*.

Chao Wang, Jie Lu, and Guangquan Zhang. 2005. A semantic classification approach for online product reviews. In *IEEE/WIC/ACM Web Intelligence*.

Literary authorship attribution with phrase-structure fragments

Andreas van Cranenburgh
Huygens ING
Royal Netherlands Academy of Arts and Sciences
P.O. box 90754, 2509 LT The Hague, the Netherlands
andreas.van.cranenburgh@huygens.knaw.nl

Abstract

We present a method of authorship attribution and stylometry that exploits hierarchical information in phrase-structures. Contrary to much previous work in stylometry, we focus on content words rather than function words. Texts are parsed to obtain phrase-structures, and compared with texts to be analyzed. An efficient tree kernel method identifies common tree fragments among data of known authors and unknown texts. These fragments are then used to identify authors and characterize their styles. Our experiments show that the structural information from fragments provides complementary information to the baseline trigram model.

1 Introduction

The task of authorship attribution (for an overview cf. Stamatatos, 2009) is typically performed with superficial features of texts such as sentence length, word frequencies, and use of punctuation & vocabulary. While such methods attain high accuracies (e.g., Grieve, 2007), the models make purely statistical decisions that are difficult to interpret. To overcome this we could turn to higher-level patterns of texts, such as their syntactic structure.

Syntactic stylometry was first attempted by Baayen et al. (1996), who looked at the distribution of frequencies of grammar productions.[1] More recently, Raghavan et al. (2010) identified authors by deriving a probabilistic grammar for each author and picking the author grammar that can parse the unidentified text with the highest probability. There is also work that looks at syntax on a more shallow level, such as Hirst and Feiguina (2007), who work with partial parses; Wiersma et al. (2011) looked at n-grams of part-of-speech (POS) tags, and Menon and Choi (2011) focussed on particular word frequencies such as those of 'stop words,' attaining accuracies well above 90% even in cross-domain tasks.

[1] A grammar production is a rewrite rule that generates a constituent.

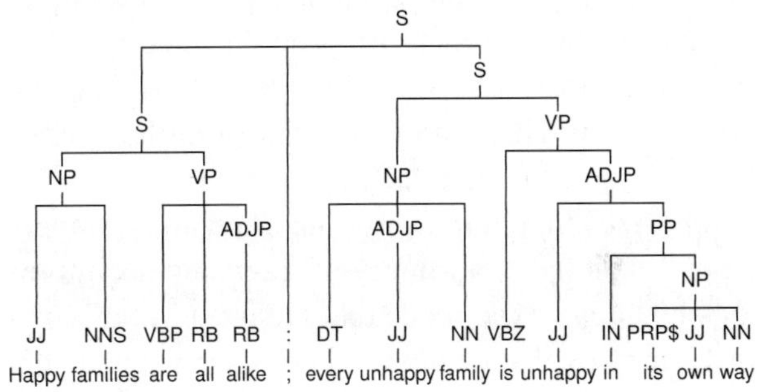

Figure 1: A phrase-structure tree produced by the Stanford parser.

In this work we also aim to perform syntactic stylometry, but we analyze syntactic parse trees directly, instead of summarizing the data as a set of grammar productions or a probability measure. The unit of comparison is tree fragments. Our hypothesis is that the use of fragments can provide a more interpretable model compared to one that uses fine-grained surface features such as word tokens.

2 Method

We investigate a corpus consisting of a selection of novels from a handful of authors. The corpus was selected to contain works from different time periods

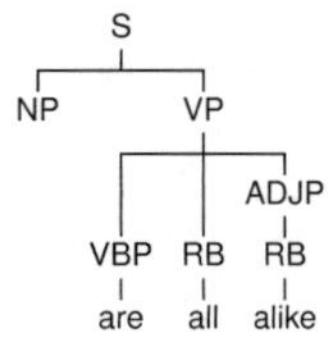

Figure 2: A phrase-structure fragment from the tree in figure 1.

from authors with a putatively distinctive style. In order to analyze the syntactic structure of the corpus we use hierarchical phrase-structures, which divide sentences into a series of constituents that are represented in a tree-structure; cf. figure 1 for an example. We analyze phrase-structures using the notion of tree fragments (referred to as subset trees by Collins and Duffy, 2002). This notion is taken from the framework of Data-Oriented Parsing (Scha, 1990), which hypothesizes that language production and comprehension exploits an inventory of fragments from previous language experience that are used as building blocks for novel sentences. In our case we can surmise that literary authors might make use of a specific inventory in writing their works, which characterizes their style. Fragments can be characterized as follows:

Definition. *A fragment f of a tree T is a connected subset of nodes from T, with $|f| \geq 2$, such that each node of f has either all or none of the children of the corresponding node in T.*

When a node of a fragment has no children, it is called a frontier node; in a parsing algorithm such nodes function as substitution sites where the fragment can be combined with other fragments. Cf. figure 2 for an example of a fragment. An important consideration is that fragments can be of arbitrary size. The notion of fragments captures anything from a single context-free production such as

(1) $S \rightarrow NP\ VP$

…to complete stock phrases such as

(2) Come with me if you want to live.

In other words, instead of making assumptions about grain size, we let the data decide. This is in contrast to n-gram models where n is an *a priori* defined sliding window size, which must be kept low because

Author (sentences)	Works (year of first publication)
Conrad, Joseph (25,889)	Heart of Darkness (1899), Lord Jim (1900), Nostromo (1904), The Secret Agent (1907)
Hemingway, Ernest (40,818)	A Farewell To Arms (1929), For Whom the Bell Tolls (1940), The Garden of Eden (1986), The Sun Also Rises (1926)
Huxley, Aldous (23,954)	Ape and Essence (1948), Brave New World (1932), Brave New World Revisited (1958), Crome Yellow (1921), Island (1962), The Doors of Perception (1954), The Gioconda Smile (1922)
Salinger, J.D. (26,006)	Franny & Zooey (1961), Nine Stories (1953), The Catcher in the Rye (1951), Short stories (1940–1965)
Tolstoy, Leo (66,237)	Anna Karenina (1877); transl. Constance Garnett, Resurrection (1899); transl. Louise Maude, The Kreutzer Sonata and Other Stories (1889); transl. Benjamin R. Tucker, War and Peace (1869); transl. Aylmer Maude & Louise Maude

Table 1: Works in the corpus. Note that the works by Tolstoy are English translations from project Gutenberg; the translations are contemporaneous with the works of Conrad.

of data-sparsity considerations.

To obtain phrase-structures of the corpus we employ the Stanford parser (Klein and Manning, 2003), which is a treebank parser trained on the Wall Street journal (WSJ) section of the Penn treebank (Marcus et al., 1993). This unlexicalized parser attains an accuracy of 85.7 % on the WSJ benchmark ($|w| \leq 100$). Performance is probably much worse when parsing text from a different domain, such as literature; for example dialogue and questions are not well represented in the news domain on which the parser is trained. Despite these issues we expect that useful information can be extracted from the latent hierarchical structure that is revealed in parse trees, specifically in how patterns in this structure recur across different texts.

We pre-process all texts manually to strip away dedications, epigraphs, prefaces, tables of contents, and other such material. We also verified that no occurrences of the author names remained.[2] Sentence and word-level tokenization is done by the Stanford parser. Finally, the parser assigns the most likely parse tree for each sentence in the corpus. No further training is performed; as our method is memory-based, all computation is done during classification.

In the testing phase the author texts from the training sections are compared with the parse trees of texts to be identified. To do this we modified the fragment extraction algorithm of Sangati et al. (2010) to identify the common fragments among two different sets of parse trees.[3] This is a tree kernel method (Collins and Duffy, 2002) which uses dynamic programming to efficiently extract the maximal fragments that two trees have in common. We use the variant reported by Moschitti (2006) which runs in average linear time in the number of nodes in the trees.

To identify the author of an unknown text we collect the fragments which it has in common with each known author. In order to avoid biases due to different sizes of each author corpus, we use the first 15,000 sentences from each training section. From these results all fragments which were found in more than one author corpus are removed. The remaining fragments which are unique to each author are used to compute a similarity score.

We have explored different variations of similarity scores, such as the number of nodes, the average number of nodes, or the fragment frequencies. A simple method which appears to work well is to count the total number of content words.[4] Given the parse trees of a known author A and those of an unknown author B, with their unique common fragments denoted as $A \sqcap B$, the resulting similarity is defined as:

$$f(A, B) = \sum_{x \in A \sqcap B} \text{content\_words}(x)$$

However, while the number of sentences in the training sets has been fixed, they still diverge in the average number of words per sentence, which is reflected in the number of nodes per tree as well. This causes a bias because statistically, there is a higher chance that some fragment in a larger tree will match with another. Therefore we also normalize for the average number of nodes. The author can now be guessed as:

$$\underset{A \in \text{Authors}}{\arg\max} \frac{f(A, B)}{1/|A| \sum_{t \in A} |t|}$$

Note that working with content words does not mean that the model reduces to an n-gram model, because fragments can be discontiguous; e.g., "he said X but Y." Furthermore the fragments contain hierarchical structure while n-grams do not. To verify this contention, we also evaluate our model with trigrams instead of fragments. For this we use trigrams of word & part-of-speech pairs, with words stemmed using Porter's algorithm. With trigrams we simply count the number of trigrams that one text shares with another. Raghavan et al. (2010) have observed that the lexical information in n-grams and the structural information from a PCFG perform a complementary role, achieving the highest performance when both are combined. We therefore also evaluate with a combination of the two.

3 Evaluation & Discussion

Our data consist of a collection of novels from five authors. See table 1 for a specification. We perform cross-validation on 4 works per author. We evaluate on two different test sizes: 20 and 100 sentences. We test with a total of 500 sentences per work, which gives 25 and 5 datapoints per work given these sizes. As training sets only the works that are not tested on are presented to the model. The training sets consist of 15,000 sentences taken from the remaining works. Evaluating the model on these test sets took about half an hour on a machine with 16 cores, employing less than 100 MB of memory per process. The similarity functions were explored on a development set, the results reported here are from a separate test set.

The authorship attribution results are in table 2. It is interesting to note that even with three different translators, the work of Tolstoy can be successfully identified; i.e., the style of the author is modelled, not the translator's.

[2] Exception: War and Peace contains a character with the same name as its author. However, since this occurs in only one of the works, it cannot affect the results.

[3] The code used in the experiments is available at `http://github.com/andreasvc/authident`.

[4] Content words consist of nouns, verbs, adjectives, and adverbs. They are identified by the part-of-speech tags that are part of the parse trees.

20 sentences	trigrams	fragments	combined	100 sentences	trigrams	fragments	combined
Conrad	83.00	87.00	94.00	Conrad	100.00	100.00	100.00
Hemingway	77.00	52.00	81.00	Hemingway	100.00	100.00	100.00
Huxley	86.32	75.79	86.32	Huxley	89.47	78.95	89.47
Salinger	93.00	86.00	94.00	Salinger	100.00	100.00	100.00
Tolstoy	77.00	80.00	90.00	Tolstoy	95.00	100.00	100.00
average:	83.23	76.16	**89.09**	average:	96.97	95.96	**97.98**

Table 2: Accuracy in % for authorship attribution with test texts of 20 or 100 sentences.

	Conrad	Hemingway	Huxley	Salinger	Tolstoy
Conrad	**94**	1		2	3
Hemingway	3	**81**		11	5
Huxley	5	2	**82**	1	5
Salinger	1	2	3	**94**	
Tolstoy	8		2		**90**

Table 3: Confusion matrix when looking at 20 sentences with trigrams and fragments combined. The rows are the true authors, the columns the predictions of the model.

Gamon (2004) also classifies chunks of 20 sentences, but note that in his methodology data for training and testing includes sentences from the same work. Recognizing the same work is easier because of recurring topics and character names.

Grieve (2007) uses opinion columns of 500–2,000 words, which amounts to 25–100 sentences, assuming an average sentence length of 20 words. Most of the individual algorithms in Grieve (2007) score much lower than our method, when classifying among 5 possible authors like we do, while the accuracies are similar when many algorithms are combined into an ensemble. Although the corpus of Grieve is carefully controlled to contain comparable texts written for the same audience, our task is not necessarily easier, because large differences within the works of an author can make classifying that author more challenging.

Table 3 shows a confusion matrix when working with 20 sentences. It is striking that the errors are relatively asymmetric: if A is often confused with B, it does not imply that B is often confused with A. This appears to indicate that the similarity metric has a bias towards certain categories which could be removed with a more principled model.

Here are some examples of sentence-level and productive fragments that were found:

(3) Conrad: [PP [IN] [NP [NP [DT] [NN sort]] [PP [IN of] [NP [JJ] [NN]]]]]

(4) Hemingway: [VP [VB have] [NP [DT a] [NN drink]]]

(5) Salinger: [NP [DT a] [NN] [CC or] [NN something]]

(6) Salinger: [ROOT [S [NP [PRP I]] [VP [VBP mean] [SBAR]] [. .]]]

(7) Tolstoy: [ROOT [SINV [`` “] [S] [, ,] ['' ”] [VP [VBD said]] [NP] [, ,] [S [VP [VBG shrugging] [NP [PRP$ his] [NNS shoulders]]]] [. .]]]

It is likely that more sophisticated statistics, for example methods used for collocation detection, or general machine learning methods to select features such as support vector machines would allow to select only the most characteristic fragments.

4 Conclusion

We have presented a method of syntactic stylometry that is conceptually simple—we do not resort to sophisticated statistical inference or an ensemble of algorithms—and takes sentence-level hierarchical phenomena into account. Contrary to much previous work in stylometry, we worked with content words rather than just function words. We have demonstrated the feasibility of analyzing literary syntax through fragments; the next step will be to use these techniques to address other literary questions.

References

Harold Baayen, H. Van Halteren, and F. Tweedie. 1996. Outside the cave of shadows: Using syntactic annotation to enhance authorship attribution. *Literary and Linguistic Computing*, pages 121–132.

Michael Collins and Nigel Duffy. 2002. New ranking algorithms for parsing and tagging: Kernels over discrete structures, and the voted perceptron. In *Proceedings of ACL*.

Michael Gamon. 2004. Linguistic correlates of style: authorship classification with deep linguistic analysis features. In *Proceedings of COLING*.

Jack Grieve. 2007. Quantitative authorship attribution: An evaluation of techniques. *Literary and Linguistic Computing*, 22(3):251–270. URL `http://llc.oxfordjournals.org/content/22/3/251.abstract`.

Graeme Hirst and Olga Feiguina. 2007. Bigrams of syntactic labels for authorship discrimination of short texts. *Literary and Linguistic Computing*, 22(4):405–417. URL `http://llc.oxfordjournals.org/content/22/4/405.abstract`.

Dan Klein and Christopher D. Manning. 2003. Accurate unlexicalized parsing. In *Proc. of ACL*, volume 1, pages 423–430.

Mitchell P. Marcus, Mary Ann Marcinkiewicz, and Beatrice Santorini. 1993. Building a large annotated corpus of English: The Penn Treebank. *Computational linguistics*, 19(2):313–330.

Rohith K Menon and Yejin Choi. 2011. Domain independent authorship attribution without domain adaptation. In *Proceedings of Recent Advances in Natural Language Processing*, pages 309–315.

Alessandro Moschitti. 2006. Making tree kernels practical for natural language learning. In *Proceedings of EACL*, pages 113–120. URL `http://acl.ldc.upenn.edu/E/E06/E06-1015.pdf`.

Sindhu Raghavan, Adriana Kovashka, and Raymond Mooney. 2010. Authorship attribution using probabilistic context-free grammars. In *Proceedings of ACL*, pages 38–42.

Federico Sangati, Willem Zuidema, and Rens Bod. 2010. Efficiently extract recurring tree fragments from large treebanks. In *Proceedings of LREC*, pages 219–226. URL `http://dare.uva.nl/record/371504`.

Remko Scha. 1990. Language theory and language technology; competence and performance. In Q.A.M. de Kort and G.L.J. Leerdam, editors, *Computertoepassingen in de Neerlandistiek*, pages 7–22. LVVN, Almere, the Netherlands. Original title: *Taaltheorie en taaltechnologie; competence en performance*. Translation available at `http://iaaa.nl/rs/LeerdamE.html`.

Efstathios Stamatatos. 2009. A survey of modern authorship attribution methods. *Journal of the American Society for Information Science and Technology*, 60(3):538–556. URL `http://dx.doi.org/10.1002/asi.21001`.

Wybo Wiersma, John Nerbonne, and Timo Lauttamus. 2011. Automatically extracting typical syntactic differences from corpora. *Literary and Linguistic Computing*, 26(1):107–124. URL `http://llc.oxfordjournals.org/content/26/1/107.abstract`.

Digitizing 18th-Century French Literature: Comparing transcription methods for a critical edition text

Ann Irvine
Computer Science Dept.
Johns Hopkins University
Baltimore, MD
anni@jhu.edu

Laure Marcellesi
French and Italian Dept.
Dartmouth College
Hanover, NH
laure.marcellesi@dartmouth.edu

Afra Zomorodian
The D. E. Shaw Group
New York, NY

Abstract

We compare four methods for transcribing early printed texts. Our comparison is through a case-study of digitizing an eighteenth-century French novel for a new critical edition: the 1784 *Lettres taïtiennes* by Joséphine de Monbart. We provide a detailed error analysis of transcription by optical character recognition (OCR), non-expert humans, and expert humans and weigh each technique based on accuracy, speed, cost and the need for scholarly overhead. Our findings are relevant to 18th-century French scholars as well as the entire community of scholars working to preserve, present, and revitalize interest in literature published before the digital age.

1 Introduction

Preparing a text for modern publication involves the following: (1) digitizing[1] a printed version of the text, and (2) supplementing the original content with new scholarly contributions such as a critical introduction, annotations, and a thorough bibliography. The second task requires a high degree of expertise and academic insight and the first does not. However, scholars working on such projects often spend large amounts of time transcribing literature from scratch, instead of focusing on skilled contributions.

In this paper, we present an analysis of our efforts using *alternative methods*, other than highly skilled scholars themselves, to transcribe a scanned image of a novel into a modifiable, searchable document. We compare four different methods of transcription with a gold standard and evaluate each for accuracy, speed, and cost-effectiveness. Choosing an appropriate transcription method may save scholars time and allow them to focus on critical contributions.

First published in 1784, Joséphine de Monbart's *Lettres taïtiennes* is an epistolary novel dramatizing the European colonial takeover of the newly-encountered island of Tahiti from the fictional point of view of a young Tahitian woman. While most works of the time painted a fictional Tahitian paradise of uninhibited sexuality, this novel offers a singular anti-colonial critique by grounding it in the suffering of the female body. We describe our work transcribing the second edition of the novel, which is written in French and was published in Paris, without date (probably 1786). The text is comprised of 156 pages, which are split into two volumes.

There are many off-the-shelf (OTS) natural language processing (NLP) tools available for French, including optical character recognition (OCR), context-sensitive spell checking, and machine translation. Additionally, French is a widely spoken language in the world today and it is often possible to recruit French speakers to do transcription and annotation. However, the early-modern (18th-century) form of the language varies substantially from the modern form, which is used to train OTS French tools and is what non-domain-expert transcribers are familiar with. Differences between the modern and early-modern forms of the language include orthography, lexical choice, and morphological patterns.

An additional challenge is that our transcriptions are based on a *copied* version of the bound text available at the Bibliothèque nationale de France. This common scenario introduces the challenge of noise, or ink marks which are not part of the text. Scattered dots of ink may result in punctuation and character accenting errors, for example.

In this paper, we compare the accuracy, speed, and

[1] In this work, *digitizing* means transcribing an image into a modifiable, searchable file of unicode characters.

cost of using several different methods to transcribe *Lettres tahitiennes*. In Section 2 we describe the transcription methods, and in Section 3 we present a detailed analysis of the types of errors made by each. We also provide a discussion of the difficulty of post-editing the output from each transcriber. Section 4 gives an overview of prior work in the area and Section 5 a practical conclusion, which may inform scholars in the beginning stages of similar projects.

2 Methods

We compare four sources of transcription for 30 pages of the novel with one gold standard:

- OTS French OCR output
- Non-expert French speakers on Amazon's Mechanical Turk (MTurk)
- Non-expert undergraduate students in the humanities, closely supervised by the expert
- Professional transcription service
- Gold standard: early-modern French literature scholar and editor of the critical edition

Given PDF images of a copy of the novel, each source transcribed the same 30 pages[2]. The pages are a representative sample from each of the two volumes of the text.

We used OTS Abbyy Finereader OCR software, which is trained on modern French text and has a fixed cost of $99.

Three MTurk workers transcribed each page of text, and the domain expert chose the best transcription of each page. In future work, we could have another round of MTurk workers choose the best transcription among several MTurk outputs, which has been shown to be effective in other NLP tasks (Zaidan and Callison-Burch, 2011). We paid each MTurk worker $0.10 to transcribe a single page.

Two closely supervised undergraduate students transcribed the novel[3], including the 30 test pages. The cost per page per student was about $0.83.

Our group also hired a professional company to transcribe the entire novel, which charged a fixed cost of $1000, or about $3.21 per page.

The early-modern French literature domain-expert also transcribed the 30 test pages from scratch, and this transcription was used as the gold standard for measuring accuracy.

Because the critical edition text should be as faithful as possible to the original text, with no alteration to the spelling, syntax, capitalization, italicization, and paragraph indentation, we define as errors to be:

- an incomplete transcription
- missing or added words, letters, or characters
- a word transcribed incorrectly
- capitalization, bold, italics not matching the original text
- incorrect formatting, including missing or added paragraph indentations and footnote distinctions

In Section 3, we present a quantitative and qualitative analysis of the types of errors made by each of our transcription methods.

3 Results and Error Analysis

Table 1 lists the error rate for each transcriber.

3.1 S/F errors

One of the most common errors made by all four transcription methods is confusing the letter ſ (or long s), which is common in early-modern French but doesn't appear in modern French, with the letter **f**. Figure 1 shows examples of phrases in the original document that include both characters. These examples illustrate how familiarity with the language may impact when transcription errors are made. All three human transcribers (MTurk workers, students, professionals) confused an **f** for an ſ in (b). Interestingly, the phrase in (b) would never be used in modern French, so the transcribers, not recognizing the overall meaning of the sentence and wary of 'missing' a ſ, incorrectly wrote *seront* instead of *feront*. In contrast, the phrase in (a) is rare but does exist in modern French. The MTurk worker and professional transcriber correctly transcribed *feront* but the student, who probably didn't know the phrase, transcribed the word as *seront*.

The OCR system trained on modern French did not recognize ſ at all. In most cases, it transcribed the letter as an **f**, but it sometimes chose other letters, such as **t**, **i**, or **v**, in order to output French words that exist in its dictionary. Although it may have been

[2] Each page is in the original duodecimo format and contains about 150 word tokens.

[3] One student transcribed volume 1, the other volume 2.

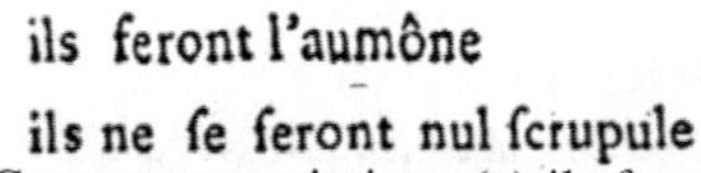

ils feront l'aumône

ils ne ſe feront nul ſcrupule

Figure 1: Correct transcription: (a) ils feront l'aumône (*give alms*). The student incorrectly transcribed *feront* as *seront*. (b) ils ne se feront nul scrupule (*they will have no qualms*). All four alternative transcription sources incorrectly transcribed *feront* as *seront*.

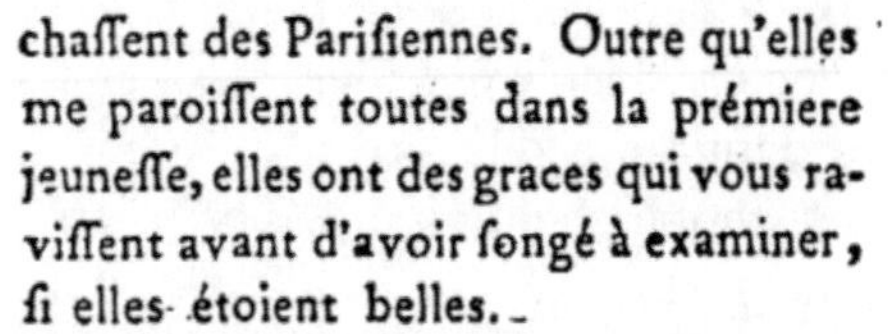

chaſſent des Pariſiennes. Outre qu'elles
me paroiſſent toutes dans la prémiere
jeuneſſe, elles ont des graces qui vous ra-
viſſent avant d'avoir ſongé à examiner,
ſi elles étoient belles.

Figure 2: Correct transcription: Outre qu'elles me paroissent toutes dans la prémiere jeunesse, elles ont des graces qui vous ravissent avant d'avoir songé à examiner, si elles étoient belles (*Besides [these women] appearing to me in the prime of youth, they have graces that delight you before you even think of considering whether they are beautiful.* Transcribers made both conjugation (*paraissent* vs. *paroissent*) and accenting (*prémiere* vs. *première*) modernization errors in this passage.

possible to train the OCR system on early-modern French, the very slight difference between the character strokes means that disambiguating between **f** and ſ would likely remain a difficult task.

3.2 Modernization errors

Eighteenth-century French is understandable by speakers of modern French, but there are a few differences. In addition to the absence of the letter ſ, modern French conjugates verbs with $-ai, -ais, -ait, -aient$ instead of $-oi, -ois, -oit, -oient$ and follows stricter rules that no longer allow for variations in spelling or accenting. Figure 2 shows examples of both. In general, the authors of modern critical editions seek to maintain original spellings so that future scholars can work as close to the original text as possible, even if the original work includes typos, which we have seen. However, our human transcribers incorrectly modernized and 'fixed' many original spellings. This is likely due to the fact that it is hard for a human transcriber who is familiar with the language to *not* 'correct' a word into its modern form. We observed this across all human transcribers. For example, our professional transcriber transcribed *première* instead of *prémiere* and one MTurk worker transcribed *chez* instead of *chés*. The OCR model, which is trained on modern French, is also biased toward modern spellings. Most of its modernization errors were related to accents. For example, it transcribed *graces* as *grâces* and *differentes* as *différentes*.

Some modernization errors occur systematically and, thus, are easy to automatically correct after the initial transcription is complete. For example, all $-aient$ word endings could be changed to $-oient$. This is not true for all modernization errors.

3.3 Errors from page noise

Since all of our transcribers worked from a scan of a copy of the original book held at the Bibliothèque nationale de France, noise in the form of small dots, originally bits of ink, appears on the pages. These small dots are easily confused with diacritics and punctuation. Our human transcribers made such errors very infrequently. However, this type of noise greatly affected the output of the OCR system. In addition to mistaking this type of noise for punctuation, sometimes it affected the recognition of words. In once instance, *visages* became *ylfygc* because of small dots that appeared below the v and a[4].

3.4 Formatting errors

We asked all transcribers to maintain the original formatting of the text, including paragraph indentations, footnotes, and font styles. However, because of limitations inherent to the MTurk task design interface, we were unable to collect anything but plain, unformatted text from those transcribers. In general, our other human transcribers were able to accurately maintain the format of the original text. The OCR output also made formatting mistakes, particularly bold and italicized words.

3.5 Other errors

Both humans and the OCR system made an assortment of additional errors. For example, two MTurk workers failed to turn off the *English* automatic spell correctors in their text editors, which resulted in *lettre* becoming *letter* and *dont* becoming *don't*.

3.6 Scholar overhead

Table 1 lists the average number of errors per page for each transcription method. In addition to consid-

[4]In this example, an ſ was also transcribed as an **f**

Error	OCR	MTurk	Prof.	Stud.
Modernization	26.29	2.82	0.71	0.46
Noise	7.68	0.0	0.32	0.21
Formatting	1.96	0.82	0.36	0.0
Total	35.93	3.86	1.39	0.71

Table 1: Mean number of errors per page, by error type and transcription method. The total includes the error types shown as well as an assortment of other errors.

ering the error rate of each, we found that it is critical to consider (a) the effort that the scholar must exert to correct, or post-edit, a non-expert's transcription, and (b) the amount of overhead required by the scholar to gather the transcriptions.

All errors are not equally serious. We found that the expert scholar had an easier time correcting some errors in post-editing than others. For example, modernization errors may be corrected automatically or in a single read through the transcription, without constantly consulting the original text. In contrast, correcting formatting errors is very time consuming. Similarly, correcting errors resulting from page noise requires the scholar to closely compare punctuation in the original text with that of the transcription and takes a lot of time.

Previous research on gathering and using non-expert annotations using MTurk (Snow et al., 2008; Callison-Burch and Dredze, 2010; Zaidan and Callison-Burch, 2011) has been optimistic. However, that work has failed to account for the time and effort required to compose, post, monitor, approve, and parse MTurk HITs (human intelligence tasks). In our exploration, we found that the time required by our expert scholar to gather MTurk annotations nearly offsets the cost savings that result from using it instead of local student or professional transcribers. Similarly, the scholar had to provide some supervision to the student transcribers. The professional transcription service, in contrast, though more expensive than the other high quality (non-OCR) methods, required no oversight on the part of the scholar. After using all methods to transcribe 30 pages of *Lettres taïtiennes* and critically comparing the costs and benefits of each, we had the professional transcription service complete the project and our expert French literature scholar has based a new critical edition of the text on this transcription.

4 Background

Snow et al. (2008) gathered annotations on MTurk in order to supervise a variety of NLP tasks. In general, they found a high degree of annotator agreement and inspired a plethora of research on using non-expert annotations for additional tasks in language processing (Callison-Burch and Dredze, 2010).

OCR has been an active area of research in NLP for decades (Arica and Yarman-Vural, 2001). Recent work has acknowledged that post-editing OCR output is an important engineering task but generally assumes large amounts of training data and does not attempt to maintain text format (Kolak et al., 2003). As we described, for our application, transcribing all content and formatting, including footnotes, references, indentations, capitalization, etc. is crucial. Furthermore, OCR output quality was so low that post-editing it would have required more work than transcribing from scratch. We did not attempt to train the OCR since, even if it had recognized ſ and learned an appropriate language model, the formatting and noise errors would have remained.

5 Future Work and Conclusions

In Section 3.2, we mentioned that it may be possible to automatically post-edit transcriptions and correct systematic modernization errors. The same may be true for, for example, some types of typos. This type of post-editing could be done manually or automatically. One potential automatic approach is to train a language model on the first transcription attempt and then use the model to identify unlikely segments of text. We plan to pursue this in future work.

Although we hoped that using MTurk or OCR would provide an inexpensive, high-quality first round transcription, we found that we preferred to use student and professional transcribers.The tradeoffs between speed and accuracy and between low cost and overhead time were not worthwhile for our project. If a scholar were working with a larger text or tighter budget, investing the time and effort to use MTurk could prove worthwhile. Using an OCR system would demand extensive training to the text domain as well as post-editing. This paper enumerates important challenges, costs, and benefits of several transcription approaches, which are worthy of consideration by scholars working on similar projects.

References

N. Arica and F. T. Yarman-Vural. 2001. An overview of character recognition focused on off-line handwriting. *Systems, Man, and Cybernetics, Part C: Applications and Reviews, IEEE Transactions on*, 31(2):216–233, May.

Chris Callison-Burch and Mark Dredze. 2010. Creating speech and language data with amazon's mechanical turk. In *Proceedings of the NAACL HLT 2010 Workshop on Creating Speech and Language Data with Amazon's Mechanical Turk*, pages 1–12, Los Angeles, June. Association for Computational Linguistics.

Joséphine de Monbart. 1786. *Lettres tahitiennes*. Les Marchands de nouveautés, Paris.

Okan Kolak, William Byrne, and Philip Resnik. 2003. A generative probabilistic ocr model for nlp applications. In *Proceedings of the NAACL*, pages 55–62. Association for Computational Linguistics.

Rion Snow, Brendan O'Connor, Daniel Jurafsky, and Andrew Y. Ng. 2008. Cheap and fast—but is it good?: evaluating non-expert annotations for natural language tasks. In *Proceedings of the Conference on Empirical Methods in Natural Language Processing*, EMNLP '08, pages 254–263, Stroudsburg, PA, USA. Association for Computational Linguistics.

Omar F. Zaidan and Chris Callison-Burch. 2011. Crowdsourcing translation: Professional quality from non-professionals. In *Proceedings of the 49th Annual Meeting of the Association for Computational Linguistics: Human Language Technologies*, pages 1220–1229, Portland, Oregon, USA, June. Association for Computational Linguistics.

A Dictionary of Wisdom and Wit: Learning to Extract Quotable Phrases*

Michael Bendersky
Dept. of Computer Science
University of Massachusetts
Amherst, MA
bemike@cs.umass.edu

David A. Smith
Dept. of Computer Science
University of Massachusetts
Amherst, MA
dasmith@cs.umass.edu

Abstract

Readers suffering from information overload have often turned to collections of pithy and famous quotations. While research on large-scale analysis of text reuse has found effective methods for detecting widely disseminated and famous quotations, this paper explores the complementary problem of detecting, from internal evidence alone, which phrases are *quotable*. These quotable phrases are memorable and succinct statements that people are likely to find useful outside of their original context. We evaluate quotable phrase extraction using a large digital library and demonstrate that an integration of lexical and shallow syntactic features results in a reliable extraction process. A study using a *reddit* community of quote enthusiasts as well as a simple corpus analysis further demonstrate the practical applications of our work.

1 Introduction

Readers have been anxious about information overload for a long time: not only since the rise of the web, but with the earlier explosion of printed books, and even in manuscript culture (Blair, 2010). One traditional response to the problem has been excerpting passages that might be useful outside their original sources, copying them into personal commonplace books, and publishing them in dictionaries such as *Bartlett's Familiar Quotations* or the *Oxford Dictionary of Quotations*. Even on the web, collection of quotable phrases continues to thrive[1], as evidenced by the popularity of quotation websites such as *BrainyQuote* and *Wikiquote*.

According to a recent estimate, there are close to 130 million unique book records in world libraries today (Taycher, 2010). Many of these books are being digitized and stored by commercial providers (e.g., Google Books and Amazon), as well as non-profit organizations (e.g., Internet Archive and Project Gutenberg).

As a result of this digitization, the development of new methods for preserving, accessing and analyzing the contents of literary corpora becomes an important research venue with many practical applications (Michel et al., 2011). One particularly interesting line of work in these large digital libraries has focused on detecting *text reuse*, i.e., passages from one source that are quoted in another (Kolak and Schilit, 2008).

In contrast, in this paper we explore the modeling of phrases that *are likely to be* quoted. This phrase modeling is done based on internal evidence alone, regardless of whether or not the phrase actually *is* quoted in existing texts.

We call such potential quotation a **quotable phrase** – a meaningful, memorable, and succinct statement that can be quoted without its original context. This kind of phrases includes aphorisms, epigrams, maxims, proverbs, and epigraphs.

* "The book is a dictionary of wisdom and wit..." *(Samuel Smiles, "A Publisher and His Friends")* This and all the subsequent quotations in this paper were discovered by the proposed quotable phrase extraction process.

[1] "Nothing is so pleasant as to display your worldly wisdom in epigram and dissertation, but it is a trifle tedious to hear another person display theirs." *(Kate Sanborn, "The Wit of Women")*

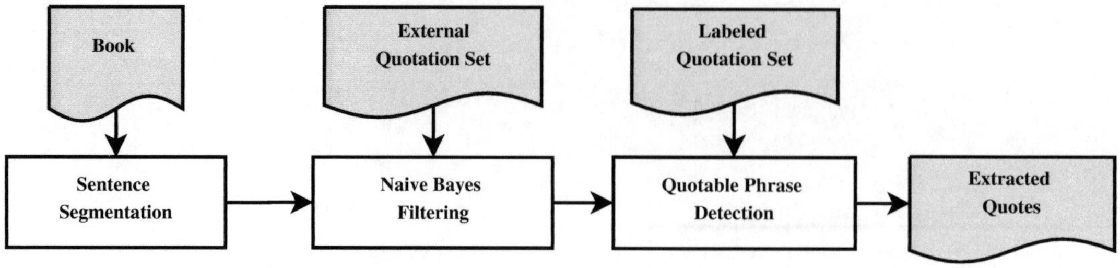

Figure 1: Diagram of the quotable phrase extraction process.

A computational approach to quotable phrase extraction has several practical applications. For instance, it can be used to recommend new additions to existing quotable phrase collections, especially focusing on lesser read and studied authors and literary works[2]. It can also generate quotable phrases that will serve as catchy and entertaining previews for book promotion and advertisement[3].

In this work, we describe such a computational approach to quotable phrase extraction. Our approach leverages the Project Gutenberg digital library and an online collection of quotations to build a *quotable language model*. This language model is further refined by a supervised learning algorithm that combines lexical and shallow syntactic features.

In addition, we demonstrate that a computational approach can help to address some intriguing questions about the nature of quotability. What are the lexical and the syntactic features that govern the quotability of a phrase? Which authors and books are highly quotable? How much variance is there in the perceived quotability of a given phrase?

The remainder of this paper is organized as follows. In Section 2 we provide a detailed description of the entire process of quotable phrase extraction. In Section 3 we review the related work. In Sections 4 and 5 we evaluate the quotable phrase extraction process, and provide some corpus quotability analysis. We conclude the paper in Section 6.

2 Quotable Phrase Extraction

There are three unique challenges that need to be addressed in the design of the process of quotable phrase extraction. The first challenge stems from the fact that the boundaries of potential quotes are often ambiguous. A quotable phrase can consist of a sentence fragment, a complete sentence, or a passage of text that spans several sentences.

The second challenge is that the occurrence of quotable phrases is a rare phenomena in literary corpora. A randomly selected book passage is unlikely to be quotable without any additional context.

The third challenge is related to the syntax and semantics of quotable phrases. For instance, consider the phrase

> "Evil men make evil use of the law, though the law is good, while good men die well, although death is an evil." *(Thomas Aquinas, "Summa Theologica")*

and contrast it with

> "Of the laws that he can see, the great sequences of life to death, of evil to sorrow, of goodness to happiness, he tells in burning words." *(Henry Fielding, "The Soul of a People")*

While both of these phrases share a common vocabulary (*law*, *death*, *good* and *evil*), the latter sentence contains unresolved pronouns (*he*, twice) that make it less amenable to quotation out of context.

Accordingly, we design a three-stage quotable phrase extraction process, with each stage corresponding to one of challenges described above. The diagram in Figure 1 provides a high-level overview of the entire extraction process on a single book. Next, we provide a brief description of this diagram. Then, in the following sections, we focus on individual stages of the extraction process.

To address the first challenge of quote boundary detection, at the first stage of the extraction process

[2] "There is life in a poet so long as he is quoted..." *(Sir Alfred Comyn Lyall, "Studies in Literature and History")*

[3] As an example, see the "Popular Highlights" feature for Kindle e-books in the *Amazon* bookstore.

(*Sentence Segmentation*) we segment the text of the input book into sentences using an implementation of the Punkt sentence boundary detection algorithm (Kiss and Strunk, 2006). In an initial experiment, we found that 78% of the approximately 4,000 quotations collected from the *QuotationsPage*[4] consist of a single sentence. From now on, therefore, we make a simplifying assumption that an extracted quotable phrase is confined within the sentence boundaries.

The second processing stage (*Naïve Bayes Filtering*) aims to address the second challenge (the rarity of quotable phrases) and significantly increases the ratio of quotable phrases that are considered as candidates in the final processing stage (*Quotable Phrase Detection*). To this end, we use a set of quotations collected from an external resource to build a *quotable language model*. Only sentences that have a sufficiently high likelihood of being drawn from this language model are considered at the final processing stage.

For this final processing stage (*Quotable Phrase Detection*), we develop a supervised algorithm that focuses on the third challenge, and analyzes the syntactic structure of the input sentences. This supervised algorithm makes use of structural and syntactic features that may effect phrase quotability, in addition to the vocabulary of the phrase.

2.1 Naïve Bayes Filtering

In order to account for the rarity of quotable phrases in the book corpus, we use a filtering approach based on a pre-built *quotable language model*. Using this filtering approach, we significantly reduce the number of sentences that need to be considered in the supervised quotable phrase detection stage (described in Section 2.2). In addition, this approach increases the ratio of quotable phrases considered at the supervised stage, addressing the problem of the sparsity of positive examples.

To build the quotable language model, we bootstrap the existing quotation collections on the web. In particular, we collect approximately 4,000 quotes on more than 200 subjects from the *QuotationsPage*. This collection provides a diverse set of high-quality quotations on subjects ranging from *Laziness* and *Genius* to *Technology* and *Taxes*.

[4]`www.quotationspage.com`

Then, we build two separate unigram language models. The first one is the quotable language model, which is built using the collected quotations ($\mathcal{L}_Q$). The second one is the background language model, which is built using the entire book corpus ($\mathcal{L}_C$). Using these language models we compute a log-likelihood ratio for each processed sentence $\mathbf{s}$, as

$$LLR_{\mathbf{s}} = \sum_{w \in \mathbf{s}} \ln \frac{p(w|\mathcal{L}_Q)}{p(w|\mathcal{L}_C)}, \qquad (1)$$

where the probabilities $p(w|\cdot)$ are computed using a maximum likelihood estimate with add-one smoothing.

A sentence $\mathbf{s}$ is allowed to pass the filtering stage if and only if $LLR_{\mathbf{s}} \in [\alpha, \beta]$, where α, β are positive constants[5]. The lower bound on the $LLR_{\mathbf{s}}$, α, requires the sentence to be highly *probable* given the quotable language model $\mathcal{L}_Q$. The upper bound on the $LLR_{\mathbf{s}}$, β, filters out sentences that are highly *improbable* given the background language model $\mathcal{L}_C$.

Finally, the sentences for which $LLR_{\mathbf{s}} \in [\alpha, \beta]$ are allowed to pass through the Naïve Bayes filter. They are forwarded to the next stage, in which a supervised quotable phrase detection is performed.

2.2 Supervised Quotable Phrase Detection

In a large corpus, a supervised quotable phrase detection method needs to handle a significant number of input instances (in our corpus, an average-sized book contains approximately 2,000 sentences). Therefore, we make use of a simple and efficient perceptron algorithm, which is implemented following the description by Bishop (2006).

We note, however, that the proposed supervised detection method can be also implemented using a variety of other binary prediction techniques. In an initial experiment, we found that more complex methods (e.g., decision trees) were comparable to or worse than the simple perceptron algorithm.

Formally, we define a binary function $f(\mathbf{s})$ which determines whether an input sentence $\mathbf{s}$ is a quotable (q) or a non-quotable ($\overline{q}$) phrase, based on:

$$f(\mathbf{s}) = \begin{cases} q & \text{if } \mathbf{w}\mathbf{x_s} > 0 \\ \overline{q} & \text{else,} \end{cases} \qquad (2)$$

[5]In this work, we set $\alpha = 1, \beta = 25$. This setting is done prior to seeing any labeled data.

Feature	Description
	Lexical
LLR	Sentence log-likelihood ratio (Eq. 1)
#word	Number of words in s.
#char	Number of characters in s.
wordLenAgg	Feature for each aggregate Agg of word length in s. Agg = {*min, max, mean*}
#capital	Number of capitalized words in s.
#quantifier	Number of universal quantifiers in s (from a list of 13 quantifiers, e.g., *all*, *whole*, *nobody*).
#stops	Number of common stopwords in s.
beginStop	True if s begins with a stopword, False otherwise.
hasDialog	True if s contains at least one of the three common dialog terms {*say*, *says*, *said*}.
#abstract	Number of abstract concepts (e.g., *adventure*, *charity*, *stupidity*) in s.
	Punctuation
hasP	Five features to indicate whether punctuation of type P is present in s. P = {*quotations, parentheses, colon, dash, semi-colon*}.
	Parts of Speech
#POS	Four features for the number of occurrences of part-of-speech POS in s. POS = {*noun, verb, adjective, adverb, pronoun*}.
hasComp	True if s contains a comparative adjective or adverb, False otherwise.
hasSuper	True if s contains a superlative adjective or adverb, False otherwise.
hasPP	True if s contains a verb in past participle, False otherwise.
#IGSeq[i]	Count of the POS sequence with the i-th highest $IG(X, Y)$ (Eq. 3) in s.

Table 1: Description of the quotability features that are computed for each sentence s .

where $\mathbf{x_s}$ is a vector of *quotability features* computed for the sentence s, and $\mathbf{w}$ is a weight vector associated with these features. The weight vector $\mathbf{w}$ is updated using stochastic gradient descent on the perceptron error function (Bishop, 2006).

Since Eq. 2 demonstrates that the supervised quotable phrase detection can be formulated as a standard binary classification problem, its success will be largely determined by an appropriate choice of feature vector $\mathbf{x_s}$. As we are unaware of any previous work on supervised detection of quotable phrases, we develop an initial set of easy-to-compute features that considers the lexical and shallow syntactic structure of the analyzed sentence.

2.3 Quotability Features

A decision about phrase quotability is often subjective; it is strongly influenced by personal taste and circumstances[6]. Therefore, the set of features that we describe in this section is merely a coarse-grained approximation of the true intrinsic qualities of a quotable phrase. Nevertheless, it is important to note that these features do prove to be beneficial in the context of the quote detection task, as is demonstrated by our empirical evaluation in Section 5.

Table 1 details the quotability features, which are divided into 3 groups: *lexical*, *punctuation-based* and *POS-based* features. All of these features are conceptually simple and can be efficiently computed even for a large number of input sentences.

Some of these features are inspired by existing text analysis tasks. For instance, work on readability detection for the web (Kanungo and Orr, 2009; Si and Callan, 2001) examined features which are similar to the *lexical* features in Table 1. *Parts of speech* features (e.g., the presence of comparative and superlative adjectives and adverbs) have been extensively used for sentiment analysis and opinion mining (Pang and Lee, 2008).

In addition, we use a number of features based on simple hand-crafted word lists. These lists include word categories that could be potential indicators of quotable phrases such as universal quantifiers (e.g., *all*, *everyone*) and abstract concepts[7].

[6]"One man's beauty another's ugliness; one man's wisdom another's folly." *(Ralph Waldo Emerson, "Essays")*

[7]For abstract concept modeling we use a list of 176 abstract nouns available at www.englishbanana.com.

The novel features in Table 1 that are specifically designed for quotable phrase detection are based on part of speech sequences that are highly indicative of quotable (or, conversely, non-quotable) phrase (features `#IGSeq[i]`). In order to compute these features we first manually label a validation set of 500 sentences that passed the Naïve Bayes Filtering (Section 2.1). Then, we apply a POS tagger to these sentences, and for each POS tag sequence of length n, seq_n, we compute its information gain

$$IG(X,Y) = H(X) - H(X|Y). \quad (3)$$

In Eq. 3, X is a binary variable indicating the presence or the absence of seq_n in the sentence, and $Y \in \{q, \overline{q}\}$.

We select k sequences seq_n with the highest value of $IG(X,Y)$[8]. We use the count in the sentence of the sequence seq_n with the i-th highest information gain as the feature `#IGSeq[i]`. Intuitively, the features `#IGSeq[i]` measure how many POS tag sequences that are indicative of a quotable phrase (or, conversely, indicative of a non-quotable phrase) the sentence contains.

3 Related Work

The increasing availability of large-scale digital libraries resulted in a recent surge of interest in computational approaches to literary analysis. To name just a few examples, Genzel et al. (2010) examined machine translation of poetry; Elson et al. (2010) extracted conversational networks from Victorian novels; and Faruqui and Padó (2011) predicted formal and informal address in English literature.

In addition, computational methods are increasingly used for identification of complex aspects of writing such as humor (Mihalcea and Pulman, 2007), double-entendre (Kiddon and Brun, 2011) and sarcasm (Tsur et al., 2010). However, while successful, most of this work is still limited to an analysis of a single aspect of writing style.

In this work, we propose a more general computational approach that attempts to extract quotable phrases. A quotability of a phrase can be affected by various aspects of writing including (but not limited to) humor and irony[9], use of metaphors[10], and hyperbole[11].

[8]In this work, we set $n = 3, k = 50$. This setting is done prior to seeing any labeled data.

Number of books	$21,492$
Number of authors	$8,889$
Total sentences	$4.45 \cdot 10^7$
After Naïve Bayes filtering	$1.75 \cdot 10^7$

Table 2: Summary of the Project Gutenberg corpus.

It is important to note that our approach is conceptually different from the previous work on paraphrase and quote detection in book corpora (Kolak and Schilit, 2008), news stories (Liang et al., 2010) and movie scripts (Danescu-Niculescu-Mizil et al., 2012). While this previous work focuses on mining popular and oft-used quotations, we are mainly interested in discovering quotable phrases that might have never been quoted by others.

4 Experimental Setup

To evaluate the quotable phrase extraction process in its entirety (see Figure 1), we use a collection of Project Gutenberg (*PG*) books[12] – a popular digital library containing full texts of public domain books in a variety of formats. In particular, we harvest the entire corpus of 21,492 English books in textual format from the *PG* website.

The breakdown of the *PG* corpus is shown in Table 2. The number of detected sentences in the *PG* corpus exceeds 44 million. Roughly a third of these sentences are able to pass through the Naïve Bayes Filtering (described in Section 2.1) to the supervised quotable phrase detection stage (Section 2.2).

For each of these sentences, we compute a set of lexical and syntactic features described in Section 2.3. For computing the features that require the part of speech tags, we use the MontyLingua package (Liu, 2004).

[9]"To be born with a riotous imagination and then hardly ever to let it riot is to be a born newspaper man." *(Zona Gale, "Romance Island")*

[10]"If variety is the spice of life, his life in the north has been one long diet of paprika." *(Fullerton Waldo, "Grenfell: Knight-Errant of the North")*

[11]"The idea of solitude is so repugnant to human nature, that even death would be preferable." *(William O.S. Gilly, "Narratives of Shipwrecks of the Royal Navy; between 1793 and 1849")*

[12]`http://www.gutenberg.org/`

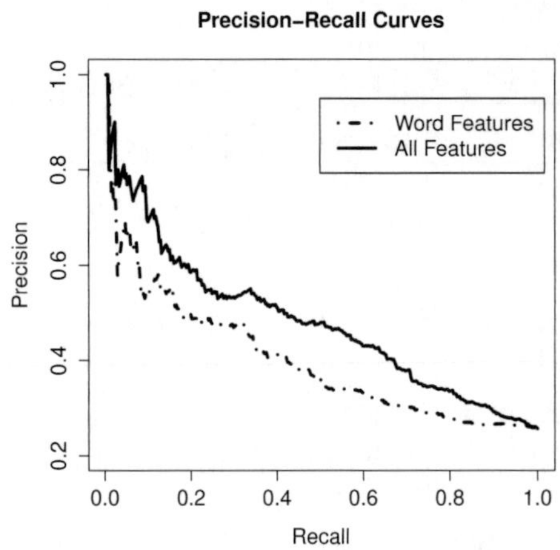

Figure 2: Prec. vs. recall for quotable phrase detection.

We find that the extraction process shown in Figure 1 is efficient and scalable. On average, the entire process requires less than ten seconds per book on a single machine.

The complete set of extracted quotable phrases and annotations is available upon request from the authors. In addition, the readers are invited to visit www.noisypearls.com, where a quotable phrase from the set is published daily.

5 Evaluation and Analysis

5.1 Naïve Bayes Filtering Evaluation

In the Naïve Bayes Filtering stage (see Section 2.1) we evaluate two criteria. First, we measure its ability to reduce the number of sentences that pass to the supervised quotable phrase detection stage. As Table 2 shows, the Naïve Bayes Filtering reduces the number of these sentences by more than 60%.

Second, we evaluate the recall of the Naïve Bayes Filtering. We are primarily interested in its ability to reliably detect quotable phrases and pass them through to the next stage, while still reducing the total number of sentences.

For recall evaluation, we collect a set of 2,817 previously unseen quotable phrases from the *Goodreads* website[13], and run them through the Naïve Bayes Filtering stage. 2,262 (80%) of the quotable phrases pass the filter, indicating a high quotable phrase recall.

[13] http://www.goodreads.com/quotes

1	#abstract	+91.64
2	#quantifier	+61.67
3	hasPP	−60.34
4	#IGSeq[16] *(VB IN PRP)*	+39.71
5	#IGSeq[6] *(PRP MD VB)*	−38.78
6	#adjective	+37.71
7	#IGSeq[14] *(DT NN VBD)*	−36.88
8	#verb	+35.22
9	beginStop	+31.73
10	#noun	+29.63

Table 3: Top quotability features.

Based on these findings, we conclude that the proposed Naïve Bayes Filtering is able to reliably detect quotable phrases, while filtering out a large number of non-quotable ones. It can be further calibrated to reduce the number of non-quotable sentences or to increase the quotable phrase recall, by changing the setting of the parameters α and β, described in Section 2.1. In the remainder of this section, we use its output to analyze the performance of the supervised quotable phrase detection stage.

5.2 Quotable Phrase Detection Evaluation

To evaluate the performance of the supervised quotable phrase detection stage (see Section 2.2) we randomly sample 1,500 sentences that passed the Naïve Bayes Filtering (this sample is disjoint from the sample of 500 sentences used for computing the IGTagSeq feature in Section 2.3). We annotate these sentences with q (*Quotable*) and $\overline{q}$ (*Non-Quotable*) labels.

Of these sentences, 381 (25%) are labeled as *Quotable*. This ratio of quotable phrases is much higher than what is expected from a non-filtered content of a book, which provides an indication that the Naïve Bayes Filtering provides a relatively balanced input to the supervised detection stage.

We use this random sample of 1,500 labeled sentences to train a perceptron algorithm (as described in Section 2.2) using 10-fold cross-validation. We train two variants of the perceptron. The first variant is trained using only the lexical features in Table 1, while the second variant uses all the features.

Figure 2 compares the precision-recall curves of these two variants. It demonstrates that using the syntactic features based on punctuation and part of speech tags significantly improves the precision of

Popular	$\Uparrow \geq 10$	12
Upvoted	$1 \leq \Uparrow \leq 10$	34
No upvotes	$\Uparrow \leq 0$	14
	$\mathbf{p}(\Uparrow > \mathbf{0}) =$	**.77**

Table 4: Distribution of *reddit* upvote scores.

quote phrase detection at all recall levels. For instance at the 0.4 recall level, it can improve precision by almost 25%.

Figure 2 also shows that the proposed method is reliable for high-precision quotable phrase detection. This is especially important for applications where recall is given less consideration, such as book preview using quotable phrases. The proposed method reaches a precision of 0.7 at the 0.1 recall level.

It is also interesting to examine the importance of different features for the quotable phrase detection. Table 3 shows the ten highest-weighted features, as learned by the perceptron algorithm on the entire set of 1,500 labeled examples.

The part of speech features `#IGTagSeq[i]` occupy three of the positions in the Table 3. It is interesting to note that two of them have a high *negative weight*. In other words, some of the POS sequences that have the highest information gain (see Eq. 3) are sequences that are indicative of non-quotable phrases, rather than quotable phrases.

The two highest-weighted features are based on handcrafted word lists (`#abstract` and `#quantifier`, respectively). This demonstrates the importance of task-specific features such as these for quotability detection.

Finally, the presence of different parts of speech in the phrase (nouns, verbs and adjectives), as well as their verb tenses, are important features. For instance, the presence of a verb in past participle (`hasPP`) is a strong *negative* indicator of phrase quotability.

5.3 The *reddit* Study

As mentioned in Section 2.3, the degree of the phrase quotability is often subjective, and therefore its estimation may vary among individuals. To validate that our quotability detection method is not biased by our training data, and that the detected quotes will have a universal appeal, we set up a verification study that leverages an online community of quote enthusiasts.

For our study, we use *reddit*, a social content website where the registered users submit content, in the form of either a link or a text post. Other registered users then upvote or downvote the submission, which is used to rank the post.

Specifically, we use the *Quotes subreddit*[14], an active *reddit* community devoted to discovering and sharing quotable phrases. At the time of this writing, the *Quotes* subreddit has more than 12,000 subscribers. A typical post to this subreddit contains a single quotable phrase with attribution. Any *reddit* user can then upvote or downvote the quote based on its perceived merit.

To validate the quality of the quotes which were used for training the perceptron algorithm, we submitted 60 quotes, which were labeled as quotable by one of the authors, to the *Quotes* subreddit. At most one quote per day was submitted, to avoid negative feedback from the community for "spamming".

Table 4 presents the upvote scores of the submitted quotes. An upvote score, denoted $\Uparrow$, is computed as

$$\Uparrow = \#\text{ upvotes } - \#\text{ downvotes}.$$

Table 4 validates that the majority of the quotes labeled as quotable, were also endorsed by the *reddit* community, and received a non-negative upvote score. As an illustration, in Table 5, we present five quotes with the highest upvote scores. Anecdotally, at the time of this writing, only one of the quotes in Table 5 (a quote by Mark Twain) appeared in web search results in contexts other than the original book.

5.4 Project Gutenberg Corpus Analysis

In this section, we briefly highlight an interesting example of how the proposed computational approach to quotable phrase extraction can be used for a literary analysis of the *PG* digital library. To this end, we train the supervised quotable phrase detection method using the entire set of 1,500 manually labeled sentences. We then run this model over all the 17.5 million sentences that passed the Naïve Bayes filtering stage, and retain only the sentences that get positive perceptron scores (Eq. 2).

[14]`http://www.reddit.com/r/quotes`

Quote	⇑
"One hour of deep agony teaches man more love and wisdom than a whole long life of happiness." *(Walter Elliott, "Life of Father Hecker")*	**49**
"As long as I am on this little planet I expect to love a lot of people and I hope they will love me in return." *(Kate Langley, Bosher, "Kitty Canary")*	**43**
"None of us could live with an habitual truth-teller; but thank goodness none of us has to." *(Mark Twain, "On the Decay of the Art of Lying")*	**40**
"A caged bird simply beats its wings and dies, but a human being does not die of loneliness, even when he prays for death." *(George Moore, "The Lake")*	**33**
"Many will fight as long as there is hope, but few will go down to certain death." *(G. A. Henty, "For the Temple")*	**30**

Table 5: Five quotes with the highest upvote scores on *reddit*.

(a) Authors			(b) Books		
1	Henry Drummond	.045	*1*	"Friendship" (Hugh Black)	.113
2	Ella Wheeler Wilcox	.041	*2*	"The Dhammapada" (Translated by F. Max Muller)	.112
3	S. D. Gordon	.040	*3*	"The Philosophy of Despair" (David Starr Jordan)	.106
4	Andrew Murray	.038	*4*	"Unity of Good" (Mary Baker Eddy)	.097
5	Ralph Waldo Emerson	.037	*5*	"Laments" (Jan Kochanowski)	.084
6	Orison Swett Marden	.034	*6*	"Joy and Power" (Henry van Dyke)	.079
7	Mary Baker Eddy	.031	*7*	"Polyeucte" (Pierre Corneille)	.078
8	'Abdu'l-Bahá	.029	*8*	"The Forgotten Threshold" (Arthur Middleton)	.078
9	John Hartley	.029	*9*	"The Silence" (David V. Bush)	.077
10	Rabindranath Tagore	.028	*10*	"Levels of Living" (Henry Frederick Cope)	.075

Table 6: Project Gutenberg (a) authors and (b) books with the highest quotability index.

This procedure yields 701,418 sentences, which we call *quotable phrases* in the remainder of this section. These quotable phrases are less than 2% of the entire Project Gutenberg corpus; however, they still constitute a sizable collection with some potentially interesting properties.

We propose a simple example of a literary analysis that can be done using this set of quotable phrases. We detect books and authors that have a high *quotability index*, which is formally defined as

$$QI(x) = \frac{\#\text{ quotable phrases}(x)}{\#\text{ total sentences}(x)},$$

where x is either a book or an author. To ensure the statistical validity of our analysis, we limit our attention to books with at least 25 quotable phrases and authors with at least 5 books in the *PG* collection.

Using this definition, we can easily compile a list of authors and books with the highest quotability index (see Table 6). An interesting observation is that many of the authors and books in Table 6 deal with religious themes: Christianity (e.g., Mary Baker Eddy, S. D. Gordon), Bahá'ísm ('Abdu'l-Bahá) and Buddhism ("The Dhammapada"). This is not surprising considering the figurative language common in the religious prose[15].

6 Conclusions

As the number of digitized books increases, a computational analysis of literary corpora becomes an active research field with many practical applications. In this paper, we focus on one such application: extraction of quotable phrases from books. Quotable phrase extraction can be used, among other things, for finding new original quotations for dictionaries and online quotation repositories, as well as for generating catchy previews for book advertisement.

We develop a quotable phrase extraction process that includes sentence segmentation, unsupervised sentence filtering based on a *quotable language model*, and a supervised quotable phrase detection using lexical and syntactic features. Our evaluation demonstrates that this process can be used for high-precision quotable phrase extraction, especially in applications that can tolerate lower recall. A study using a *reddit* community of quote enthusiasts as well as a simple corpus analysis further demonstrate the practical applications of our work.

[15]"If a man speaks or acts with an evil thought, pain follows him, as the wheel follows the foot of the ox that draws the carriage."(*"The Dhammapada", translated by F. Max Muller*)

7 Acknowledgments

This work was supported in part by the Center for Intelligent Information Retrieval, in part by NSF grant IIS-0910884 and in part by ARRA NSF IIS-9014442. Any opinions, findings and conclusions or recommendations expressed in this material are those of the authors and do not necessarily reflect those of the sponsor.

References

Christopher M. Bishop. 2006. *Pattern Recognition and Machine Learning*. Springer.

Ann M. Blair. 2010. *Too Much to Know: Managing Scholarly Information before the Modern Age*. Yale University Press.

Cristian Danescu-Niculescu-Mizil, Justin Cheng, Jon Kleinberg, and Lillian Lee. 2012. You had me at hello: How phrasing affects memorability. In *Proc. of ACL*, page To appear.

David K. Elson, Nicholas Dames, and Kathleen R. McKeown. 2010. Extracting social networks from literary fiction. In *Proc. of ACL*, pages 138–147.

Manaal Faruqui and Sebastian Padó. 2011. "I thou thee, thou traitor": predicting formal vs. informal address in English literature. In *Proceedings of ACL-HLT*, pages 467–472.

Dmitriy Genzel, Jakob Uszkoreit, and Franz Och. 2010. "Poetic" Statistical Machine Translation: Rhyme and Meter. In *Proc. of EMNLP*, pages 158–166.

Tapas Kanungo and David Orr. 2009. Predicting the readability of short web summaries. In *Proc. of WSDM*, pages 202–211.

Chloe Kiddon and Yuriy Brun. 2011. That's What She Said: Double Entendre Identification. In *Proc. of ACL-HLT*, pages 89–94.

T. Kiss and J. Strunk. 2006. Unsupervised multilingual sentence boundary detection. *Computational Linguistics*, 32(4):485–525.

Okan Kolak and Bill N. Schilit. 2008. Generating links by mining quotations. In *Proc. of 19th ACM conference on Hypertext and Hypermedia*, pages 117–126.

Jisheng Liang, Navdeep Dhillon, and Krzysztof Koperski. 2010. A large-scale system for annotating and querying quotations in news feeds. In *Proc. of SemSearch*.

Hugo Liu. 2004. Montylingua: An end-to-end natural language processor with common sense. Available at: `web.media.mit.edu/~hugo/montylingua`.

Jean-Baptiste Michel, Yuan Kui Shen, Aviva Presser Aiden, Adrian Veres, Matthew K. Gray, The Google Books Team, Joseph P. Pickett, Dale Hoiberg, Dan Clancy, Peter Norvig, Jon Orwant, Steven Pinker, Martin A. Nowak, and Erez Lieberman Aiden. 2011. Quantitative analysis of culture using millions of digitized books. *Science*, 331(6014):176–182.

Rada Mihalcea and Stephen Pulman. 2007. Characterizing humour: An exploration of features in humorous texts. In *Proc. of CICLing*, pages 337–347.

Bo Pang and Lillian Lee. 2008. Opinion mining and sentiment analysis. *Foundations and Trends in Information Retrieval*, 2(1-2):1–135.

Luo Si and Jamie Callan. 2001. A statistical model for scientific readability. In *Proc. of CIKM*, pages 574–576.

Leonid Taycher. 2010. Books of the world, stand up and be counted! All 129,864,880 of you. *Inside Google Books blog*.

Oren Tsur, Dimitry Davidov, and Avi Rappoport. 2010. ICWSM–A great catchy name: Semi-supervised recognition of sarcastic sentences in online product reviews. In *Proc. of ICWSM*, pages 162–169.

A Pilot PropBank Annotation for Quranic Arabic

Wajdi Zaghouani
University of Pennsylvania
Philadelphia, PA USA
wajdiz@ldc.upenn.edu

Abdelati Hawwari and **Mona Diab**
Center for Computational Learning Systems
Columbia University, NYC, USA
{ah3019,mdiab}@ccls.columbia.edu

Abstract

The Quran is a significant religious text written in a unique literary style, close to very poetic language in nature. Accordingly it is significantly richer and more complex than the newswire style used in the previously released Arabic PropBank (Zaghouani et al., 2010; Diab et al., 2008). We present preliminary work on the creation of a unique Arabic proposition repository for Quranic Arabic. We annotate the semantic roles for the 50 most frequent verbs in the Quranic Arabic Dependency Treebank (QATB) (Dukes and Buckwalter 2010). The Quranic Arabic PropBank (QAPB) will be a unique new resource of its kind for the Arabic NLP research community as it will allow for interesting insights into the semantic use of classical Arabic, poetic literary Arabic, as well as significant religious texts. Moreover, on a pragmatic level QAPB will add approximately 810 new verbs to the existing Arabic PropBank (APB). In this pilot experiment, we leverage our knowledge and experience from our involvement in the APB project. All the QAPB annotations will be made freely available for research purposes.

1 Introduction

Explicit characterization of the relation between verbs and their arguments has become an important issue in sentence processing and natural language understanding. Automatic Semantic role labeling [SRL] has become the correlate of this characterization in natural language processing literature (Gildea and Jurafsky 2002). In SRL, the system automatically identifies predicates and their arguments and tags the identified arguments with meaningful semantic information. SRL has been successfully used in machine translation, summarization and information extraction. In order to build robust SRL systems there is a need for significant resources the most important of which are semantically annotated resources such as proposition banks. Several such resources exist now for different languages including FrameNet (Baker et al., 1998), VerbNet (Kipper et al. 2000) and PropBank (Palmer et al., 2005). These resources have marked a surge in efficient approaches to automatic SRL of the English language. Apart from English, there exist various PropBank projects in Chinese (Xue et al., 2009), Korean (Palmer et al. 2006) and Hindi (Ashwini et al., 2011). These resources exist on a large scale spearheading the SRL research in the associated languages (Carreras and Marquez, 2005), Surdeanu et al. (2008). However, resources created for Arabic are significantly more modest. The only Arabic Propank [APB] project (Zaghouani et al., 2010; Diab et al., 2008) based on the phrase structure syntactic Arabic Treebank (Maamouri et al. 2010) comprises a little over 4.5K verbs of newswire modern standard Arabic. Apart from the modesty in size, the Arabic language genre used in the APB does not represent the full scope of the Arabic language. The Arabic culture has a long history of literary writing and a rich linguistic heritage in classical Arabic. In fact all historical religious non-religious texts are written in Classical Arabic. The ultimate source on classical Arabic language is the Quran. It is considered the Arabic language reference point for all learners of Arabic in the Arab and Muslim world. Hence understanding the semantic nuances of Quranic Arabic is of significant impact and value to a large population. This is apart from its significant difference from the newswire genre, being closer to poetic language and more creative linguistic expression. Accordingly, in this paper, we present a pilot annotation project on the creation a Quranic Arabic PropBank (QAPB) on layered above the Quranic Arabic Dependency Treebank (QATB) (Dukes and Buckwalter 2010).

2 The PropBank model

The PropBank model is a collection of annotated propositions where each verb predicate is annotated with its semantic roles. An existing syntactic treebank is typically a prerequisite for this shallow semantic layer. For example consider the following English sentence: 'John likes apples', the predicate is 'likes' and the first argument, the subject, is 'John', and the second argument, the object, is 'apples'. 'John' would be semantically annotated as the *agent* and 'apples' would be the *theme*. According to PropBank, 'John' is labeled ARG0 and 'apples' is labeled ARG1. Crucially, regardless of the adopted semantic annotation formalism (PropBank, FrameNet, etc), the labels do not vary in different syntactic constructions, which is why proposition annotation is different from Treebank annotation. For instance, if the example above was in the passive voice, 'Apples are liked by John', John is still the agent ARG0, and Apples are still the theme ARG1.

3 Motivation and Background

The main goal behind this project is to extend coverage of the existing Arabic PropBank (APB) to more verbs and genres (Zaghouani et al. 2010; Diab et al. 2008). APB is limited to the newswire domain in modern standard Arabic (MSA). It significantly lags behind the English PropBank (EPB) in size. EPB consists of 5413 verbs corresponding to 7268 different verb senses, the APB only covers 2127 verb types corresponding to 2657 different verb senses. According to El-Dahdah (2008) Arabic Dictionary, there are more than 16,000 verbs in the Arabic language. The Quran corpus comprises a total of 1466 verb types including 810 not present in APB. Adding the 810 verbs to the APB is clearly a significant boost to the size of the APB (38% amounting to 2937 verb types).

In the current paper however we address the annotation of the Quran as a stand alone resource while leveraging our experience in the APB annotation process. The Quran consists of 1466 verb types corresponding to 19,356 verb token instances. The language of the Quran is Classical Arabic (CA) of 77,430 words, sequenced in chapters and verses, dating back to over 1431 years. It is considered a reference text on both religious as well as linguistic matters. The language is fully specified with vocalic and pronunciation markers to ensure faithful oration. The language is poetic and literary in many instances with subtle allusions (Zahri 1990). It is the source of many other religious and heritage writings and a book of great importance to muslims worldwide, including non speakers of Arabic.

Dukes and Buckwalter (2010) started the Quranic Arabic Corpus, an annotated linguistic resource which marks the Arabic grammar, syntax and morphology for each word. The QATB provides two levels of analysis: morphological annotation and syntactic representation. The syntax of traditional Arabic grammar is represented in the Quranic Treebank using hybrid dependency graphs as shown in Figure 1.[1] To the best of our knowledge, this is the first PropBank annotation of a religious and literary style text.

The new verbs added from the Quran are also common verbs widely used today in MSA but the Quranic context adds more possible senses to these verbs. Having a QAPB allows for a more semantic level of analysis to the Quran. Currently the Quranic Corpus Portal[2] comprises morphological annotations, syntactic treebanks, and a semantic ontology. Adding the QAPB will render it a unique source for Arabic language scholars worldwide (more than 50,000 unique visitors per day).

Linguistic studies of the Quranic verbs such as verbal alternations, verb valency, polysemy and verbal ambiguity are one of the possible research directions that could be studied with this new resource. On the other hand, the Arabic NLP research community will benefit from the increased coverage of the APB verbs, and the new domain covered (religious) and the new writing style (Quranic Arabic). Furthermore, Quranic citations are commonly used today in MSA written texts (books, newspapers, etc.), as well as Arabic social media intertwined with dialectal writings. This

[1] This display is different from the other existing Arabic Treebank, the Prague Arabic Dependency Treebank (PADT) (Smrž et al., 2008).

[2] http://corpus.quran.com/

makes the annotation of a Quranic style a rare and relevant resource for the building of Arabic NLP applications.

4 Methodology

We leverage the approach used with the previous APB (Zaghouani et al. 2010; Diab et al. 2008). We pay special attention to the polysemic nature of predicates used in Quranic Arabic. An Arabic root meaning tool is used as a reference to help in identifying different senses of the verb. More effort is dedicated to revision of the final product since unlike the APB, the QAPB is based on a dependency Treebank (QATB) not a phrase structure Treebank.[3]

For this pilot annotation experiment, we only annotate the 50 most frequent verbs in the corpus corresponding to 7227 verbal occurrences in the corpus out of 19,356 total verbal instances. In the future plans, the corpus will cover eventually all the 1466 verbs in the whole Quranic corpus. Ultimately, it is our plan to perform a merging between the new frame files of the QAPB and the existing 1955 Frame files of the Arabic PropBank

4.1 The annotation process

The PropBank annotation process is divided into two steps: a. creation of the frame files for verbs occurring in the data, and b. annotation of the verbal instances with the frame file ids. During the creation of the Frame Files, the usages of the verbs in the data are examined by linguists (henceforth, "framers"). During the frameset creation process, verbs that share similar semantic and syntactic characteristics are usually framed similarly). Once a predicate (in this case a verb) is chosen, framer-look at an average sample size of 60-70 instances per predicate found in the Quranic corpus in order to get an idea of its syntactic behavior. Based on these observations and their linguistic knowledge and native-speaker intuition, the framers create a Frame File for each verb containing one or more framesets, which correspond to coarse-grained senses of the predicate lemma. Each frameset specifies the PropBank core labels (i.e., ARG0, ARG1,...ARG4) corresponding to the argument structure of the verb. Additionally, illustrative examples are included for each frameset, which will later be referenced by the annotators. Note that in addition to these core, numbered roles, PropBank also includes annotations of a variety of modifier roles, prefixed by ARGM labels from a list of 15 arguments (ARGM-ADV, ARGM-BNF, ARGM-CAU,ARGM-CND, ARGM-DIR, ARGM-DIS, ARGM-EXT, ARGM-LOC, ARGM-MNR, ARGM-NEG, ARGM-PRD, ARGM-PRP, ARGM-REC, ARGM-TMP, ARGM-PRD). Unlike the APB frame files creation, where no specific Arabic reference is used, for this project, an Arabic root meaning reference tool developed by Swalha (2011) is used by the framers to ensure that all possible meanings of the verbs in the corpus are covered and all various senses are taken into account. The Arabic root-meaning search tool is freely available online.[4] The search is done by root, the tool displays all possible meanings separated by a comma with citation examples from many sources including the Quran. Once the Frame files are created, the data that have the identified predicate occurrences are passed on to the annotators for a double-blind annotation process using the previously created framesets. Each PropBank entry represents a particular instance of a verb in a particular sentence in the Treebank and the mapping of numbered roles to precise meanings is given on a verb-by-verb basis in a set of frames files during the annotation procedure. To ensure consistency, the data is double annotated and finally adjudicated by a third annotator. The adjudicator resolves differences between the two annotations if present to produce the gold annotation. A sample Frameset and a related annotation example from the QAPB are shown in Table 1. During the annotation process, the data is organized by verb such that each verb with all its instances is annotated at once. In doing so, we firstly ensure that the framesets of similar verbs, and in turn, the annotation of the verbs, will both be consistent across the data. Secondly, by tackling annotation on a verb-by-verb basis, the annotators are able to concentrate on a single verb at a time, making the process easier and faster for the annotators.

[3] The Propbank style of annotation are already used with other languages on top of dependency Treebank structures such as the Hindi Treebank project (Ashwini et al., 2011).

[4] Available at :<http://www.comp.leeds.ac.uk/cgi-bin/scmss/arabic_roots.py>

FrameSet Example	**Annotation Example**
Predicate: wajadaوَجَدَ Roleset id: f1, to find **Arg0: the finder** **Arg1: thing found**	**Rel:** wajada, **وَجَدَ** **Arg0: -NONE- *** **Gloss: You** **Arg1: هُ** **Gloss: it** **ArgM-LOC: عِنْدَ اللَّهِ** **Gloss: with Allah** **Example in Arabic:** **وَمَا تُقَدِّمُوا لِأَنْفُسِكُمْ مِنْ خَيْرٍ تَجِدُوهُ عِنْدَ اللَّهِ** **Gloss: and whatever good you put forward for yourselves - you will find it with Allah**

Table 1. The frameset / Annotation of wajada

4.2 Tools

Frameset files are created in an XML format. We use tools used in the APB project. The Frame File editing is performed by the Cornerstone tool (Choi et al., 2010a), which is a PropBank frameset editor that allows creation and editing of PropBank framesets without requiring any prior knowledge of XML. Moreover, we use Jubilee[5] as the annotation tool (Choi et al., 20010b). Jubilee is a recent annotation tool which improves the annotation process of the APB by displaying several types of relevant syntactic and semantic information simultaneously. Having everything displayed helps the annotator quickly absorb and apply the necessary syntactic and semantic information pertinent to each predicate for consistent and efficient annotation. Both tools are currently being modified in order to handle the Dependency TreeBank structure, originally the tool was designed specifically to handle phrase structure Tree format. Moreover, since the file formats and the tree formats in the dependency Treebank are different from the previous APB effort, a revision in the Quranic Treebank output had to be done. This involves mainly a change in the annotated data format in order to add the role labels in the annotation file. For the moment, all of the 50 XML Frame files have been created and some manual annotation is performed to illustrate the feasibility of the experiment.

[5] Cornerstone and Jubilee are available as Open Source tools on Google code.

4.3 Impact of the dependency structure Treebank

Having The Quran corpus annotated using a dependency structure Treebank has some advantages. First, semantic arguments can be marked explicitly on the syntactic trees (such as the Arg0 Pron. In Figure 1), so annotations of the predicate argument structure can be more consistent with the dependency structure as shown in Figure 1.

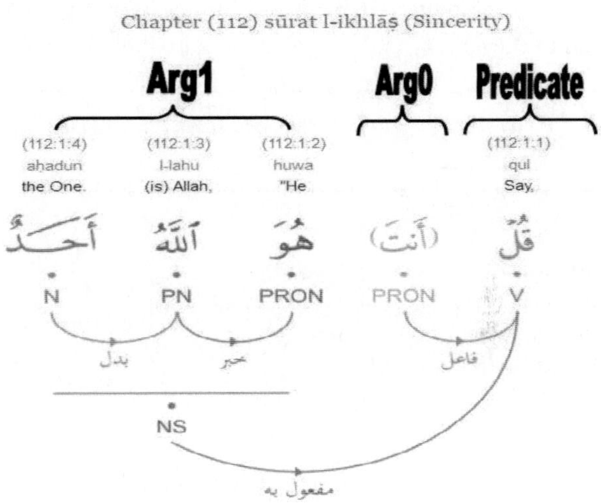

Figure 1. Semantic role labels to the QATB

Secondly, the Quranic Arabic Dependency Treebank (QATB) provides a rich set of dependency relations that capture the syntactic-semantic information. This facilitates possible mappings between syntactic dependents and semantic arguments. A successful mapping would reduce the annotation effort.

It is worth noting the APB comprises 1955 verbal predicates corresponding to 2446 framesets with an ambiguity ratio of 1.25. This is in contrast to the QAPB where we found that the 50 verbal predicate types we annotated corresponded to 71 framesets thereby an ambiguity ratio of 1.42. Hence these results suggest that the QAPB is more ambiguous than the newswire genre annotated in the APB. By way of contrast, the EPB comprises 6089 verbal predicates corresponding to 7268 framesets with an ambiguity ratio of 1.19.

21 verb types of the 50 verbs we annotated are present in both corpora corresponding to 31 framesets in QAPB (a 1.47 ambiguity ratio) and 25 framesets in APB (1.19 ambiguity ratio). The total verbal instances in the QAPB is 2974. 29 verb

types with their corresponding 40 framesets occur only in the QAPB (58% of the list of 50 verbs). This translated to a 1.38 ambiguity ratio.

In the common 21 verb types shared between APB and QAPB corpora we note that 12 predicates share the same exact frame sets indicating no change in meaning between the use of the predicates in the Quran and MSA. However, 9 of the verbal predicates have more framesets in QAPB than APB. None of the verbal predicates have more framesets in APB than QAPB. Below is an example of a verbal predicate with two different framesets.

FrameSet Example	**Annotation Example**
Predicate: >anozal أنْزَل Roleset id: f1, to reveal Arg0: revealer Arg1: thing revealed Arg2: start point Arg3: end point, recipient	Rel: >anozal Arg0: نَا Gloss: we Arg1: آيَاتٍ بَيِّنَاتٍ Gloss: *clear verses* Arg3: إلَيْكَ Gloss: to you Example in Arabic: وَلَقَدْ أنْزَلْنَا إلَيْكَ آيَاتٍ بَيِّنَاتٍ *We have certainly revealed to you verses [which are] clear proofs*

Table 2. The frameset / Annotation of >anozal (QAPB)

FrameSet Example	**Annotation Example**
Predicate: >anozal أنْزَل **Roleset id*: f1, to release*** Arg0: *agent releasing* Arg1:*thing released*	Rel: >anozal Arg0: زياد Gloss: Zyad **Arg1:NONE-*** Gloss: He ARGM-TMP: منتصف الثمانينات Gloss: the mid-eighties Example in Arabic: عودة الطلب على أغاني شريط أنا مش كافر الذي أنزله زياد منتصف الثمانينات The songs of the Album I am not a disbeliever released by Ziad during the eighties are popular again.

Table 3. The frameset / Annotation of >anozal (APB)

The two frames of verb '' >anozal " can clarify the meaning differences between MSA and QA as used in the Quran. Although both APB and QAPB have this verb, they have different senses leading to different semantic frames. In the QAPB the sense of revealed is only associated with religious texts, while in MSA it has the senses of released or dropped.

5 Conclusion

We have presented a pilot Quranic Arabic PropBank experiment with the creation of frame files for 50 verb types. At this point, our initial study confirms that building a lexicon and tagging the Arabic Quranic Corpus with verbal sense and semantic information following the PropBank model is feasible. In general, the peculiarities of the Quranic Arabic language did not seem to cause problems for the PropBank annotation model. We plan to start the effective annotation of the resource in order to finalize the creation of a QAPB that covers all 1466 verbal predicates. Once released, the data will be freely available for research purpose.

References

Vaidya Ashwini, Jinho Choi, Martha Palmer, and Bhuvana Narasimhan. 2011. Analysis of the Hindi Proposition Bank using Dependency Structure. In *Proceedings* of the fifth Linguistic Annotation Workshop. ACL 2011, pages 21-29.

Collin F. Baker, Charles J. Fillmore, and John B. Lowe. 1998. The Berkeley FrameNet project. In *Proceedings* of COLING-ACL '98, the University of Montreal, pages 86–90.

Xavier Carreras and Lluıs Marquez. 2005. Introduction to the CoNLL-2005 shared task: Semantic role labeling. In *Proceedings* of the Ninth (CoNLL-2005), pages 152–164.

Jinho Choi, Claire Bonial, and Martha Palmer.2010a. PropBank Instance Annotation Guidelines Using a Dedicated Editor, Cornerstone.In *Proceedings* of the (LREC'10), pages 3650-3653.

Jinho Choi, Claire Bonial, and Martha Palmer.2010b. PropBank Instance Annotation Guidelines Using a Dedicated Editor, Jubilee.In *Proceedings* of the (LREC'10), pages 1871-1875.

Mona Diab, Aous Mansouri, Martha Palmer, Olga Babko-Malaya,Wajdi Zaghouani, Ann Bies, and Mohammed Maamouri. 2008. A Pilot Arabic PropBank. In *Proceedings* of the (LREC'08), pages 3467-3472.

Kais Dukes and Tim Buckwalter. 2010. A Dependency Treebank of the Quran using Traditional Arabic Grammar. In *Proceedings* of the 7th International Conference on Informatics and Systems (INFOS).

Antoine El-Dahdah. 2008. *A Dictionary of Arabic Verb Conjugation*. Librairie du Liban, Beirut, Lebanon.

Daniel Gildea, and Daniel Jurafsky. 2002. Automatic-Labeling of Semantic Roles. *Computational Linguistics* 28:3, 245-288

Karin Kipper, HoaTrang Dang, and Martha Palmer. 2000. Class-Based Construction of a Verb Lexicon. In *Proceedings* of the AAAI-2000 Seventeenth National Conference on Artificial Intelligence, pages 691-696.

Mohamed Maamouri, Ann Bies, Seth Kulick, Fatma-Gaddeche, Wigdan Mekki, Sondos Krouna, Basma-Bouziri, and Wajdi Zaghouani. 2011. Arabic Treebank: Part 2 v 3.1. LDC Catalog No.:LDC2011T09

Martha Palmer, Dan Gildea, and Paul Kingsbury. 2005. The proposition bank: A corpus annotated with semantic roles. *Computational Linguistics Journal*, 31:1

Martha Palmer, Shijong Ryu, Jinyoung Choi, Sinwon Yoon, and Yeongmi Jeon. 2006. LDC Catalog LDC2006T03.

Otakar Smrž, Viktor Bielický, IvetaKouřilová, Jakub Kráčmar, Jan Hajič and Petr Zemánek. 2008. Prague Arabic Dependency Treebank: A Word on the Million Words.In *Proceedings* of the Workshop on Arabic and Local Languages (LREC 2008).

Mihai Surdeanu, Richard Johansson, Adam Meyers, Lluıs Marquez, and Joakim Nivre. 2008. The CoNLL-2008 shared task on joint parsing on syntactic and semantic dependencies. In *Proceedings* of CoNLL'08, pages 159–177.

Majdi Swalha. 2011. *Open-source Resources and Standards for Arabic Word Structure Analysis: Fine Grained Morphological Analysis of Arabic Text Corpora*. PhD thesis, Leeds University.

Nianwen Xue and Martha Palmer. 2004. Calibrating features for semantic role labeling. In Dekang Lin and Dekai Wu, editors, *Proceedings* of EMNLP 2004, pages 88–94.

Wajdi Zaghouani , Mona Diab, Aous Mansouri, Sameer Pradhan, and Martha Palmer. 2010. The revised Arabic PropBank. In *Proceedings* of the Fourth Linguistic Annotation Workshop (LAW IV '10), ACL, pages 222-226.

Maysoon Zahri. 1990. *Metaphor and translation*. PhD thesis, University of Salford.

Trend Analysis in Harper's Bazaar

Sophie Kushkuley, B.S.
Brandeis University
415 South St
Waltham, MA 02453, USA
sophiek@brandeis.edu

Abstract

Topic modeling of fashion trends were analyzed using the MALLET toolkit. Harper's Bazaar magazines from 1860-1899 were used (freely available online). This resulted in 20 topics with 4 characterizing words each. Trends over time were analyzed in several different ways using 100-topics and 20-topics.

1 Introduction

Using trend analysis to extract topics from a fashion magazine may finally put to rest the question of the cyclicality of fashion. Entire issues of Harper's Bazaar from the 19th century are freely available online [1]. Preliminary data analysis using the NLTK toolkit in Python [2] did not yield promising results. Bigram collocations were extracted for the first three years of data. The collocations were extracted on a monthly basis, however the bigrams were extremely non-specific and contained no relevant information. Topic modeling is the natural choice for large amounts of historical data, so this was the strategy implemented for the second attempt. Extracting this data and applying the MALLET toolkit [3] for topic modeling provided a good start and a novel way of looking at fashion trends.

2 Data Extraction

For every year from 1867 through 1900 roughly 52 volumes (one volume per week) per year of Harper's Bazaar are available in text format online. Most volumes from 1867 - 1899 contain an article entitled 'New York Fashions'. For consistency, this is the article that was scraped from every volume for the purposes of topic modeling. Volumes from year 1890 only go up to April 28th and do not contain the 'New York Fashions' article, hence 1890 was excluded from the analysis. 1867 was a short year as well, volumes started in November. A Python script was used to extract the articles from every volume, however, the data is not entirely uniform and contains errors. Despite significant post-processing, noise in the data has caused some imprecision.

3 Topic Modeling

MALLET uses latent Dirichlet allocation [5] to produce a topic distribution over any given text. Stop words were removed automatically, and a distribution of a user specified number of topics was produced together with a user specified number of topic keys associated with every topic.

3.1 100-Topic Model

First, 100 topics were distributed over all the data, each with 4 topic keys. Many of the resulting topics were uninformative (e.g. 'cost made black ladies' and 'good made make great'). Below is a sample of the topic keys for the first 20 topics:

black satin green jet; trimmed satin skirt dress; skirt made skirts hips; silk black long jet; brown gray blue dark; white tulle dress low; worn ladies young made; de black white soie; flannel worn warm skirts; dress costumes white blue; blue pink white pale; satin velvet lace brocade; price shown centre set; plain figures shown designs; yard cents sold cost ;

capes back long jackets; cambric tucks linen french; girls years white children; costumes costume style trimming; collar high pointed front.

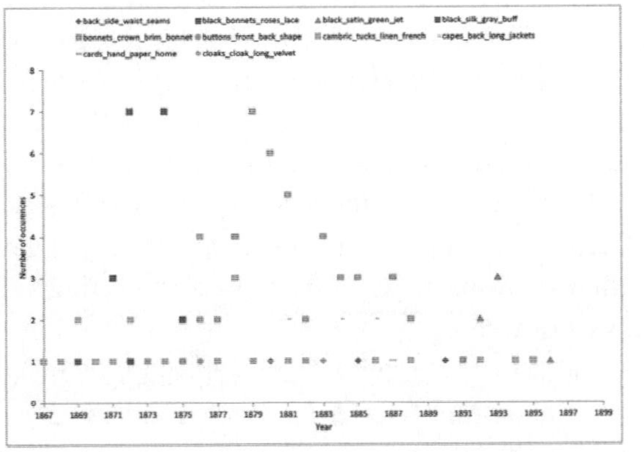

Figure 1: Occurrences of topic by year: first 10

At first, the topic with the highest percentage for each volume was chosen, along with its topic keys. Then every year for which this is the number one topic was found. Some topics will be associated with the same year a number of times, because each year contains roughly 52 volumes each of which has a topic distribution. The number of times each year shows up in each number one topic was counted and plotted (Figure 1). This allows one to see which topics are strongly correlated with a particular year or set of years, and from here it may be possible to deduce which topics are most representative of trends by year.

Some keys (e.g. 'cost made black ladies') are very general, uninformative and infrequent. Others occur several times in one year and not in any other year (e.g. 'costumes costume style trimming'). Then there are topics that occur frequently over a short range of years (e.g. 'dresses skirt plain wool'). And still other, such as 'fur seal skin black' that occur infrequently over a vast range of years, vs those that occur infrequently over a short range of years, 'flannel worn warm skirts'.

The most relevant topics are the ones that occur frequently over a short range of time. These are topics that may be representative of trends, and it would be helpful to plot the distribution of such topics over time.

3.2 20-Topic Model

Due to the large amount of data generated by the 100-topic model, a 20-topic model was generated to provide a more thorough analysis of the data. Twenty topics are more easy to manually look at, and 20 is not too few topics but it's also not an overwhelmingly large number of topics. For each of the 20 topics 4 topic keys were generated. Below is the list of all 20 topic keys:

fur seal black long; made gown skirt gowns; hair ladies made worn; yard price cents suits; velvet cloth red made; made girls waist dresses; crape black mourning worn; white dress dresses silk; white lace blue made; satin lace black jet; skirt front back side; silver gold diamonds large; black blue color brown; designs wood cost small; worn suits white black; stripes colors blue designs; text px hearth td; bonnets crown hats brim; silk long made back; back waist sleeves skirt.

It is evident that one topic ('text px hearth td') is due to bad post processing, so it has been thrown out from further analyses. Topics in the 20-topic model have much higher counts than those in the 100-topic model. This might lead to less fine-grained topics for the data. Some topics clearly stand out as having a very high frequency for a short range of years (e.g. 'made gown skirt gowns').

Next, the distribution of a sample of topics was plotted by year. This was done by following each topic separately over time; the percent of the topic in the distribution for each year was plotted by year. Since every year has many topic distributions (corresponding to each of the 52 volumes per year for most years) a bootstrapping sampling method was performed to determine the percentage associated with a specific topic and year. Bootstrapping provides the advantage of a weighted average that correctly preserves the original distribution. A percent from the topic percent-pool for the year was chosen randomly 1,000 times and averaged to produce one single percent associated with that topic and year.

The most frequently occurring topics are 'Silk long made back'; 'Skirt front back side'; 'Velvet cloth red made'; 'White lace blue made'; 'Yard price cents suits'; 'Made gown skirt gowns'; 'Back waist sleeves skirt'; 'Black blue color brown').

Four of these topic percentages are plotted by year

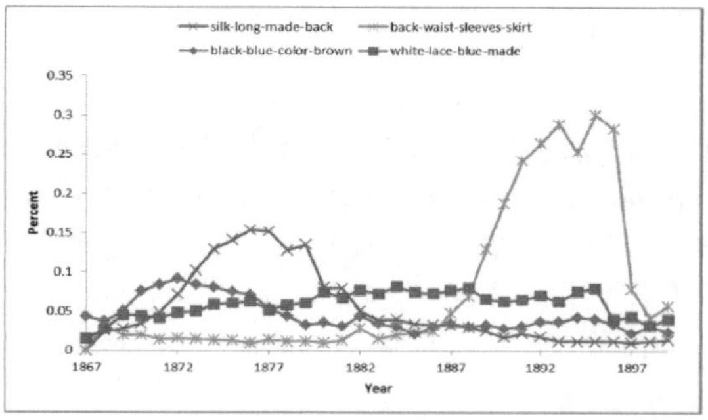

Figure 2: Topics by year

(Figure 2). This yields a view of the topics in which specific trends can be spotted based on frequency (e.g. long and silk items peaked around 1872-1882, velvet and red characteristics peaked around 1882-1887). In addition, a certain amount of cyclicality can be seen in Figure 2. Two of the topics have a topic key in common, 'back'. The first topic 'silk long made back' peaks around 1877, and 'back waist sleeves skirt' peaks around 1895, and these two topics have a topic key in common, 'back'. Given a context, meaning can be found in such trending topics.

3.3 Project Refinement

It appears that the topic keys generated by the 100-topic model are more relevant and contain more information than those generated by the 20-topic model. On the other hand the 20-topic model is simpler to analyze. Therefore, inspired by the work on Martha Ballard's diary [4] another model was generated with 20 topic keys for each of 20 topics.

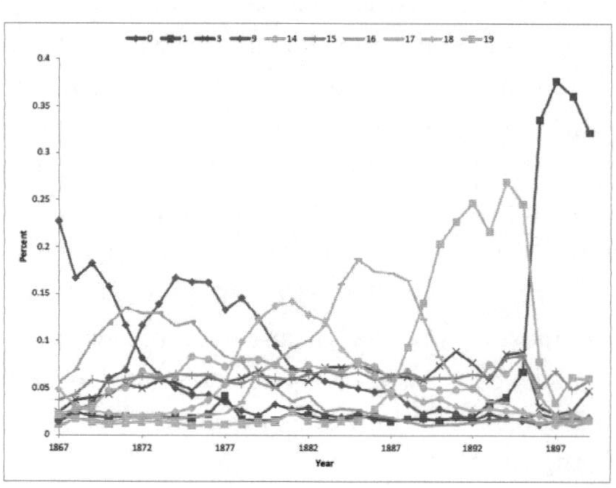

Figure 3: Trend-predicting topics by year

These labels were plotted by year, and topics with the most movement are shown (Figure 3). There are trends here that clearly stand out, but there does not seem to be enough data to follow the trends through to the end. Certain topics rise in popularity and fall again, however, it is impossible to know from 30 years of data if they rise again further in time. Similarly to the 20-topic model with 4 topic keys, many topics stand out due to their cyclic nature. However unlike the 4-topic keys model, rises and dips in frequency are more dramatic, suggesting that more topic keys leads to a more thorough analysis of trends.

An additional analysis was performed using not only the most highly probable topic associated with every year but the top three such topics. The number of occurrences of the top three topics of every month were counted and divided by the total number of months to obtain a percent of occurrence for the year. A heat map was then generated for this data (Figure 4). Some specific trends are discernible, and even a potentially cyclic topic (topic 7 is frequent in 1867 and resurfaced in 1896).

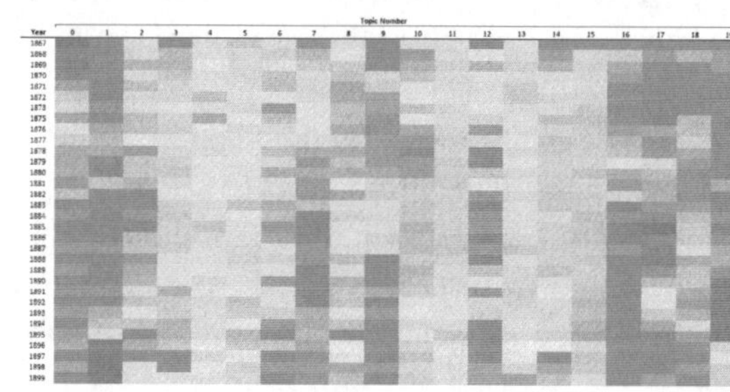

Figure 4: Heat map of topic occurrence by year

The high frequency topics are presented below. Types of garments, accessories, colors, materials and fabric stylings have been highlited:

0 **black** yard **silk** wide **dress** price worn half gros sold **fringe** folds **trimming** grain cents inches yards trimmed centre amp

1 made **gown** gowns **lace black silk** worn **white** style wear put **satin** trimmed waist fashion effect great year smart women

7 **skirt** front **belt** skirts waist cut narrow side back long material short **ruffles** bands band **flounce trimmed** trimming full upper

9 **silk black skirt dresses basque** back long front

side **pleating** trimmed pleated **flounces** pleatings dress **apron** polonaise plain trimming sleeves

16 **suits** worn made ladies cost **gray** suit blue stylish amp imported fashion shown **linen brown** garment soft yard cents **braid**

17 **skirt dresses** made waist front full side plain **red** dress **drapery** foot **wool** skirts line **gathered** surah **pleats basque vest**

18 **satin red lace gold** plush colors beads **velvet** large made small **brocaded** plain **trimmings embroidery** imported great shown shades dark

19 **black** sleeves waist **gowns skirt silk** back **ribbon satin** full front **white** collar large **green bodice belt yellow** foot gown

These topics include many descriptive terms (in bold) that could depict broad scale fashion trends. Highlighted topic keys describe real trends and provide a starting point for further analysis. Not surprisingly, frequent topics coincide with the most highly peaking and oscillating topics in Figure 3. These frequent topics also depict more fashion trends, as defined by the categories mentioned above. For example, below is a non-frequent topic, and it does not include a single topic key that falls into the categories defined above:

2 hair head price natural cents large fancy pretty long ladies hand lady box made cards dolls water children good dressed.

4 Conclusion

Topic modeling for 19th century magazine data does not automatically yield relevant topics that can be plotted and analyzed. Extensive post-processing and generalization is necessary for useful results. It is important to correctly classify topic keys and identify useless topics.

It seems to be the case that more topics and more topic keys yield better results; which may then be obtained by carefully sorting through the 100-topic model and categorizing topic keys into topic labels, then plotting them by year to analyze trends. It may be possible with more detailed analyses to deduce topic keys that are cyclic in nature when put in context (e.g. 'back' in Figure 2). A heat map can be a good way to weed out uninteresting topics. It also provides an excellent visualization method for the rise and fall of topics, as well as topic cyclicality. Based on these highlighted topics, it is interesting to group the topic keys by characteristic (e.g., color, article of clothing, construction, technique, material etc).

Trends have been discerned in this analysis, and with this wealth of freely available data specific fashion trends can be searched for and analyzed.

5 Future Work

The fashion trend analysis of the 19th century according to Harper's Bazaar presented here is incomplete. Further refinement of the topics will yield the identification of more specific trends that can then be analyzed over time.

Honing in on specific topic categories (e.g. articles of clothing, materials, colors and styles) can help illuminate trends. Topic analysis can then be performed for every category for a cross-sectional view of trends.

Post-processing of the keys is another necessary step to focus in on trends. For example, stemming the topic keys is necessary to avoid repetitive keys.

Additional data will also be helpful to fully analyze trends and assess cyclicality. Shared topic keys among the topics may provide insight into the problem, if a method of linking them contextually can be deduced.

This paper provides an initial insight into fashion trends using topic modeling with MALLET, but it also leaves room for further directed analyses.

References

1. Albert R. Mann Library. 2012. *Home Economics Archive: Research, Tradition and History (HEARTH).* Ithaca, NY: Albert R. Mann Library, Cornell University. http://hearth.library.cornell.edu (Version January 2005).
2. Bird, Steven. *NLTK: Natural Language Toolkit.* http://www.nltk.org/.
3. McCallum, Andrew Kachites. 2002. *MALLET: A Machine Learning for Language Toolkit.* http://mallet.cs.umass.edu.
4. Cameron Blevins. 2010. *historying. Topic Modeling Martha Ballard's Diary,* http://historying.org/2010/04/01/topic-modeling-martha-ballards-diary/.
5. Blei, David M. Ng, Andrew Y. Jordan, Michael I. 2003. *Latent Dirichlet Allocation.* Journal of Machine Learning Research 3 (2003) 993-1022.

Social Network Analysis of *Alice in Wonderland*

Apoorv Agarwal[1]* **Augusto Corvalan[1]**** **Jacob Jensen[1]†** **Owen Rambow[2]‡**

[1] **Department of Computer Science, Columbia University, New York, NY, USA**
[2] **Center for Computational Learning Systems, Columbia University, New York, NY, USA**
* apoorv@cs.columbia.edu ** ac3096@columbia.edu
†jej2120@columbia.edu ‡rambow@ccls.columbia.edu

Abstract

We present a network analysis of a literary text, *Alice in Wonderland*. We build novel types of networks in which links between characters are different types of *social events*. We show that analyzing networks based on these social events gives us insight into the roles of characters in the story. Also, static network analysis has limitations which become apparent from our analysis. We propose the use of dynamic network analysis to overcome these limitations.

1 Introduction

In recent years, the wide availability of digitized literary works has given rise to a computational approach to analyzing these texts. This approach has been used, sometimes in conjunction with more traditional literary analysis techniques, to better grasp the intricacies of several literary works. As the field matured, new approaches and ideas gave rise to the use of techniques, like social networks, usually reserved for quantitive fields in order to gain new insights into the works. Recently, Elson et al. (2010) extracted networks from a corpus of 19th century texts in order to debunk long standing hypotheses from comparative literature (Elson et al., 2010). Moretti (2011) examined a social event network constructed from Hamlet in order to delve deeper into its infamously dense character network.

While this approach is clearly powerful, it is not without drawbacks. As Moretti (2011) points out, undirected and unweighted networks are blunt instruments and limited in their use. While, as discussed below, some researchers have sought to rectify these limitations, few have done so with a strict and specific rubric for categorizing interactions.

In this paper, we annotate Lewis Carroll's *Alice in Wonderland* using a well-defined annotation scheme which we have previously developed on newswire text Agarwal et al. (2010). It is well suited to deal with the aforementioned limitations. We show that using different types of networks can be useful by allowing us to provide a model for determining point-of-view. We also show that social networks allow characters to be categorized into roles based on how they function in the text, but that this approach is limited when using static social networks. We then build and visualize dynamic networks and show that static networks can distort the importance of characters. By using dynamic networks, we can build a fuller picture of how each character works in a literary text.

Our paper uses an annotation scheme that is well-defined and has been used in previous computational models that extract social events from news articles (Agarwal and Rambow, 2010). This computational model may be adapted to extract these events from literary texts. However, the focus of this paper is not to adapt the previously proposed computational model to a new domain or genre, but to first demonstrate the usefulness of this annotation scheme for the analysis of literary texts, and the social networks derived from it. All results reported in this paper are based on hand annotation of the text. Furthermore, we are investigating a single text, so that we do cannot draw conclusions about the usefulness of our methods for validating theories of literature.

We summarize the contributions of this paper:

- We manually extract a social network from *Al-*

ice in Wonderland based on the definition of *social events* as proposed by us in (Agarwal et al., 2010).

- We use static network analysis (in a bottom-up approach) for creating character sketches. We show that exploiting the distinction between different types of social events (*interaction* and *observation*), we are able to gain insights into the roles characters play in this novel.

- We point certain limitations of the static network analysis and propose the use of dynamic network analysis for literary texts.

The rest of the paper is organized as follows. In Section 2, we present previous work. In Section 3, we present a brief overview of social events. In Section 4, we discuss the data and annotation scheme. In Section 6, we present results on static network analysis, and results on dynamic network analysis in Section 7. We conclude and present future direction of research in Section 8.

2 Literature Review

The power of network analysis in the field of literature is evidenced by the rapid rise of work and interest in the field in recent years. Network extraction and analysis has been performed on subjects as varied as the Marvel universe (Alberich et al., 2002), *Les Misérables* (Newman and Girvan, 2004), and ancient Greek tragedies (Rydberg-Cox, 2011). Elson et al. (2010) has looked at debunking comparative literature theories by examining networks for sixty 19th-century novels. Elson et al. (2010) used natural language processing techniques to attribute quoted speech to characters in the novels, and then used this data to create networks that allowed the researchers to make novel observations about the correlation between setting and the number of characters. Because the study was limited to quoted speech, however, a large chunk of interactions (such as non-quoted dialog, observations and thoughts) were missing from the network and subsequent analysis. Our work specifically addresses these missed cases, and in that sense our technique for creating social networks is complementary to that of Elson et al. (2010).

Several other researchers have found network theory to be useful in the study of literature. In his study of Dicken's *Bleak House*, Sack refines the granularity of interaction types by breaking down links by the purpose of the interaction, differentiating between conversations meant, for example, for legal investigation vs. philanthropy. Sack (2006) also expands on the definition of ties, including face-to-face interaction as well as what he terms "weak ties", which includes interactions like being involved in the same legal suit. His links are a hybrid of quantitative and qualitative. Characters are linked by interaction, but how these interactions are then classified are subjective according to Sack (2006). Thus, they do not follow a strictly defined rubric. Celikyilmaz et al. (2010) have also worked along a similar track, analyzing networks built based on topical similarity in actor speech.

A theorist who has grappled with the limitations of network analysis is Franco Moretti. In *Network Theory Plot Analysis*, Moretti (2011) takes a similar path as Elson et al. (2010), where the act of speech signifies interaction. Moretti (2011) points out that his close reading of the network extracted from *Hamlet* is limited by several factors. First, edges are unweighted, giving equal importance to interactions that are a few words and long, more involved conversations. Second, edges have no direction, which eliminates who initiated each interaction. Moretti (2011) concludes that more rigorous network analysis tools are needed in order to make further headway in the field. In this paper we extract two types networks from *Alice in Wonderland*, one directed and the other undirected, both of which are weighted. We show that indeed discriminating between uni-directional and bi-directional linkages gives us insight into the character profiles and their role in the novel.

Overall, the previous work has primarily focused on turning time into space, flattening out the action in order to bring to light something that was obfuscated previously. However, time and its passage plays a crucial role in literature. Literature is, after all, built in layers, with successive scenes stacking up on each other. Texts reveal information not all at once, like a network, but in spurts. This is not merely an unfortunate side-effect of the medium, but a central element that is manipulated by authors and is central in extracting "meaning" (Perry, 1979).

However, the static social network (SSN) medium itself is not suited to clearly reveal these changes. Dynamic social networks (DSN), on the other hand, can go beyond the summary statistics of SSN. Moreover, because of their flattening effect, SSNs can lead to inaccurate or inexact information (Berger-Wolf et al., 2006). The DSN approach has many applications, from analyzing how terrorist cells evolve over time (Carley, 2003), to mapping the interactions in the writing community (Perry-Smith and Shalley, 2003). One of the obstacles to using DSNs is that they are not as straight-forward to visualize as SSNs. In this paper, we use a visualization outlined in Moody et al. (2005). While the visualization may not be novel, to the best of our knowledge, DSNs have not yet been used to observe networks extracted from literary texts. Our goal is to push beyond the limitations of static network analysis of literature by adding the crucial element it lacks: dynamism.

3 Social Events

A text may describe a social network in two ways: explicitly, by stating the type of relationship between two individuals (e.g. *Mary is John's wife*), or implicitly, by describing an event whose repeated instantiation may lead to a stronger social relationship (e.g. *John talked to Mary*). These latter types of events are called *social events* (Agarwal et al., 2010). Agarwal et al. (2010) defined two broad types of social events: **interaction** (**INR**), in which both parties are aware of each other and of the social event, e.g., a conversation, and **observation** (**OBS**), in which only one party is aware of the other and of the interaction, e.g., thinking of or talking about someone. An important aspect of annotating social events is taking into consideration the intention of the author: does the author want us to notice an event between characters or is he/she simply describing a setting of a plot? Since our definition of social events is based on cognitive states of characters, as described by the author, we do not annotate a social event in Example (2) below since there is no evidence that either *Alice* or the *Rabbit* are aware of each other. However, in Example (1), there is clear evidence that *Alice* notices the *Rabbit* but there is no evidence that the *Rabbit* notices *Alice* as well. Therefore, there in only a one-directional social event between these entities called the **observation** (**OBS**) event.

1. (1) Then [Alice] {saw} the [White Rabbit] run by her. OBS

2. (2) The [White Rabbit] ran by [Alice]. No social event

Agarwal et al. (2010) have defined finer sub-types of these two coarse types of events. These sub-types include recording physical proximity of characters, verbal and non-verbal interactions, recording if the thought process of thinking about the other entity is initiated by a previous event or by reading a magazine or other social medium. Many of these sub-types are irrelevant for this literary text simply because it does not describe use of technology. There are no emails being sent (which would be a verbal interaction which does not happen in close physical proximity), no one is watching the other on television etc. Therefore, for this paper, we only focus on two broad social event types: **interaction** versus **observation**. For details and examples of other subcategories please refer to (Agarwal et al., 2010).

4 Data

We annotate an abridged version of *Alice in Wonderland* from project Gutenberg.[1] This version has ten chapters, 270 paragraphs and 9611 words.

Agarwal et al. (2010) trained two annotators to annotate social events in a well known news corpus – Automated Content Extraction (ACE2005, (Walker, 2005)). Once trained, we used one of the annotators to annotate the same events in *Alice in Wonderland*. Unlike the ACE corpus, we did not have previous gold annotations for entity mentions or mention resolution. However, since we are primarily interested only in social events, we instructed the annotator to all and only record entity mentions that participate in a social event.

Since the text is fairly short, the authors of this paper checked the quality of annotations during the annotation process. After the annotation process was complete, one of the authors went over the annotations as an adjudicator. He did not propose deletion of any annotation. However, he proposed adding a

[1] http://www.gutenberg.org/ebooks/19551

couple of annotations for chapter 3 for the *mouse drying ceremony*. In this scene, the *mouse* instructs a group of birds to dry themselves. Lewis Carroll refers to groups of birds using *them, they*. Our annotation manual does not handle such group formations. Do we introduce a *part-of* relation and associate each bird in the group with the group mention (marking the group mention as a separate entity) or not? If yes, and if the group loses one entity (bird in this case), do we mark another group entity and associate the remaining birds with this new group or not? In general, the problem of such groups is hard and, to the best of our knowledge, not handled in current entity recognition manuals. We postpone handling the annotation of such groups for future work.

Another point that the adjudicator raised, which is out of scope for our current annotation manual, is the way of handling cases where one entity interacts with the other but mistakenly thinking that the entity is someone else. For example, the *Rabbit* interacts with *Alice* thinking that she is *Mary Ann*.

5 Social Network Analysis (SNA) metrics

In this section we briefly describe some of the widely used SNA metrics that we use throughout the paper for drawing conclusions about the social network of *Alice in Wonderland*.

Notation: A network or graph, $G = (N, E)$ is given by a set of nodes in the network, N and a set of edges, E. G can be represented as an adjacency matrix A such that $A_{i,j} = I((i,j) \in E)$. Following are the metrics we use:

Degree centrality (Newman, 2010): A node's degree centrality is equal to the total number of its incoming and outgoing edges. The number of connections is often a good proxy for a node's importance.

In-degree centrality (Newman, 2010): Degree centrality, but summing only a node's incoming edges. In the undirected case, this reduces to Degree centrality.

Out-Degree centrality (Newman, 2010): Degree centrality, but summing only a node's outgoing edges. In the undirected case, this reduces to Degree centrality.

Hubs (Kleinberg, 1999): A node's hub score is its element in the largest eigenvector of AA'. This quantifies how well it reliably points to high-scoring authorities. Intuitively, a high Hub score means a good directory of important nodes.

Authorities (Kleinberg, 1999): A node's authority score is its element in the largest Eigenvector of $A'A$. This quantifies how much attention it gets from high-scoring hubs. Intuitively, a high authority score means a node of importance.

6 Static Network Analysis

In this section we present results for static network analysis of the different types of networks extracted from *Alice in Wonderland*. We use a bottom-up approach. We extract different types of social networks and look at the profiles of characters based on these networks and network analysis metrics. We observe that the profiles of some characters are strikingly different. In this paper, we discuss three characters whose profiles we found most interesting. We are able to show that making a distinction between types of networks based on directionality (who is observing whom) is indeed useful.

6.1 Data Visualization

We calculate hubs and authority weights of all the characters in *Alice in Wonderland*. Since we are using a bottom-up approach, there is a lot of data to look at along different dimensions. We develop a data visualization scheme that makes it easy for us to compare profiles of characters along different dimensions and to compare their profiles with each other.

Following are the different dimensions that we are interested in: 1) type of network, denoted by set $N = \{\text{OBS, INR}\}$, 2) network analysis metric, denoted by the set $M = \{\text{Hub weight, Authority weight}\}$, 3) rank of a character based on type of network and network analysis metric used, denoted by the set $R = \{1, 2, 3, \ldots 52\}$, and 4) absolute separation of consecutively ranked characters for a particular network analysis metric, denoted by a continuous set $S = [0, 1]$. We need this last dimension since one character may be ranked higher than another, yet the separation between the absolute values of the network analysis metric is fairly small. We treat characters with such small separations in absolute values as having the same rank. There are a to-

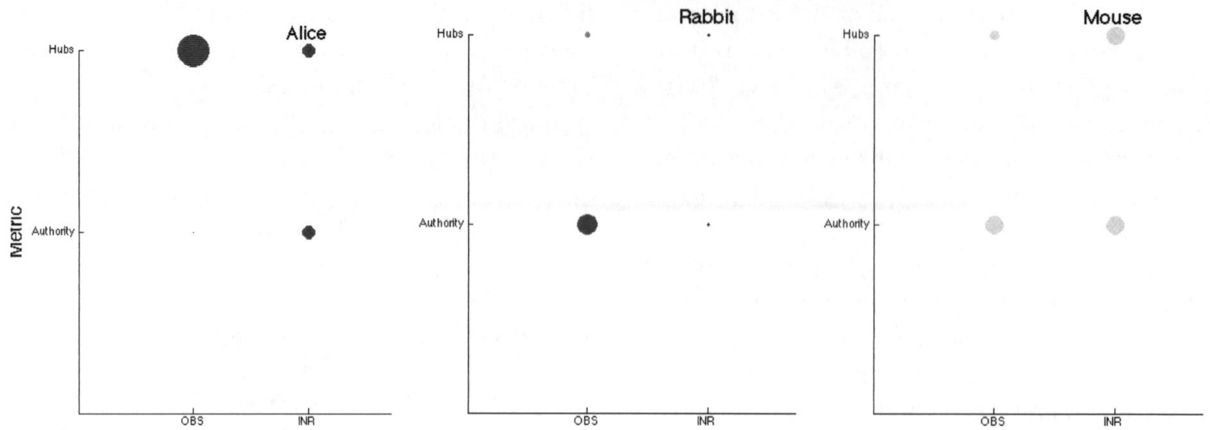

(a) Alice (b) White Rabbit (c) Mouse

Figure 1: Static networks analysis plots for three characters of *Alice in Wonderland*. X-axis denotes network types, OBS, INR, Verbal and Non-verbal (inorder), Y-axis denotes network analysis metrics, Authority weight and Hub weight. Color coding: Blue = rank 1, Green = rank 2, Red = rank 3 and all other ranks are color Black. Size of the dot is directly proportional to separation from next lower rank, in terms of the network analysis value.

tal of four dimensions for each character, and a total of $2 * 2 * 52 = 208$ data points to look at (ignoring the last dimension, absolute separation from the consecutively ranked character). We represent these four dimensions dimensions in a 2-D scatter plot as follows:

X-axis: We plot the network types along the X-axis.

Y-axis: We plot the network analysis metric along the Y-axis.

Color: Color of a dot denotes the rank of the character. We choose the following color coding. Blue denotes rank one, Green denotes rank two, Red denotes rank three and all the remaining ranks are denoted by color Black. After rank three the absolute value of the metrics plummet and are very close to one another i.e. the separation between absolute values (of network analysis metrics) for consecutively ranked characters is less than 0.001.

Size: The size of a dot denotes the fourth dimension i.e. the absolute separation in network analysis metric of the character under consideration to the next lower ranked character. For example, in Figure 1, rank of the *Rabbit* for network type OBS when looking at the authority weight is 1 and the separation from ranked 2 character, the *Mouse*, is high, as denoted by the larger circle. Alternatively, when looking at rank for *Rabbit* as a hub for network type OBS, he is ranked 3, but there is very little separation between him and the next lowest ranked character.

This visualization enables us to compare a lot of numbers conveniently, out of which arise three interesting character profiles. These profiles yield information as to how each character functions in the story.

6.2 Point-of-View

Alice: Alice has the highest centrality for every network which, using the definition of protagonist given by Moretti (2011), makes her the protagonist of the text. However, from our analysis we are also able to conclude that the story is being told from Alice's perspective. Note that protagonist and perspective-holder are not always the same. For example, *The Great Gatsby* is narrated by Nick Carraway, but the protagonist is Jay Gatsby. Even though to a reader of the text, the perspective holder(s) might be easy to identify, to the best of our knowledge there are no network analysis approaches that can do this. We show that by treating interaction and observation events in isolation, we are able to conclude that *Alice* is the only perspective holder in the story.

The perspective, or point of view, is the "mode (or modes) established by an author by means of which the reader is presented with the characters, dialog, actions, setting and events" (Abrams, 1999). There are four of these:

1. First-Person: The story is being told from the perspective of a narrator that refers to itself as "I" (or "we").

2. Second-Person: Similar to first-person, but the narrator refers to a character(s) in the story as "you". This form of narration is not common.

3. Third-Person Limited: Here, the narrator is not a character in the story, but an outside entity that refers to other characters as "he/she/it/they". However, in limited, this entity is limited to one focal character that the narrator follows.

4. Third-Person Omniscient: A type of third-person narration where the narrator has access to the thoughts and actions of multiple characters.

For first, second and third-person limited, it is expected that the character who is observing other characters is the perspective holder. In order to isolate observations from mentions, the OBS network should be built ignoring quoted speech. Computationally, we believe this would be a fairly easy task. In terms of the terminology we introduce, the perspective holder will have *observation* links pointing to other characters but will not receive *observation* links. In a first-person narration, this character will be an "I" or a name if the "I" is named. The same case for second-person and "you." In third-person limited, while an entity is narrating the story, there is one focal character whose perspective limits and sometimes colors the narration. Thus, that character will still be the one with *observation* links emanating but not receiving. In third-person omniscient, since the narrator has access to every character's thoughts and actions, it is expected that many characters would receive and emanate *observation* links, while there would be an absence of characters who are emanating *observation* links but not receiving any. Therefore, the behavior of perspective holding character is consistent across different types of narrations – it is the character that emanates *observation* type of links but does not receive any. This analysis extends to the case where there are multiple character perspectives being used by seeing which characters are sending but not receiving OBS links and which are not. However, in the rare case where an actor whose point-of-view is being received overhears himself being mentioned, this will be annotated as having him receive a OBS link, thereby throwing off the categorization. We ignore this rare case for now.

Looking at hub and authority weights of *Alice's* **OBS** network (Figure 1(a)), it is apparent that all the *observation* links are pointing outwards from *Alice*. *Alice* is ranked one (color of the dot is blue) and has a high separation from the second ranked entity (size of the dot) for Hub-weight metric. A high hub-weight rank means that most of the links are emanating from this character. In comparison, *Alice's* authority-weight of **OBS** network is low. This means that other characters are not talking about *Alice*. Thus, the story must be being told from the point-of-view of *Alice*.

It should be noted that for concluding who is the perspective holder, it is important to only look at the **OBS** network. The same conclusion cannot be made if we look at the **INR** network. This supports our effort to make a distinction between uni-directional versus bi-directional links.

6.3 Character Sketch for Minor Characters

White Rabbit: The *White Rabbit* has a very different profile when we look at its **OBS** network in comparison to *Alice* (figure 1(b)). *Rabbit* is ranked one but as an authority, instead of as a hub, in the **OBS** network. This means that most of the *observation* links are leading to *Rabbit* i.e. *Rabbit* is being observed or talked about by other characters. On the other hand *Rabbit* is ranked third in **INR** (for which hub and authority have the same value, since INR is non-directional). Thus, *Rabbit* is frequently observed and talked about, yet remains insular in his interactions with other characters. This suggests that *Rabbit* is playing some sort of unique role in the text, where importance is being placed on his being observed rather than his interactions.

Mouse: *Mouse* has yet another kind of profile. For *Mouse*, both hub and authority weights are ranked two and have a clear separation from the next ranked character. We may observe that *Mouse* not only interacts with many characters, but mentions and is mentioned in abundance as well. This makes him a very important and well-connected character in the story, behind only *Alice*. Thus, we can suggest that his role in the text is as a connector between many characters. *Mouse* mentions many characters to other characters, interacts with them and is in turn mentioned by them.

6.4 Need for Dynamic Analysis

The need for a dynamic analysis model is made clear in the case of *Mouse*. His huge importance (overshadowing more traditionally popular characters such as *the Queen* and *Mad Hatter*) was an unexpected result. However, this is not the whole story: *Mouse* actually only appears in one scene in chapters 2-3. In the scene, Alice has created a large lake with her tears and meets *Mouse*, who introduces her to many minor characters during a drying ceremony. Outside of this ceremony, *Mouse* does not reappear in the text. This one scene, while important, should not be enough to overshadow characters such as *the Queen*, who is responsible for Alice's life or death during the climax of the text. Thus, it is clear from the formation of these character profiles that certain information is being skewed by static network analysis. Most notably, the importance of time as it flows in text is being lost. This observation is the impetus for a new model that addresses these issues, as outlined in the following section.

7 Dynamic Network Analysis

Figure 2 presents plots for dynamic network analysis of the different types of networks extracted from *Alice in Wonderland*. We look at interaction (INR) and observation (OBS) networks, as we did for the previous section, except we do this for each of the 10 chapters independently of all other chapters. The social network metrics we consider are: degree, in-degree and out-degree centrality. Note that for an undirected network (i.e. INR), all three network analysis metrics are the same. In this section we present insights about the three characters considered in the previous section (Alice, Mouse and Rabbit), that are lost in static network analysis.

From Figure 2, it is clear that *Alice* (dotted blue line) is *not* the most central character in every chapter, something that is lost in the static network. Consider figure 2(a) i.e. degree centrality of INR network. *Alice* ranks 2 in chapters 3, 4 (the drying ceremony mentioned above) and 9. In chapter 9, *Alice* is overshadowed by *The Hatter* and *Rabbit*. This makes sense, as this chapter concerns *Rabbit* and *The Hatter* being witnesses at *Alice's* trial. By breaking the story down chapter by chapter like this, it becomes evident that although *Alice* is a very active character throughout, there are moments, such as the trial, where she is inactive, indeed powerless. Yet as soon as the trial is over and *Alice* is back in her own world in chapter 10, we see a spike as she again takes an active role in her fate.

Figure 2(b) shows in-degree centrality for the OBS network. This represents how often a character is thought about or talked about by another character. Notice that *Alice* is completely absent in this network: no one thinks about or mentions her. This is to be expected, as *Alice* is our guide through Wonderland. No one mentions her because she is present in every scene, thus any dialog about her will become an interaction. Likewise, no one thinks of her because the reader is not presented with other character's thoughts, only *Alice's*. This is consistent with earlier observations made in the static network. Interestingly, *Queen* (solid black line) comes to dominate the later chapters, as she becomes the focus of *Alice's* thoughts and mentions. Again, this spike in *Queen's* influence (Figure 2(b)) is lost in the static network. But it is *Queen* who ultimately has the power to decide the final punishment for *Alice* at the end of the trial, so it is fitting that *Alice's* thoughts are fixated with her.

Figure 2(c) shows the out-degree centrality of the OBS network, a starkly different picture. Here, we see why *Mouse* (dashed red line) has such importance in the static network. Over the course of the drying ceremony in chapter 2 and 3, he mentions a very large number of characters. The dynamic network allows us to see that while *Mouse* does play a key role at one point of the story, his influence is largely limited to that one section. Other characters overshadow him for the rest of the text. Comparing *Mouse's* role in the in-degree centrality graph (figure 2(b)) vs. out-degree centrality (figure 2(c)), we can see that much of *Mouse's* influence comes not from entities referring to him (in-degree), but rather the number of entities he mentions. His importance

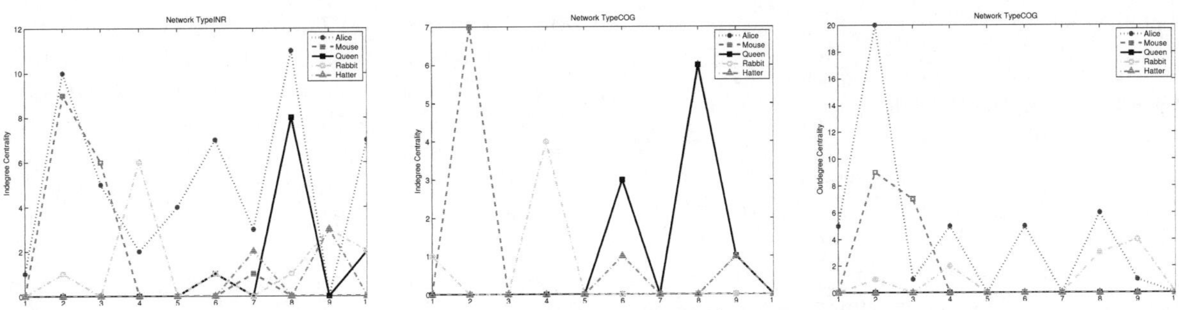

(a) Degree centrality measure for INR network (b) In-degree centrality measure for OBS network (c) Out-degree centrality measure for OBS network

Figure 2: Dynamic network analysis plots for all 10 chapters of *Alice in Wonderland*. Each plot presents the change of centrality values (Degree, In-degree, Out-degree) in different types of network (INR and OBS). X-axis has the chapter numbers (one through ten) and Y-axis has the value of the relevant centrality measure.

in the piece, then, appears to be isolated to a key chapter where he acts as a guide to introduce many entities to the reader.

Likewise, tracing *Rabbit* (dash-dotted green line) across in- and out-degree centrality of the OBS network (figure 2(b) and 2(c)) gives a more fine-grained view of how he works in the text. He is the most mentioned in chapters 1 and 4, chapters that sandwich a big event, the drying ceremony of chapters 2 and 3. Likewise, he reemerges for another big event, Alice's trial (chapter 8, 9, 10). As previously mentioned, *Queen* is the primary concern in *Alice's* mind during the length of the trial. However, *Queen* is absent from the out-degree graph–she makes no reference to off-screen characters. *Rabbit*, who has a large spike in out-degree links during these chapters, is the one who actually mentions a large number of characters, while *Queen* focuses on interacting with those already present. Thus, *Rabbit* is a character that concerns Alice during large set-pieces, one whose primary purpose comes in noticing and being noticed.

We see that using a dynamic network can provide a more subtle view than using a static network. Characters who are key in certain sections are no longer overshadowed, like *Queen*, nor are their importance exaggerated, like *Mouse*. It can also provide us with a better view of when and how a protagonist is most important throughout the text. Finally, analyzing across data dimensions can provide a very specific idea of how a character is functioning, as seen with *Rabbit*.

8 Conclusion

In this paper we have motivated a computational approach to dynamic network analysis. We have hand-annotated Lewis Carrol's *Alice in Wonderland* using a strict and well-defined annotation scheme and created social event networks from these annotations. From these, we have shown the usefulness of using different types of networks to analyze different aspects of a text. We derive point-of-view from a social network. We also break down important characters into certain roles that describe how they function in the text. Ultimately, we find that these roles are limited by the static nature of social networks and create dynamic networks. From these, we extract a clearer picture of how these roles work, as well as other characters overshadowed in the static network. Having shown the value of such analysis, future work will focus on adapting our computational model (Agarwal and Rambow, 2010) for extracting social events from a different domain (news articles) to this new domain (literary text). We will then investigate a large number of literary texts and investigate how we can use our machinery to empirically validate theories about literature.

Acknowledgments

We would like to thank three anonymous reviewers for very useful comments and suggestions, some of which we intend to pursue in future work. This work is supported by NSF grant IIS-0713548.

References

M.H. Abrams. 1999. *A Glossary of Literary Terms*. Harcourt Brace College Publisher.

Apoorv Agarwal and Owen Rambow. 2010. Automatic detection and classification of social events. In *Proceedings of the 2010 Conference on Empirical Methods in Natural Language Processing*.

Apoorv Agarwal, Owen C. Rambow, and Rebecca J. Passonneau. 2010. Annotation scheme for social network extraction from text. In *Proceedings of the Fourth Linguistic Annotation Workshop*.

R. Alberich, J. Miro-Julia, and F. Rossello. 2002. Marvel universe looks almost like a real social network. *eprint arXiv:cond-mat/0202174*, February.

Berger-Wolf, Tanya Y., and Jared Saia. 2006. A framework for analysis of dynamic social networks. In *Proceedings of the 12th ACM SIGKDD international conference on Knowledge discovery and data mining*, KDD '06, pages 523–528, New York, NY, USA. ACM.

K. M. Carley. 2003. Dynamic network analysis. In R. Breiger, K. M. Carley, and P. Pattison, editors, *Dynamic Social Network Modeling and Analysis: Workshop Summary and Papers*, pages 133–145, Washington, DC.

Asli Celikyilmaz, Dilek Hakkani-Tur, Hua He, Greg Kondrak, and Denilson Barbosa. 2010. The actor-topic model for extracting social networks in literary narrative. *Proceedings of the NIPS 2010 Workshop – Machine Learning for Social Computing*.

David K. Elson, Nicholas Dames, and Kathleen R. McKeown. 2010. Extracting social networks from literary fiction. *Proceedings of the 48th Annual Meeting of the Association for Computational Linguistics*, pages 138–147.

Jon M. Kleinberg. 1999. Authoritative sources in a hyperlinked environment. *J. ACM*, 46(5):604–632, September.

James Moody, Daniel McFarland, and Skye Benderde-Moll. 2005. Dynamic network visualization. *American Journal of Sociology*, 110(4):1206–1241, January.

Franco Moretti. 2011. Network theory, plot analysis. *New Left Review*.

M. E. J. Newman and M. Girvan. 2004. Finding and evaluating community structure in networks. *Phys. Rev. E*, 69(2), February.

Mark Newman. 2010. *Networks: An Introduction*. Oxford University Press, Inc., New York, NY, USA.

Jill E. Perry-Smith and Christina E. Shalley. 2003. The social side of creativity: A static and dynamic social network perspective. *The Academy of Management Review*, 28(1):89–106.

Menakhem Perry. 1979. Literary dynamics: How the order of a text creates its meanings [with an analysis of faulkner's "a rose for emily"]. *Poetics Today*, 1(1/2):35–361, October.

Jeff Rydberg-Cox. 2011. Social networks and the language of greek tragedy. *Journal of the Chicago Colloquium on Digital Humanities and Computer Science*, 1(3).

Alexander Graham Sack. 2006. Bleak house and weak social networks. *unpublished thesis, Columbia University*.

Christopher R Walker, 2005. *ACE (Automatic Content Extraction) English Annotation Guidelines for Events Version 5.4.3 2005.07.01*. Linguistic Data Consortium.

Towards a computational approach to literary text analysis

Antonio Roque
Computer Science Department
University of California, Los Angeles
antonio@roque-brown.net

Abstract

We consider several types of literary-theoretic approaches to literary text analysis; we describe several concepts from Computational Linguistics and Artificial Intelligence that could be used to model and support them.

1 Problem Statement

Consider the first sentence of the novel *Finnegan's Wake* (Joyce, 1939):

> riverrun, past Eve and Adam's, from swerve of shore to bend of bay, brings us by a commodius vicus of recirculation back to Howth Castle and Environs.

To computationally analyze this sentence as literature, we must understand that its meaning is more than the combination of its semantic components. The rubric of "who did what to whom, when, where, and why" will at best lead us only to understand that somewhere, probably in Ireland, a river is flowing.

Some obvious low-level tasks to improve our reading include: exploring the meaning of non-standard capitalization and spacing, as in "riverrun"; resolving allusions, such as "Eve and Adam's," and considering the significance of variations from common phrasings[1]; identifying alliterated phrases such as "swerve of shore" and "bend of bay" and considering their effect; recognizing tone shifts such as "commodius vicus of recirculation," and resolving any allusions they may indicate; identifying the significance of named entities such as "Howth Castle and Environs"[2]; exploring the effect of the line's syntax on reception, as described by writing scholars (Tufte, 2006).

But becoming absorbed in these admittedly interesting questions threatens to distract us from the larger questions that literary theorists have been studying for over a century. Those questions include:

- what interpretation is the "gold standard" by which others should be judged? Is it the meaning intended by the author? Is it the significance of the text to the readers (and if so, which readers?) Or is the meaning of a literary text inherent in how it takes part in a system and process of language use?
- what metrics can tell us whether one interpretation is better than another?
- how should we model the literary text as it relates to the larger body of language use, which includes both literary and nonliterary texts as well as everyday situated language use by intelligent agents? What features are necessary and sufficient to represent the way meaning (both literary and non-literary) is created and established among language-using populations? How is this meaning tied both to an intelligent

[1] For example, the quotation-delimited phrase "Adam and Eve" returns over 12 million Google results but "Eve and Adam" only returns around 200,000 (as of March 28, 2012.)

[2] For example: do they have an appearance or other attribute that would commonly be brought to mind? Are there associations that would normally be suggested to members of a given community of language use? *cf.* the significance of the Watergate office complex in American communities of political discourse.

agent's abstract beliefs as well as that agent's moment-to-moment understanding of its environment?

The wording of these questions is slanted to suggest their utility to computational linguistics. First, we may want to know how much of the meaning of a literary text comes from the author as opposed to from our situated interpretation of the text or from a language system[3]. Second, evaluation metrics would help us determine whether or not the performance of an automated literary system is improving. Finally, we would benefit from the explanations of a computational model of a literary text's meaning as it emerges from the situated reading of an authored artifact in the context of a multi-agent language system; if nothing else, it would tell us how to design algorithms that both consume and produce literary artifacts in human-like ways.

2 Approach

Computationally, the questions in Section 1 are likely to be answered over the course of decades rather than years. Contemporary relevant research from the fields of Computational Linguistics (CL) and Artificial Intelligence (AI) includes: semantic analysis of narratives (Elson and McKeown, 2009, Finlayson, 2011); summarizing fiction (Mani, 2005; Kazantseva and Szpakowicz, 2010) and performing information-extraction on fiction (Elson et al, 2010); modeling affect and reader-response in narrative (Mani, 2010; McQuiggan, 2010; Mohammad, 2011; Francisco et al., 2011); properties of narrative such as novelty (Peinado et al., 2010) and irony (Utsumi, 2004); models of discourse in narrative (Polanyi et al., 2004; Goyal et al., 2010); computational models of aesthetic creativity (Gervás et al., 2009); and the automatic generation of prose (Callaway and Lester, 2002) and poetry (Manurung, 2003; Gervás, 2007; Greene et al., 2010).

However, these disparate research traditions consider questions closer to the low-level tasks described in Section 1 than to the theoretical questions of interpretation ranking, evaluation, and computational modeling of meaningful human language use. This is possibly because of the empirical methods which have become dominant in AI/CL in recent history (Cohen, 1995). A field whose methods are tuned to empirical evaluation will naturally shy from an area with few clear empirical tasks, whose humanities practitioners are likely to indulge in analyses assuming human levels of knowledge and language-processing capabilities.

Because of this we will turn instead for inspiration from the **digital humanities** (Schreibman, 2004). With its roots in humanities computing (Hockey, 2004) which constituted the earliest use of computers in the humanities, digital humanities took shape with the advent of the Internet. Digital humanities researchers currently apply computers to research questions such as authorship attribution (Jockers and Witten, 2010), statistical word-use analysis (Burrows, 2004), and the development of resources for classical lexicography (Bamman and Crane, 2009), often collaborating with statisticians or computer scientists.

Digital humanities has always had detractors among more traditional humanities scholars, but scholars sympathetic to the overall goals of digital humanities have also critiqued some of its practices. Consider the technological constraints imposed by projects in which texts are digitized, annotated, and statistically analyzed. Those constraints make tacit assumptions about the objectivity of knowledge and the transparency of its transmission (Drucker, 2009). Those assumptions may be contrary to a literary theorist's understanding of how literary text analysis actually works.

For example, in the case of scholar/artist Johanna Drucker, knowledge is seen as partial, subjective, and situated. Subjectivity in this context has two components: a point of view inscribed in the possible interpretations of a work, and "inflection, the marked presence of affect and specificity, registered as the trace of difference, that inheres in material expressions" (Drucker, 2009). To Drucker, subjectivity of knowledge is evident in the fact that interpretation occurs in modeling, encoding, processing, and accessing knowledge.

Drucker's focus is on humanities tools in digital contexts rather than digital tools in humanities contexts. We will proceed in a similar spirit, considering the tasks and approaches of literary text analysis as practiced by literary theorists and considering what kinds of models and approaches from contemporary AI/CL research they might find useful,

[3] We may be interested in user modeling of the author, versus modeling our own interpretative techniques, versus performing sentiment analysis on a particular community of language use, for example.

rather than starting with the tasks and approaches that AI/CL researchers are most familiar with and asking how they can be applied to literary text analysis.

As a specific goal to guide our thought, we will adopt a statement from another scholar who emphasizes the importance of keeping the humanities central to computational text analysis. In *Reading Machines: Toward an Algorithmic Criticism*, Stephen Ramsay develops the notion of adapting the constraints imposed by computation to intentionally create "those heightened subjectivities necessary for critical work" (Ramsay, 2011). While doing so, Ramsay states that from a humanist's perspective:

> Tools that can adjudicate the hermeneutical parameters of human reading experiences - tools that can tell you whether an interpretation is permissible - stretch considerably beyond the most ambitious fantasies of artificial intelligence.

The rest of this paper will attempt to respond to Ramsay's claim by developing such ambitious fantasies. We will strive to consider literary text analysis as it is understood by literary theorists of recent history, and we will describe how representative processes from each of these theories could be modeled computationally using techniques from the AI/CL research communities.

3 Literary Text Analysis

3.1 Expressive Realism

Human judgments on the nature of literature and the way literature is best read have changed frequently since classical times. The last century in particular has provided numerous, often contradictory, notions of how we should determine the meaning of a story, leaving us with no consensus. Even within a school of thought there may be significant differences of opinion, and evaluation is typically no more empirical than how persuasive the interpretation of a given text may be. Still, we may identify certain key ideas and use them to imagine ways they could involve computation.

We may begin by considering **expressive realism**, an approach to literary theory which developed in the late 19th and early 20th centuries, and is a combination of the classical Aristotelian notions of art as *mimesis* (reproducing reality) and the Romantic-era view of poetry as an outpouring of strong emotions produced by an artist whose percepts and affective processing are unusually well-tuned[4] (Belsey, 1980). The task of the reader in this formulation is to faithfully create in their minds the realities being represented by the work, and to enrich themselves by following the thoughts and feelings that the artist experienced.

Computationally, we may frame this as a knowledge engineering task: the writer is a subject matter expert in perceiving the world, and has developed knowledge about the world and innovative ways of emotionally relating to the world. The literary critic's task is to identify which writers have produced knowledge and affective relationships that are most worth adopting. The reader's task is to be guided by the critics to the best writers, and then strive to adopt those writers' knowledge and affective relations as their own.

It may seem difficult to perform such a task with a text such as *Finnegan's Wake*, which is not easy to translate into propositions. But consider a writer's understanding of what happens when reading expressive realist fiction (Gardner, 1991):

> If we carefully inspect our experience as we read, we discover that the importance of physical detail is that it creates for us a kind of dream, a rich and vivid play in the mind. We read a few words at the beginning of a book or the particular story, and suddenly we find ourselves seeing not only words on a page but a train moving through Russia, an old Italian crying, or a farmhouse battered by rain.

Gardner describes fiction as producing an immersive experience in which the reader's sensations are empathically aligned with those of the writer. This alignment produces an understanding unlike that of propositional knowledge:

> [The writer] at the very least should be sure he understands the common objection summed up in the old saw "Show, don't tell." The reason, of course, is that set beside the complex thought achieved by drama, explanation is thin gruel,

[4] Belsey, who is critical of this approach, quotes the poet William Wordsworth's view of artists as "possessed of more than usual organic sensibility." In fact, Wordsworth believed a Poet was "endowed with more lively sensibility; more enthusiasm and tenderness, who has a greater knowledge of human nature, and a more comprehensive soul, than are supposed to be common among mankind..." (Wordsworth, 1802.)

> hence boring. ... After our [reading] experience, which can be intense if the writer is a good one, we know why the character leaves when finally she walks out the door. We know in a way almost too subtle for words...

The subtletly described by Gardner's explains how a text such as *Finnegan's Wake* may be read without recourse to a detailed exegesis producing propositional content. The reader need only become suggestible to the text, and allow themselves to experience the "complex thought" suggested by the writer. Of course, this "intense" experience may lead one to a further study of the writer's mind-set, which would then create an even fuller understanding of that writer's approach.

Such a description may seem like an unlikely candidate for computational modeling, but consider the neurolinguistic implications of models of the mirror neuron system (Rizzolatti and Craighero, 2004): hypothetically, a reader's neural structure might literally copy that of the writer's, provided the stimulus of the text. In this way we might model the transmission of knowledge "almost too subtle for words."

3.2 New Criticism

Later literary theories found expressive realism problematic in various ways. For example, the Anglo-American **New Criticism** defined the *intentional fallacy*, which states that "the design or intention of the author is neither available nor desirable as a standard for judging the success of a work of literary art" (Wimsatt and Beardsley, 1954)[5]. Wimsatt and Beardsley proposed to avoid "author psychology" by focusing on the *internal evidence* of the text, which they defined as

> public evidence which is discovered through the semantics and syntax of a poem, through our habitual knowledge of the language, through grammars, dictionaries, and all the literature which is the source of dictionaries, in general through all that makes a language and culture...

The language knowledge and resources were used to identify the "technique of art". New Critic John Crowe Ransom provided examples of what *devices* should be used in analyzing poetry (Ransom, 1938):

> its metric; its inversions; solecisms, lapses from the prose norm of language, and from close prose logic; its tropes; its fictions, or inventions, by which it secures 'aesthetic distance' and removes itself from history...

However, these devices were not studied for their own sake. Ransom continued: "the superior critic is not content with the compilation of the separate devices; the suggest to him a much more general question." The question in this case is "what [the poem] is trying to represent" and why it does so using those particular devices. This was worth understanding because the New Critics believed that "great works of literature are vessels in which humane values survive" (Selden and Widdowson, 1993) and which reinforce those values in the diligent reader.

Computationally, the list of language resources described by Wimsatt and Beardsley recalls the corpus- and knowledge-based resources promoted by textbook approaches to CL (Jurafsky and Martin, 2000). The low-level tasks in analyzing *Finnegan's Wake* described in Section 1 align with the New Critical identification of literary devices. Much of the CL/AI research described in Section 2 is in this vein.

However, to create a complete computational model of literary reading from this perspective we would also need a model of the types of "humane values" that New Critics revered. Unfortunately, the New Critics themselves did not explicitly provide such a model, as doing so was considered irrelevant. But we ourselves could adapt a computational model of culture to develop a representation of the New Critic's cultural values. AI researchers develop computational model of culture by, for example, implementing Cultural Schema Theory and Appraisal Theory in cognitive architectures to describe how culture emerges from an individual's cognitive processes (Taylor et al., 2007). There is room here to adapt the system of perceived affordances (Gorniak and Roy, 2006) in which language understanding is represented as the process of filtering real-world devices in a way analogous to how the New Critics filter literary devices.

[5] Note that Wimsatt and Beardsley did not not deny the scholarly value of "literary biography," and New Critic John Crowe Ransom stated "Without [historical studies] what could we make of Chaucer, for instance?" (Ransom, 1938) New Critics merely believed that *close readings* of the text should take precedence during literary text analysis.

3.3 Russian Formalism

The New Criticism developed independently of **Russian formalism**, which similarly focused on the text and the literary devices present, rather than the author's intentions or the context of the text's production. Because of this, most of the computational representations used in discussion of the New Critics could also be applied to the Russian formalists.

However, unlike the New Critics, the Russian formalists believed that art existed to create a sense of *defamiliarization*:

> art exists that one may recover the sensation of life; it exists to make one feel things... The technique of art is to make objects 'unfamiliar,' to make forms difficult, to increase the difficulty and length of perception because the process of perception is an aesthetic end in itself and must be prolonged. *Art is a way of experiencing the artfulness of an object: the object is not important.*[6]

The defamiliarizing force of literature is easy to see in a text such as *Finnegan's Wake,* whose second sentence reads:

> Sir Tristram, violer d'amores, fr'over the short sea, had passencore rearrived from North Armorica on this side the scraggy isthmus of Europe Minor to wielderfight his penisolate war: nor had topsawyer's rocks by the stream Oconee exaggerated themselse to Laurens County's gorgios while they went doublin their mumper all the time: nor avoice from afire bellowsed mishe mishe to tauftauf thuartpeatrick: not yet, though venissoon after, had a kidscad buttended a bland old isaac: not yet, though all's fair in vanessy, were sosie sesthers wroth with twone nathandjoe.

This is not a text that can easily be read rapidly. A more methodical reading is most obviously rewarded by the portmanteaux (which are created by combining words in new ways) along with the other literary devices. Computationally, as before this can be seen as another set of devices to be automatically processed. However it may be more productive to see this as an example of how writers strive to invent new devices and combine devices in new ways, which may be resistant to automated analyses. From this perspective, defamiliarization has its effect on the computational linguist who is developing the algorithms. The perception of the researcher is thus shifted and prolonged, creating in them a recovery of the sensation for language.

[6] First published in 1917, this translation is from (Shlovsky, 1988). Emphasis from the original.

3.4 Structuralism and Post-Structuralism

Linguist Roman Jakobson was central figure in both Russian formalism and **structuralism**, two mutually influential schools of thought. A key difference between the two is their understanding of the relation between aesthetic products and their cultural context. To Russian formalists (as well as to New Critics), literary text existed apart from other cultural phenomena, whereas structuralism provided a formal framework which studied systems of arbitrary signs which could be built at different *levels*, (Schleifer, 1993) so that literary structures could be built with reference to cultural structures.

With roots in the semiotics of linguist Ferdinand de Saussure and of philosopher Charles Sanders Peirce, structuralism aimed at systematically uncovering the way that meaning arises from systems of signs forming linguistic elements such as sentences and paragraphs as well as higher levels of narrative discourse.

Continued scholarship on structuralism exposed a number of difficulties. Besides its lack of interest in individual cases or in the way systems change over time, the arbitrary nature of structuralist signs contradicted its aspirations to systematic representation (Schleifer, 1993). This was leveraged by philosopher Jacques Derrida, who argued that one could not study structures from "outside," in the way that an objective study requires.

Derrida was a **post-structuralist**, who used structuralism as a starting point but did not limit themselves with structuralism's constraints. Another post-structuralist, literary theorist Roland Barthes, used the phrase *death of the author* in a way reminiscent of the New Critics' intentional fallacy. Barthes, however, used the the arbitrariness of signs to go beyond the New Critics and reject the existence of any "ultimate meaning" of a text. Barthes saw the source of understanding as the reader:

> [A] text consists of multiple writings, issuing from several cultures and entering into dialogue with each other, into parody, into contestation;

> but there is one place where this multiplicity is collected, united, and this place is not the author, as we have hitherto said it was, but the reader... (Barthes, 1967)

To Barthes, readers are not important in terms of their personal history or their state of mind, but rather that they are the one who "holds gathered into a single field all the paths of which the text is constituted." (Barthes, 1967) In other words, the text's meaning is dependent on the structures of signs in which the reader exists. And because signs are arbitrary, the reading produced by any reader must likewise be arbitrary, at least in terms of any objective measure of quality.

Another post-structuralist, psychologist Jacques Lacan, maintained that humans entered systems of signs in which they found or were provided roles, such as child/parent or male/female (Selden and Widdowson, 1993). This process is directed by the unconscious, and the only way it is able to take on comprehensible meaning is in expression through a system of language signs.

These are but a few of the influential structuralist and post-structuralist scholars, but they suffice to consider applicable computational techniques.

We begin by considering the concept of language as a complex adaptive system (Beckner et al., 2009). This provides a model that brings together language, interpretation, and intelligent agents (Steels, 2007) in a way that allows experiments with both sets of software agents and language-using robots (Steels, 2006). As in the structuralist view, meaningful language use is dependent on complex systems involving signification.

But this complex system is made up of language-using agents, who must work together to determine norms as well as actually use language for real-world tasks and abstract reasoning. The model must work not only at the system level, but also at the individual level. CL/AI research in societal grounding (DeVault et al., 2006), dialogue grounding (Traum, 1994), semantic alignment (Pickering and Garrod, 2004), and relational agency (Bickmore and Picard, 2005) provide ways of representing how populations of agents use language meaningfully, and how pairs of human-like intelligent agents coordinate language in situated dialogues, while developing social relationships. As in the Lacanian subject, these agents are created or trained in terms of their difference or similarity from the other agents, adopting and being defined by their roles in the structured societies of agents.

When considering *Finnegan's Wake*, an intelligent agent would bring with it an algorithm for identifying features in stories, as well as resources such as language model data and its model of the role it fits in its social structures. Reading the text, the agent identifies literary devices that it uses as affordances to react with its emotions and its social perceptions, as well as to weigh the semantics of the text. When reading the text, the agent's interpretation of the story will be based on its gendered identity and personal history. In this way, the literary analysis of the agent is highly dependent on its sense of identity, as well as the localized nature of its language resources.

4 Conclusions

We began by describing some of the larger questions that literary theorists have been working with for over a century. We described some ideas from the digital humanities, including an expressed skepticism in artificial intelligence's ability to model human-like readings of literary texts. In response to that skepticism, we have described several major approaches to literary text analysis, and for each we have suggested ways in which state-of-the-art CL/AI techniques could be applied to model or support their approach.

Of course this is by no means an exhaustive survey of either literary theoretical approaches or applicable CL/AI techniques. Rather, we are suggesting that a great number of possibilities remain unexplored between the two.

References

David Bamman and Gregory Crane. 2009. Computational Linguistics and Classical Lexicography, *Digital Humanities Quarterly*, Volume 3 Number 1.

Roland Barthes. 1967. The Death of the Author. *Aspen*. No. 5-6.

Clay Beckner, Nick C. Ellis, Richard Blythe, John Holland, Joan Bybee, Jinyun Ke, Morten H. Christiansen, Diane Larsen-Freeman, William Croft, Tom Schoenemann. 2009. Language Is a Complex Adaptive System: Position Paper. *Language Learning*, 59:Suppl 1, December 2009, pp 1-26.

Catherine Belsey. 1980. *Critical Practice*. Routledge. London, UK.

Timothy Bickmore and Rosalind Picard. 2005. Establishing and maintaining long-term human-computer relationships. *ACM Transactions on Computer-Human Interaction (ToCHI)*.

John Burrows. 2004. Textual Analysis. In *A Companion to Digital Humanities*, ed. S. Schreibman, R. Siemens, and J. Unsworth, Oxford: Blackwell Publishing.

Charles B. Callaway and James C. Lester. 2002. Narrative Prose Generation, Artificial Intelligence. Volume 139 Issue 2, Elsevier Science Publishers Ltd. Essex, UK

Paul R. Cohen. 1995. *Empirical Methods for Artificial Intelligence*. Bradford Books. Cambridge, MA.

David DeVault, Iris Oved, and Matthew Stone. 2006. Societal Grounding is Essential to Meaningful Language Use. In *Proceedings of the Twenty-First National Conference on Artificial Intelligence (AAAI-06)*

Johanna Drucker. 2009. *SpecLab: Digital Aesthetics and Projects in Speculative Computing*. University Of Chicago Press.

David K. Elson, Nicholas Dames, Kathleen R. McKeown. 2010. Extracting Social Networks from Literary Fiction. In *Proceedings of the 48th Annual Meeting of the Association for Computational Linguistics* (ACL 2010), Uppsala, Sweden

David K. Elson and Kathleen R. McKeown. 2009. Extending and Evaluating a Platform for Story Understanding. *Papers from the 2009 AAAI Spring Symposium: Intelligent Narrative Technologies II*. The AAAI Press, Menlo Park, California.

Mark A. Finlayson. 2011. Corpus Annotation in Service of Intelligent Narrative Technologies, *Proceedings of the 4th Workshop on Intelligent Narrative Technologies*, Stanford, CA.

Virginia Francisco, Raquel Hervás, Federico Peinado, and Pablo Gervás. 2011. EmoTales: creating a corpus of folk tales with emotional annotations. *Language Resources & Evaluation*.

John Gardner. 1991. *The Art of Fiction: Notes on Craft for Young Writers*. Vintage, New York, NY.

Pablo Gervás. 2009. Computational Approaches to Storytelling and Creativity. *AI Magazine*, Fall, p 49-62.

Pablo Gervás, Raquel Hervás, Jason R Robinson. 2007. "Difficulties and Challenges in Automatic Poem Generation: Five Years of Research at UCM". in *Papers presented at e-poetry* 2007, Université Paris8.

Peter Gorniak and Deb Roy. 2007. Situated Language Understanding as Filtering Perceived Affordances. *Cognitive Science*, Volume 31, Issue 2, pages 197–231.

Amit Goyal, Ellen Riloff, Hal Daumé, III. 2010. Automatically producing plot unit representations for narrative text. In *Proceedings of the 2010 Conference on Empirical Methods in Natural Language Processing*.

Erica Greene, Tugba Bodrumlu, and Kevin Knight. 2010. Automatic Analysis of Rhythmic Poetry with Applications to Generation and Translation. In *Proceedings of the 2010 Conference on Empirical Methods in Natural Language Processing*, pages 524–533.

Susan Hockey. 2004. The History of Humanities Computing. In *A Companion to Digital Humanities*. Blackwell, Oxford, UK.

Matthew L. Jockers and Daniela M. Witten, 2010 "A comparative study of machine learning methods for authorship attribution", *Literary and Linguistic Computing* 25(2):215-223

James Joyce. 1939. *Finnegan's Wake*. Faber and Faber, London, UK.

Daniel Jurafsky and James H. Martin. 2000. *Speech and Language Processing*. Pearson Prentice Hall. Upper Saddle River, New Jersey.

Anna Kazantseva and Stan Szpakowicz. 2010. Summarizing Short Stories. In *Computational Linguistics*, 36(1), pp. 71-109.

Scott W. McQuiggan, Jennifer L. Robison, and James C. Lester. 2010. Affective Transitions in Narrative-Centered Learning Environments. In *Educational Technology & Society*. 13 (1): 40–53.

Inderjeet Mani. 2005. Narrative Summarization. *Journal Traitement automatique des langues (TAL)*: Special issue on Context: Automatic Text Summarization.

Inderjeet Mani. 2010. Predicting Reader Response in Narrative. In *Proceedings of the Intelligent Narrative Technologies III Workshop*.

Hisar Maruli Manurung. 2003. *An Evolutionary Algorithm Approach to Poetry Generation*. PhD thesis, University of Edinburgh. College of Science and Engineering. School of Informatics.

Saif Mohammad. 2011. From Once Upon a Time to Happily Ever After: Tracking Emotions in Novels and Fairy Tales, In *Proceedings of the ACL 2011 Workshop on Language Technology for Cultural Heritage, Social Sciences, and Humanities (LaTeCH)*, June, Portland, OR.

Federico Peinado, Virginia Francisco, Raquel Hervás, Pablo Gervás. 2010. Assessing the Novelty of Computer-Generated Narratives Using Empirical Metrics. *Minds & Machines*, 20:565–588.

Martin J. Pickering and Simon Garrod. 2004. Towards a mechanistic Psychology of dialogue. *Behavioral and Brain Sciences*, 27:169-22.

Livia Polanyi, Chris Culy, Martin van den Berg, Gian Lorenzo Thione, David Ahn, 2004. Sentential Structure and Discourse Parsing. In *ACL2004 - Workshop on Discourse Annotation*.

Stephen Ramsay. 2011. *Reading machines: Towards an Algorithmic Criticism*. University of Illinois Press, Urbana, IL

John Crowe Ransom. 1938. Criticism, Inc. Anthologized in *The Norton Anthology of Theory & Criticism.* 2010. WW Norton & Company, New York, NY.

Giacomo Rizzolatti and Laila Craighero. 2004. The Mirror Neuron System. In *Annual Review of Neuroscience*. 27:169–92.

Ronald Schleifer. 1993. Structuralism. in *The Johns Hopkins Guide to Literary Theory and Criticism*. Michael Groden and Martin Kreiswirth, eds. The Johns Hopkins University Press. Baltimore, USA.

Susan Schreibman, Ray Siemens, John Unsworth, eds. 2004. *A Companion to Digital Humanities*. Blackwell, Oxford, UK.

Raman Selden and Peter Widdowson. 1993. *A Reader's Guide to Contemporary Literary Theory*. University Press of Kentucky. Lexington, KY.

Luc Steels. 2006. How to do experiments in artificial language evolution and why. *Proceedings of the 6th International Conference on the Evolution of Language*. pp 323-332.

Luc Steels. 2007. Language Originated in Social Brains. *Social Brain Matters: Stances of Neurobiology of Social Cognition*, pages 223-242, Editions Rodopi. Amsterdam NL.

Glenn Taylor, Michael Quist, Steve Furtwangler, and Keith Knudsen. 2007. *Toward a Hybrid Cultural Cognitive Architecture*. CogSci Workshop on Culture and Cognition.

David Traum. 1994. *A Computational Theory of Grounding in Natural Language Conversation*, TR 545 and Ph.D. Thesis, Computer Science Dept., U. Rochester, NY.

Virginia Tufte. 2006. *Artful Sentences: Syntax as Style*. Graphics Press, Chesire, CT.

Akira Utsumi. 2004. Stylistic and Contextual Effects in Irony Processing. In *Proceedings of the 26th Annual Meeting of the Cognitive Science Society*.

W.K. Wimsatt, Jr., and Monroe C. Beardsley. 1954. The Intentional Fallacy. From *The Verbal Icon: Studies in the Meaning of Poetry*. University of Kentucky Press, Lexington, KY.

William Wordsworth. 1802. Preface to *Lyrical Ballads*. Anthologized in *The Norton Anthology of Theory & Criticism.* 2010. WW Norton & Company, New York, NY.

Author Index

Association for Computational Linguistics
209 N. Eighth Street
Stroudsburg, Pennsylvania 18360

CURRAN ASSOCIATES INC
proceedings.com